D1564606

Heads above Water

KATHIE AND ED COX JR. BOOKS ON

CONSERVATION LEADERSHIP,

sponsored by

 THE MEADOWS CENTER
FOR WATER AND THE ENVIRONMENT
TEXAS STATE UNIVERSITY

Andrew Sansom, General Editor

A list of other titles in this series may be found at the back of the book.

Heads above Water

THE INSIDE STORY OF
THE EDWARDS AQUIFER
RECOVERY IMPLEMENTATION
PROGRAM

ROBERT L. GULLEY

*Forewords by Andrew Sansom
and Glenn Hegar*

TEXAS A&M UNIVERSITY PRESS

College Station

Library of Congress Cataloging-in-Publication Data

Gulley, Robert L., 1945– author.
    Heads above water: the inside story of the Edwards Aquifer Recovery
  Implementation Program / Robert L. Gulley; foreword by Andrew
  Sansom. — First edition.
      pages cm — (Conservation leadership series)
    Includes bibliographical references and index.
    ISBN 978-1-62349-268-7 (cloth: alk. paper) — ISBN 978-1-62349-269-4
  (ebook) 1. Edwards Aquifer Recovery Implementation Program. 2. Water-
  supply—Texas—Edwards Aquifer Region—Management. 3. Edwards
  Aquifer (Tex.) 4. Endangered species—Texas—Edwards Aquifer Region.
  5. Water quality management—Texas—Edwards Aquifer Region.
  6. Environmental law—Texas. 7. Water rights—Texas—Edwards Aquifer
  Region. I. Title. II. Series: Conservation leadership series.
  TD224.T4G85 2015
  333.91'04153097643—dc23

                             2014032569

*To the members of the
Edwards Aquifer Recovery
Implementation Program and
the future generations that
will benefit from their efforts*

CONTENTS

SERIES EDITOR'S FOREWORD

It is fitting that this fifth title in the Conservation Leadership Series, jointly presented by Texas A&M University Press and The Meadows Center for Water and the Environment at Texas State University, covers a transformational breakthrough in our ability to provide leadership examples for the benefit of emerging conservation leaders, mentors, professionals, philanthropists, and volunteers across the country.

Heads Above Water: The Inside Story of the Edwards Aquifer Recovery Implementation Program is the first book to carry the series new title: The Kathie and Ed Cox Jr. Books on Conservation Leadership. Mr. and Mrs. Cox, who are among Texas' most distinguished conservationists, have generously endowed the series and thus ensured that it will continue to provide the excellence and worth demonstrated in the initial volumes for generations of conservationists to come.

Just as fitting is the indisputable fact that Dr. Robert Gulley's engaging account on these pages chronicles one of the most successful conservation projects in American history, an initiative that, by consensus reached by very diverse stakeholders, has created a framework that ensures both the preservation of the biological diversity of one of the United States' most unique aquatic resources and continued economic prosperity for the nation's fastest growing region.

If there were ever a natural resource worthy of global recognition, it would be the Edwards Aquifer that lies beneath the fabled Hill Country of Texas. This unique hydrogeological feature is one of the world's most abundant artesian underground reservoirs, providing life-giving water to more than two million people in Central Texas for agriculture, industry, residential consumption, and recreation. The presence of springs arising from the aquifer were among the earliest phenomena recorded by Spanish explorers who laid the groundwork for the establishment of the first European settlements in Texas, including the iconic missions and presidios such as the Alamo in San Antonio. For the next two centuries, the Alamo City and others in the Texas Hill Country were able to grow and prosper without relying on any other water source other than the prolific Edwards Aquifer.

Today, San Antonio is the seventh largest city and one of the fastest growing in America. As a result, the voracious appetite created by this boom has far exceeded the capacity of the Edwards Aquifer to meet contemporary demands for water. The aquifer is also home to eight federally listed endangered or threatened species whose very existence is at risk as a result of the increasing demand.

With federal and state institutions failing to address the risk to these eight species, a federal judge threatened in a landmark lawsuit styled *Sierra Club v. Babbitt* that, unless the state of Texas created a regulatory authority to protect the aquifer-dependent endangered species in the San Marcos and Comal springs, it would face federal control of the aquifer. This was an extraordinary move that resulted in the creation of the Edwards Aquifer Authority. Nonetheless, fourteen years later, adequate protections were not in place, the threat of drought was increasing, and the threat of federal intervention realistic.

Enter Robert Gulley.

In 2006, with the reality that the survival of the eight critically endangered or threatened species remained at risk, the US Fish and Wildlife Service called for stakeholders to collaboratively develop a plan to ensure recovery of the aquifer's rare organisms. Among them were the cities of San Marcos and New Braunfels and Texas State University, which not only use the aquifer, but they are also the location of magnificent springs that are home to the species themselves. The Texas Legislature followed by directing thirty-nine stakeholder groups to accomplish this difficult task by 2012, and Dr. Gulley was recruited to facilitate the process. Dr. Gulley, having served as a senior attorney with the US Department of Justice, had extensive experience in legal matters related to water and endangered species. He managed the process to its successful conclusion and by all accounts achieved that success with remarkable skill, grace, patience, knowledge, and enthusiasm. He has been repeatedly honored for the accomplishment. Thus, it is appropriate that Dr. Gulley's account of this remarkable conservation achievement, which at its heart is a balance of economic and environmental interests, carry the Kathie and Ed Cox Jr. Books on Conservation Leadership name.

Mr. Cox, who served as chairman and vice chairman on the Texas Parks and Wildlife Commission from 1979 to 1988, by virtue of appointments from both Democratic and Republican governors, was one of the most influential and effective leaders in the department's history.

During his tenure, the Texas Legislature declared the Red Drum a game species, ending its commercial exploitation and leading to the establishment of the first Redfish fingerlings in the world produced in a hatchery. As chairman, he directed the creation of a resource protection program in the Parks and Wildlife Department that became the most effective defense mechanism for safeguarding fish and wildlife in the state. In the mid-1980s, Cox led consolidation efforts in the Department of Wildlife Regulation that had been shared by county governments across Texas with the passage of the Wildlife Conservation Act. He capped this extraordinary legacy as chairman of the Texas Parks and Wildlife Foundation with the launch of the most ambitious conservation land acquisition program in Texas history and the establishment of the Texas Freshwater Fisheries Center in Athens. Kathie Cox, an accomplished equestrian, has made magnificent contributions throughout the years to wildlife art with her acclaimed photography and sculptures.

And so the narrative that follows here is not only the story of one of the most important conservation projects ever accomplished in Texas, it is a celebration of two remarkable and generous Texas citizens who have devoted their lives to the natural resources of the state and an extraordinary environmental leader who made it happen.

—Andrew Sansom
General Editor, Kathie and Ed Cox Jr.
Books on Conservation Leadership

FOREWORD

Everyday our lives are filled with moments and events that we can rarely recall later in the day, much less years later. Every so often, something sticks in our minds as if it happened seconds ago. A vivid memory of mine is from the time I spent as a first year law student in San Antonio, when the daily news would report the exact level of the Edwards Aquifer. At first I thought it was odd that the news would update the public on the aquifer level every single day, let alone multiple times a day. As a sixth generation Texan who grew up on a family farm in an area of Texas with more rainfall, I came to appreciate the value of water to my family's livelihood very early in life. Even with this backdrop to my life, I remember thinking as the days, weeks, and months passed, that the people in San Antonio are absolutely and strangely obsessed with the level of this aquifer.

For the most part, Texans and Americans take for granted that cheap, fresh water will always run abundantly from the taps of their homes. It is hard for people in our country to grasp the fact that over one-third of the world's population does not have access of adequate sanitation and almost eleven percent does not have access to clean water. These two facts certainly put into perspective the often cited Mark Twain quote: "Whiskey is for drinking; water is for fighting over!" Although no one can prove that Twain is the author of the quote, the most basic fact in life is that water is essential to our wellbeing, which is why this quote puts into perspective the decades of struggles among the various interest groups in the Edwards Aquifer region.

After leaving law school, I returned home where rain is typically plentiful and water is not as scarce as the arid Edwards region, however, those daily news reports stuck in the back of my mind. Within six years of my graduation and leaving San Antonio, I found myself serving in the Texas House of Representatives and watched as the legislators from the Edwards Aquifer region debated and fought over this cheap and clean resource. The pieces slowly filled in as to who were the interest groups in this regional Texas fight. What made the matter even more complex was the looming axe of federal intervention if the diverse residents of the aquifer could not agree on how to best protect the endangered species that also depended on this unique aquifer.

In 2007, after only four years in the Texas House, I was sworn in to represent a state senate district that was vast and diverse. This district was home to downstream portions of five major Texas river basins, a third of the Texas coast, and the western portion of the district that was very dependent on the waters of the Edwards Aquifer. It is an understatement to say that I found myself immersed in water fights all over my senate district. An important fact is that I was filling the shoes of the senate author of the legislation that created the Edwards Aquifer Authority (EAA), which was created to solve the endangered species issue. Unfortunately for the EAA, the hurdle was too complex and 2007 was building up as another major legislative session for the Edwards Aquifer fight.

My new district depended on the waters of the Edwards, which in years of normal rainfall would freely flow from two springs upstream from my district. The problem for my district was in the years of below normal rainfall or when those above us would over pump the aquifer, the springs would then cease to flow freely. I was asked by my constituents, which included downstream agricultural, municipal, and industrial users, to play a major role in the looming legislative struggle. The end user was the bays and estuaries that depended upon the fresh water inflows. I was keenly aware that so many had worked on the problem over the prior decades, not to mention the multitude of issues that were entangled together and the years of animosity, mistrust, and sheer exhaustion on the part of this region of Texas to find a solution to the web of vexing issues.

The fights in the Edwards Aquifer are as legendary as Texas itself, and in understanding the details of this fight, a person can quickly understand why each person and interest group had some form of right on his and her side. As one reads the pages of this book, you can quickly see that the decades of fighting, lawsuits, threats of federal intervention, state legislative intervention, false starts, delays, more lawsuits, and negotiations wore on the leadership in the region, yet through it all, Texas and the region continued to survive and prosper.

After months of working with stakeholders, countless hours of negotiations, and lots of political jockeying, a deal was struck on legislation that had many pieces, yet the center piece was the creation of a Recovery Implementation Program (RIP) with carefully crafted timelines. The RIP was modeled from successes in other parts of our nation that ultimately achieved a habitat conservation plan that could be approved by the United States Fish & Wildlife Service, and the timelines were designed to build trust and momentum among the stakeholders. Unfortunately, the deal was made as the legislative clock was rapidly ticking to a close and it looked as though another stalemate for the Edwards region was inevitable, which in turn would mean another round of lawsuits that would consume this region of Texas for years to come. I remember lying down in bed and being so exhausted from days without much sleep, yet my mind was racing at 2:30 a.m. It seemed like an eternity as I laid there wondering what I could have done differently and finally concluded that despite the inevitable fate of more lawsuits being filed over how to protect the endangered species of the Edwards Aquifer, Texas was a great place to call home. When the sun comes up in a few hours, life will continue to survive and prosper.

When the sun came up, I spent a few hours with my family before returning to the capitol. Remarkably, a rare legislative miracle occurred that put the RIP deal back on track in the waning hours of session, and the journey to reach a consensus was once again afloat. New hurdles would exist, yet the path forward was possible if we could take small victories and build a relationship of trust among the players of the Edwards region. This book details the water fights of the Edwards Aquifer region and the seemingly endless effort to avoid the blunt axe of federal intervention. After reading this book, I have become even more amazed that the diverse interests of this region were able to finally come up with a solution to the complex web of issues that had plagued the region for so long.

—Glenn Hegar
Texas State Senator

PREFACE

On an evening in November 2011 I was being honored on the rooftop terrace of the Texas River Center at Texas State University for my contribution to a truly historic achievement. After four and one-half years, thirty-nine diverse stakeholders had reached consensus on the use of the Edwards Aquifer in ways that balanced the needs of the region for water with the needs of eight species protected by the federal Endangered Species Act (ESA). The agreement ended a half century of rancor and litigation over the use of the water in the Edwards Aquifer.

As state senator Glenn Hegar lauded the achievements of the stakeholders gathered there, my thoughts wandered back to the beginning of this extraordinary process. I had been hired by the stakeholders as the program manager for a process known as the Edwards Aquifer Recovery Implementation Program. No one had explained exactly what the job entailed. The only hint I had was from Bob Shaw at Texas A&M University, who told me not to worry because, regardless of what I did, I would have a brief honeymoon period after which the stakeholders would return to their old ways and blame the failure of the process on me.

The history of the Edwards dispute certainly supported Shaw's view. The Edwards Aquifer is the primary source of water for more than two million people in south-central Texas. It serves much of the domestic and industrial water needs of the cities of San Antonio, San Marcos, and New Braunfels and the agricultural needs of primarily the western part of the aquifer region. It is the source of the springs that feed the Comal and San Marcos Rivers, which are used for recreational activities that are a large part of the economies of San Marcos and New Braunfels. Further, these rivers are tributaries of the Guadalupe River, which provides water to the downstream surface water rights holders such as the Guadalupe-Blanco River Authority, the City of Victoria, and several Gulf Coast chemical plants, as well as freshwater inflows to San Antonio Bay and estuaries along the Gulf Coast.

Since the 1950s the different interests in the Edwards Aquifer region had been at war over the use of the aquifer. For many years, few, if any, regulatory mechanisms existed to manage the use of the aquifer. Like all other groundwater in the state, the use of the aquifer was governed almost exclusively by the "rule of capture," under which a landowner was free to pump and use as much water as could be beneficially used without waste. The aquifer users also had no legal obligation to limit the use of the aquifer to protect surface water interests downstream of the San Marcos and Comal Springs. It was the wild, wild West, and the person with the biggest pump prevailed.

The competing interests in the Edwards region tried many times to resolve their differences. Some efforts came close to succeeding, but all ultimately failed. Alliances in these efforts frequently shifted, and, even on good days, trust was nonexistent. Litigation was rampant, lawyers abundant, and legislators unable to agree on an acceptable solution.

Finally, in 1991, the Sierra Club filed suit in federal court against the US Fish and Wildlife Service (USFWS) for violations of the Endangered Species Act with respect to the Edwards Aquifer. In early 1993, the court ruled that the Fish and Wildlife Service had failed to protect federally listed species in the Comal and San Marcos Springs ecosystem as required by the act. While the court did not specifically order the State of Texas to take any action, it made abundantly clear that, if the Texas Legislature did not take immediate action to protect the federally listed species, the "blunt axes of federal intervention would have to be dropped."

In response, in 1993 the Texas Legislature put an end to the rule of capture for the Edwards Aquifer and created the Edwards Aquifer Authority to manage the aquifer and to protect the federally listed species. It took more than three years for litigation over the creation of the authority to subside long enough for it to begin to function. Meanwhile, severe drought struck the region, prompting the federal court to attempt to take over the management of the aquifer to protect the species. However, the US Court of Appeals for the Fifth Circuit halted that attempt.

Once the Edwards Aquifer Authority began to function, its attempts to protect the species fell short of the requirements of the legislature and the expectations of many stakeholders in the region. If possible, trust among the stakeholders worsened, tensions increased, and discord prevailed. By 2007 it appeared that once again the Edwards Aquifer dispute was heading back to federal court.

To avoid again risking federal control, the legislature required the

Edwards Aquifer Authority and four state agencies to participate in a facilitated, consensus-based stakeholder process—the Edwards Aquifer Recovery Implementation Program (EARIP)—to create a plan to ensure that the federally listed species were adequately protected. The plan had to be approved by the US Fish and Wildlife Service and take effect by December 31, 2012.

This book tells the story of how the EARIP overcame years of hostility, mistrust, and litigation over the use of the aquifer and resolved, by consensus, one of the most intractable and long-standing water problems in the nation. The story of how the EARIP solved the problem, where so many earlier efforts failed, cannot be understood without reviewing the events that set the stage for this achievement. As you work through the story, you will see in the earlier failures the essential tools, information, and understandings being developed that ultimately the EARIP was able to put to use successfully.

The history leading up to the creation of the EARIP may be a bit long and, at times, detailed, but it will not be boring. After all, this is Texas. Private property interests are third only in importance to God and pickup trucks, being ornery is a state tradition, and the Endangered Species Act and federal control are slightly less popular than a liberal at a Tea Party rally.

After a brief, but important introduction to the Edwards Aquifer, we will begin the story of the Edwards Issue back where it all began, with the attempts of the City of San Antonio to develop surface water supplies after a severe drought from 1947 through 1956 referred to as the "drought of record."

ACKNOWLEDGMENTS

The opportunity to write a book about the Edwards Aquifer Recovery Implementation Program (EARIP) is truly a gift. A big bonus was the opportunity to work with the individual stakeholders in that group. They are fine people, and I will always cherish memories of them, that experience, and the time we spent together.

I owe special thanks to Jerry James, Weir Labatt, Todd Votteler, and Jim Bower, who spent countless hours listening to me talk about my latest discovery while doing research for this book and who read the initial draft to see if I got the facts right. There are few things an attorney hates more than someone trying to keep him honest. In their case, I have to make an exception. Jerry, Weir, and Todd each spent years working on the "Edwards Issue" and brought tremendous knowledge and experience to the task. Jim participated in the EARIP and evinced a comprehensive understanding of the importance of the process and procedures. In addition, while I was writing this book, he constantly reminded me to keep things simple and stop writing like a lawyer.

When I started writing this book, I had little more to guide me than access to the Edwards Aquifer Habitat Conservation Plan website. That changed quickly. Through the Freedom of Information Act, I was able to gain access to seven file cabinets full of documents on the Edwards Aquifer from the Austin field office of the US Fish and Wildlife Service (USFWS). Adam Zerrenner and Kevin Connally helped guide me through these documents. Both spent considerable time providing me their perspectives on the EARIP and its significance. Adam arranged for me to have access to former and current USFWS employees, including Mike Spear, Alisa Shull, and Steve Cullinan, and for me to have lunch with John Hall, which was quite informative and helpful.

Mary Q. Kelly gave me nine boxes of documents from her time as an attorney for the Edwards Underground Water District. These documents and her voluminous notes were invaluable to me. While I did not formally interview her, we talked while I was writing this book, and her insights were quite valuable. Todd Votteler and Roger Nevola gave me access to many documents from the Sierra Club cases, including transcripts of the trial and some of the hearings. Over time, I got other documents from Cindy Loeffler, Tyson Broad, Dianne Wassenich, Jerry James, the San Antonio River Authority, and Velma Danielson that filled many important gaps about the EARIP, particularly regarding the period before I became the program manager.

Velma Danielson of Blanton & Associates graciously provided the map of the Edwards Aquifer region.

I hope the book is about more than the lifeless pages of documents. Over nine months, I was able to interview many people involved in the Edwards Issue, including Joe Aceves, Colette Barron, Tyson Broad, Luana Buckner, Rebecca Cedillo, Lila Cockrell, Steve Cullinan, John Donahue, Calvin Finch, John Hall, Robert Hasslocher, Stuart Henry, Myron Hess, Anna Munoz, Roger Nevola, Fred Pfeiffer, Robert Puente, Rodney Reagan, Greg Rothe, Andrew Sansom, M. J. Spear, Tom Taggart, Adam Zerrenner, and Larry Zinn. I deeply appreciate the time they spent with me and the insights they were able to provide. All of them shared their thoughts and perspectives, which I hope breathed life into the book.

I am particularly grateful to Dr. Andy Sansom, executive director of The Meadows Center for Water and the Environment, and Shannon Davies, editor-in-chief and Louise Lindsey Merrick Editor for the Natural Environment at Texas A&M University Press, for the opportunity to write this book. It is the latest in a series of books that Andy has written or sponsored with Texas A&M University Press.

My gratitude to my wife, Carol, daughter, Annalee, and clumber spaniel, Topee, for their patience and support goes without saying. Carol has been the love of my life for fifty-six years, since I sat behind her in middle school. I am sure we have talked through every idea in this book more than once. We decided to come back to Texas when Annalee had grown tired of the political life in Washington, DC, and moved to San Antonio, where Carol and I grew up. Annalee gave me encouragement as I tried to piece together the story. Her most frequent advice was "you can't say that." Topee was my companion for the last ten years. She listened attentively and growled at all the right times; she will be missed.

PARTIAL CAST OF CHARACTERS

MAYORS OF SAN ANTONIO

Phil Hardberger	June 17, 2005–May 31, 2009
Nelson W. Wolff	June 1, 1991–May 31, 1995
Lila Cockrell	June 1, 1989–May 31, 1991
	May 1, 1975–April 30, 1981
Henry G. Cisneros	May 1, 1981–May 31, 1989
Charles Becker	May 1, 1973–April 30, 1975
Walter W. McAllister	May 1, 1961–April 30, 1971

The **EDWARDS AQUIFER AUTHORITY** (EAA) is a water conservation district and political subdivision of the State of Texas. The Texas Legislature created it in 1993 with Senate Bill 1477 in response to the *Sierra Club v. Babbitt* decision. The authority includes all of Uvalde, Medina, and Bexar Counties and the parts of Comal, Hays, Atascosa, Caldwell, and Guadalupe Counties overlying the Edwards Aquifer.

The **EDWARDS UNDERGROUND WATER DISTRICT** was created by the Texas Legislature in 1959. Five counties—Bexar, Medina, Uvalde, Comal, and Hays—were included in the district, with each county having three members on the district board of directors. The legislature authorized it "to conserve, preserve, protect and increase the recharge of and prevent pollution of the underground water." But it did not authorize the Edwards Underground Water District to restrict the rights of landowners to pump water from beneath their land. The legislature amended the enabling statute of the district in 1983 to give it the authority to limit the transportation of water from the aquifer out of the district. Medina and Uvalde Counties withdrew from the district in 1989. In 1993, the Texas Legislature dissolved the Edwards Underground Water District and replaced it with the Edwards Aquifer Authority.

The **GUADALUPE-BLANCO RIVER AUTHORITY** (GBRA) is a water conservation and reclamation district created by the Texas Legislature in 1933. It consists of a ten-county statutory district, which begins near the headwaters of the Guadalupe and Blanco Rivers and ends at San Antonio Bay. It includes Kendall, Comal, Hays, Caldwell, Guadalupe, Gonzales, DeWitt, Victoria, Calhoun, and Refugio Counties. The primary responsibilities of the authority include managing, developing, conserving, distributing, and protecting the water resources of the Guadalupe River Basin.

The **NUECES RIVER AUTHORITY** was created by the Texas Legislature in 1935. It has broad authority to preserve, protect, and develop surface water resources, and it is thus involved in flood control, irrigation, navigation, water supply, wastewater treatment, and water quality control. The Nueces River Authority serves all or parts of twenty-two counties in South Texas and has responsibility for more than seventeen thousand square miles generally constituting the drainage area of the Nueces River, the tributaries of the river, and the adjoining coastal basins.

The **SAN ANTONIO RIVER AUTHORITY** (SARA) is a special-purpose district. It was created by the Texas Legislature in 1937 as the San Antonio River Canal and Conservancy District. At that time, the board for the district was made up of members entirely from Bexar County. Its mission focused on the creation of a barge canal from the Gulf Coast to San Antonio. Flood control in the San Antonio Basin was added to its mission in 1941. The legislature changed the name of the district to the San Antonio River Authority in 1953. The authority was reorganized in 1961 and its jurisdiction expanded to include Wilson, Karnes, and Goliad Counties. Its mission was expanded to include planning, managing, and implementing water-related programs and projects in the San Antonio River Basin and protecting and managing the resources and ecology of the San Antonio River. The board for the authority consists of members representing Bexar, Wilson, Karnes, and Goliad Counties.

The **SAN ANTONIO WATER SYSTEM** (SAWS) is a public utility owned by the City of San Antonio. It was created in May 1992 through the consolidation of three predecessor agencies: the City Water Board (water supply utility), City Wastewater Department (sewage collection and treatment), and the Alamo Water Conservation and Reuse District (reuse of treated wastewater).

The **TEXAS PARKS AND WILDLIFE DEPARTMENT** was created in 1963 through the merger of the State Parks Board and the Game and Fish Commission. It is responsible for managing and protecting wildlife and wildlife habitat and managing parklands and historic areas.

The **TEXAS WATER COMMISSION** during the relevant time frame was the primary regulatory agency for water resources in the state. It was the successor to the Texas Board of Engineers, created by the Texas Legislature in 1913. From 1965 to 1977, it was known as the Texas Water Rights Commission and was exclusively responsible for water rights issues. All other water-related functions were transferred to the Texas Water Development Board. In 1977, the Texas Department of Water Resources was created with responsibility for most water-related functions and the Texas Water Rights Commission was renamed the Texas Water Commission. In 1985, the Texas Department of Water Resources was dissolved, with regulatory enforcement being transferred to the re-created Texas Water Commission and planning and finance responsibilities, to the re-created Texas Water Development Board. In 1993, the Texas Water Commission was combined with the Texas Air Control Board and parts of the Texas Department of Health related to drinking water, municipal solid waste, and radioactive materials and was renamed the Texas Natural Resource Conservation Commission. In 2002, it was renamed the Texas Commission on Environmental Quality (TCEQ). With respect to water, the TCEQ is the principal agency responsible for protecting surface and groundwater water quality, managing water conservation and pollution control, and allocating and enforcing surface water rights.

The **UNITED STATES FISH AND WILDLIFE SERVICE** (USFWS), sometimes referred to as "the service," is a federal agency within the Department of the Interior that is responsible for enforcing federal wildlife laws, protecting endangered species, managing migratory birds, and handling related functions.

Heads above Water

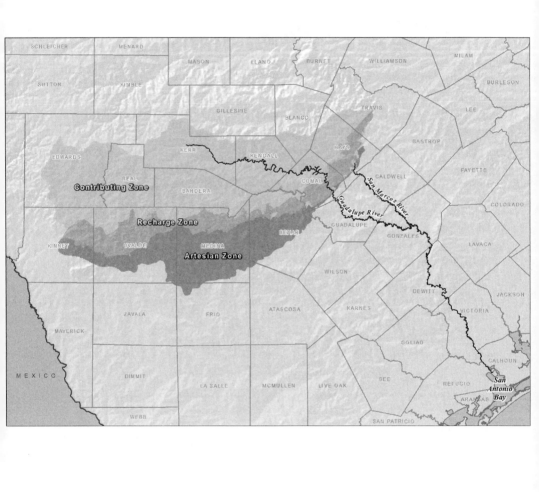

PART I

THE "EDWARDS ISSUE"

> The "Edwards Issue" is characterized by competing interests represented principally by irrigation demand in the West, municipal pumpage demands in the central area, and recreational based industries and other "downstream users" in the East. The issue is further complicated by environmental and federal interests in the protection of endangered species dependent on spring habitat. Lack of agreement among these disparate interests has prevented the development of a comprehensive management plan for the area.
> — Committee of Natural Resources, Texas House of Representatives Interim Report (1992)

The San Antonio segment of the Edwards Aquifer is a unique aquifer flowing 180 miles through channels and pathways in a highly porous limestone formation known as karst. The aquifer flows southwest to northeast, from near Brackettville, Texas, in the west to Buda, Texas, in the east.

The aquifer is divided into three zones: the contributing zone, the recharge zone, and the artesian zone. The contributing zone covers about fifty-four hundred square miles on the Edwards Plateau in the Texas Hill Country. Runoff, primarily from rainfall in the contributing zone, feeds streams that flow over relatively impermeable limestone until it reaches the recharge zone.

The recharge zone is a 1,250-square-mile area where the highly faulted and fractured Edwards limestone outcrop allows large quantities of water to flow into the aquifer. About 75 percent of the recharge occurs where streams and rivers cross this permeable formation. The remaining recharge occurs when precipitation falls directly on the outcrop. Most of the recharge occurs in the western counties of Medina and Uvalde, where the Edwards outcrop is at the surface.

The artesian zone of the Edwards is confined between two relatively impermeable geological formations. New water entering the aquifer in the recharge zone puts pressure on water that is already confined in the formation, thus forcing it up to the surface through springs.

This artesian flow occurs, for example, at the San Marcos Springs and Comal Springs in the northeastern part of the aquifer.

The springs at Comal and San Marcos feed the Comal River and the San Marcos River, which are tributaries of the Guadalupe River. As water from the Edwards Aquifer is discharged at the Comal and San Marcos Springs, it loses the legal status of groundwater and becomes surface water. The right to divert flows of the Guadalupe River and tributaries to it has been fully allocated by the Texas Commission on Environmental Quality. Because the river is fed by the Comal and San Marcos Springs, surface water permits issued to users of the Guadalupe River are based in part on the flows from the aquifer.

A geological constriction known as the Knippa Gap separates a pool of water under Uvalde County from the San Antonio pool under Medina, Bexar, and Comal Counties. The J-17 index well in northeastern Bexar County near Fort Sam Houston is used to monitor the water levels in the artesian zone of the San Antonio pool. The J-27 index well in Uvalde County is used to monitor the water levels in the artesian zone of the Uvalde pool.

In total, the aquifer is estimated to hold between twenty-five million and fifty-five million acre-feet of water.[1] However, most of that water is not legally available for pumping. To ensure springflow essential to protect the federally listed species in the Comal and San Marcos Springs and surface water flows in the Guadalupe River, the Edwards Aquifer must be managed to the upper 5 to 10 percent of the formation. This means that the aquifer is still 90 to 95 percent full when all of the springs stop flowing. The Comal and San Marcos Springs orifices are at a higher elevation than most of the confined artesian zone. This situation is analogous to a bucket of water with holes near the top. Although water is available at the bottom of the bucket, it cannot be extracted without affecting the flow through the holes at the top.

Prior to 1993, the State of Texas did not regulate the amount of groundwater that could be pumped from the Edwards Aquifer.[2] Further, the users of the Edwards Aquifer had no legal obligation to limit their use to protect the surface water interests downstream of the San Marcos and Comal Springs. This was a matter of great concern to the downstream interests, who realized that increased pumping of the Edwards Aquifer would reduce the discharge of water from the spring systems and potentially interfere with their established surface water rights in the Guadalupe River. The concerns of the downstream water users boiled over after a ten-year period of severe drought from 1947 through 1956.

From 1947 through 1956, the Edwards Aquifer experienced the most severe, prolonged drought in the historical record. This drought is referred to as the drought of record. Recharge, largely from rainfall, during this period averaged 229,000 acre-feet per year—far less than the historic average recharge of 711,000 acre-feet over the period from 1934 through 2011.[3] Pumping from the aquifer averaged 219,000 acre-feet per year from 1947 through 1956. However, from 1950 through 1956, the average recharge was only 169,000 acre-feet while the average pumping was 240,000 acre-feet. By pumping more water from the aquifer than was being replaced by recharge, the aquifer was being "overdrafted" or "mined" during this period.

Beginning on June 13, 1956, flows from the Comal Springs ceased for 144 consecutive days.[4] As a result, the entire population of a small fish, the fountain darter, in the Comal Springs system was extirpated. The San Marcos Springs never completely stopped flowing, allowing fountain darters from the San Marcos River to be successfully reintroduced into the Comal River in the mid-1970s. However, beginning in 1970, the fountain darter and seven other species living in those two spring systems were listed as threatened or endangered under the federal Endangered Species Act.[5]

The severity of the drought of record made it clear that, to have a reliable water supply and sustain growth in the San Antonio area, the city had to obtain a surface water supply.[6] This conclusion was reinforced over the ensuing years by a series of severe droughts of shorter duration, in 1962–64, 1981–84, 1988–89, and 1994–96. These droughts were characterized by significantly below average recharge, overdrafting of the aquifer, and diminished springflows and, thus, diminished flows in the Guadalupe River. For example, in 1984, recharge during the two preceding years had been well below average and pumping that year was very high: 530,000 acre-feet.[7] As a result, Comal Springs almost stopped flowing (28 cubic feet per second). In 1984, the flow of the Guadalupe River at Victoria was "barely adequate to meet the demands of existing water rights, and was less than that required to sustain the productivity of the San Antonio Bay System."[8] As noted in one report, "While the 1984 drought was not the most severe by historical standards, it was a major concern to the people and businesses of the region."[9]

1 : "WHAT'S PAST IS PROLOGUE"

Those who cannot remember the past are condemned to repeat it.
— George Santayana, *The Life of Reason*, volume 1 (1905)

The first well known to have been drilled into the Edwards Aquifer was the work of the Judson Brothers Well Drilling Company, in 1888.[1] Until that time, San Antonio had been dependent on water from the San Antonio River. Soon thereafter, George W. Brackenridge, president of the San Antonio National Bank and the San Antonio Water Works Company, had the Judson Brothers drill a well into the Edwards Aquifer on his property in what is now known as Brackenridge Park. Brackenridge was seeking a source of pure water for the Water Works Company to replace the algae-laden water from the San Antonio River.[2] That well was successful, but the flow from the well was not adequate for use in Brackenridge's water works system. Three years later, Brackenridge partnered with M. C. Judson to drill a well into the Edwards Aquifer on property Brackenridge had acquired south of Market Street. That well and subsequent wells in the aquifer produced millions of gallons of water per day that were used to supply drinking water to the city of San Antonio. By 1900, the city's use of water from the San Antonio River for its drinking water supply was virtually replaced by water from the aquifer as the city continued to grow.

But with the continued growth of the city, and mindful of the effects of the drought of record, in the early 1960s both the US Study Commission and the Texas State Water Plan (1961) found that for the City of San Antonio to meet long-term municipal and industrial water requirements, "it will be necessary for San Antonio to obtain surface-water supplies."[3]

In response, the City of San Antonio attempted to develop new alternative water supplies. None of the attempts were successful—in many instances because the political will was not there to invest in the future absent an immediate demand for additional water and because of the readily available supply of inexpensive water in the aquifer. The efforts to find alternative water supplies for the city have been fraught with disputes with the downstream interests, which contributed to the often acrimonious tone of most of the later debates.

Attempting to Develop Alternative Water Supplies for the San Antonio Area

During the drought of the 1950s the City of San Antonio adopted a master plan that recommended that the city participate in the construction of the Canyon Reservoir to develop additional water supplies to support the growth of the city.[4]

In the 1930s, the US Army Corps of Engineers (ACOE) and the Guadalupe-Blanco River Authority began planning the construction of the Canyon Dam on the Guadalupe River.[5] Severe flooding on the river and the onset of the drought of record accelerated that planning process. The dam and reservoir would provide both flood control and water for the river authority to provide to customers. Under the plan, the ACOE would own the dam and manage the reservoir. It would be entitled to the water in the flood control storage pool of the reservoir. The Guadalupe-Blanco River Authority would pay 35 percent of the cost of the dam and would be entitled to the water in the conservation storage pool.

In 1953, the City of San Antonio tendered a "presentation" to the Board of Water Engineers (predecessor to the Texas Water Commission) to determine the feasibility of participating in the construction and cost of the project. The city wanted to have the height of the dam raised to allow the city to obtain one hundred thousand acre-feet of water from the reservoir that it would then transport to San Antonio to supplement the municipal supply.[6] The Guadalupe-Blanco River Authority opposed including the city in the project because it believed the dam should provide water to meet the demands of the Guadalupe Basin rather than the water demands of the City of San Antonio.[7]

In 1956, the Guadalupe-Blanco River Authority and the City of San Antonio filed competing applications with the Board of Water Engineers requesting water from the Canyon Reservoir.[8] The city sought to obtain one hundred thousand acre-feet from the reservoir for municipal use. The Guadalupe-Blanco River Authority sought fifty thousand acre-feet of water annually for municipal use, thirty-two thousand acre-feet for manufacturing and industrial use, and twenty thousand acre-feet for irrigation. On July 5, 1957, the Board of Water

Engineers granted the application of the Guadalupe-Blanco River Authority and denied that of the City of San Antonio. The city appealed both decisions. In 1966, the Texas Supreme Court affirmed the decisions of the Board of Water Engineers.[9]

While the dispute over the Canyon Reservoir was still raging, the Guadalupe-Blanco River Authority partnered with the San Antonio River Authority to build a dam and develop a reservoir on the Guadalupe River near Cuero, Texas.[10] The project was a part of a larger plan, referred to as the SARA-GBRA Exchange, in which the authorities would exchange water from their respective basins and share proportionately in the cost of constructing two dams, one in the Guadalupe River Basin, known as the Cuero Dam, and the other in the San Antonio River Basin, known as the Goliad Dam. The construction of Cuero Dam was to be phase I of the project. This phase was to be completed in stages. In the first stage, the dam would be built on the main stem of the Guadalupe River. In exchange for sharing in the cost of the Cuero Dam, the San Antonio River Authority could remove up to 123,500 acre-feet of water annually from the Cuero Reservoir and provide it to municipalities in Bexar County through a pipeline that would be paid for by the City of San Antonio. The second stage would be built on Sandies Creek, a tributary of the Guadalupe, when the demand for additional water existed. This stage would make available an additional 56,500 acre-feet of water for the city.

The city was left out of the negotiations, however, because the City Water Board made "persistent" attempts to inject the Canyon project into the discussions, and the San Antonio River Authority was thus designated as the "proper negotiating agent."[11] The San Antonio River Authority would have to work out any disagreements with the city. Both river authorities approved the project in June 1963.

The mayor of San Antonio, Walter McAllister, a strong political figure in the city, opposed the project. According to Lila Cockrell, who was on the city council at that time, Mayor McAllister opposed the project because much less expensive water was available from the Edwards Aquifer, because he did not favor partnering with the Guadalupe-Blanco River Authority (with which the city was locked into a dispute about the Canyon project), and because the City Water Board had alternative, non-Edwards supplies that it believed could be developed.[12]

On July 9, 1963, the City Water Board, probably influenced by the mayor's opposition, rejected participating in the project. Shortly afterwards, the San Antonio City Council supported the decision of the City Water Board and withdrew from the project.[13] Instead, the city chose to pursue alternative reservoir sites on the Pedernales River in the Colorado River Basin and on the upper Guadalupe River in the Comfort area and the Blanco River near the Clopton Crossing in Wimberley, both in the upper Guadalupe River Basin.[14] The Guadalupe-Blanco River Authority "lawyered up" and vowed to fight the development of the alternative projects in the upper Guadalupe River watershed.[15] Although discussions continued, neither the exchange project nor the alternatives adopted by the city were ever built.

In 1968, the Texas Water Plan called for the development of the Cibolo and Goliad Reservoirs in the San Antonio River Basin to meet water needs of the municipal and industrial users in the San Antonio area by 2020.[16] The San Antonio River Authority had already begun discussions with the Bureau of Reclamation regarding federal funding for the construction of the Cibolo Reservoir. The San Antonio City Water Board expressed a strong interest in participating in the project.[17] The San Antonio River Authority and City Water Board began discussions with Representatives Abraham "Chick" Kazen Jr. and Henry B. González to garner congressional support for the project.

The Cibolo project would have constructed a reservoir on Cibolo Creek in Wilson County just southeast of San Antonio with a firm yield of approximately twenty-four thousand acre-feet annually. The Bureau of Reclamation would pay for and construct the project under a contract with the San Antonio River Authority. The City of San Antonio would obtain approximately twenty thousand acre-feet of water annually from the reservoir, with the remaining four thousand acre-feet going to Karnes City and Kenedy in Wilson County.

In 1974, Congress appeared poised to authorize funding for the project, subject to the approval of the contract by the San Antonio City Council. However, the city had elected a new mayor, Charles Becker, and the trustees on the City Water Board had changed; John Schaefer, a local real estate developer, had become chair of the City Water Board Trustees. Mayor Becker opposed the project, and, in April 1974, Schaefer, only three months into the job, was called on to make a recommendation to the council regarding the position that the city should take on the pending congressional action. Schaefer, damning the project with faint praise and addressing the mayor indecorously as "Charlie," told the council that the board did not oppose the Cibolo

Reservoir but that it should be built after the construction of another project, the Applewhite Reservoir.[18]

The decision regarding whether to move forward with the congressional authorization prompted significant debate in the city council. Council member Lila Cockrell strongly supported moving forward with the Cibolo effort rather than waiting for the Applewhite project, which was only in the early stages of the planning process. "Time keeps marching on and we keep postponing and postponing. We still need the surface water and we still haven't got it," she stated.[19] Ultimately, the City Water Board notified Congress and the Bureau of Reclamation that the city was interested in the Cibolo project but would continue to explore other options.[20] Despite this less-than-enthusiastic support, Congress authorized the project in November 1974.[21]

In 1975, the water board told the council that it did not intend to pursue the Cibolo project but instead would begin negotiations with the Guadalupe-Blanco River Authority to lease water from the authority's Canyon Reservoir. At that point, the Cibolo project was relegated to the stygian fate of San Antonio surface water projects.

In the mid-1970s, the Guadalupe-Blanco River Authority faced the first annual payment on the project: $308,890.[22] Cities in the Guadalupe Basin had been reluctant to purchase Canyon Lake water, and the authority was not authorized by the legislature to raise revenues through taxes.[23] Accordingly, the Guadalupe-Blanco River Authority offered the City of San Antonio an opportunity to purchase thirty thousand acre-feet of water from Canyon Lake in 1976, with an option to obtain an additional twenty thousand acre-feet. However, the contract was controversial. Some opposed the contract because of their belief that the water would be delivered to the more affluent north side of the city and be used to support development there.[24] They favored the moribund Cibolo project, which would deliver water to the less affluent south and southeast side of the city.

On May 27, 1976, after approval by the Guadalupe-Blanco River Authority Board of Directors and the San Antonio City Water Board, the Canyon Lake water contract was presented to the San Antonio City Council.[25] Mayor Cockrell strongly supported accepting the contract. The chair of the City Water Board of Trustees, John Schaefer, told the council, "I think the consequences [of not approving the contract] could be disastrous."[26]

Opposition to the contract was led by Mayor Pro Tem Glen Hartman. He opposed the contract because it was a "take or pay" contract and there was no evidence that San Antonio would need the surface water being offered.[27] Council member Henry Cisneros, who would become mayor in 1981, also voted against the project. Cisneros explained that, before he made a decision on the Guadalupe-Blanco River Authority contract, he wanted an update on the status, cost, and timetable for completing the Cibolo Dam that Congress had authorized in 1974.

The city council rejected the contract by a 5-to-4 vote. Years later, Mayor Cockrell observed, "Had we gone ahead with it[,] as of now, in 1992, we would have spent $17 million to $18 million. If you compared that to all the money already spent on the (now halted Applewhite Reservoir), you could see we'd have made a wise investment."[28]

On November 15, 1977, the city council created the Water Resources Task Force, which comprised the City Planning Commission, Citizens Advisory Committee, and Technical Advisory Committee. The task force submitted its report to the city council in 1979.[29] The report included three principal recommendations: (1) implement a water conservation program; (2) acquire fifty thousand acre-feet of water per year in order of priority from the upper Guadalupe River Basin, the Applewhite project, or the Cibolo project; and (3) establish a regional conservancy district to implement a "total management plan." The regional conservancy district would allocate Edwards Aquifer water and manage the aquifer, including implementing a strategy for conjunctive management of both surface water and groundwater. The report recognized that legislation would be needed to create such a district. Finally, the report recommended that negotiations with the Guadalupe-Blanco River Authority be renewed and that a regional forum be established to discuss the recommended strategies, with the Edwards Underground Water District taking the lead in the forum.

After discussing the recommendation, the San Antonio City Council on July 19, 1979, approved by a vote of 9 to 1, a three-part management plan that included conservation, recycling, and the construction of a surface water reservoir in Bexar County known as the Applewhite Reservoir.[30]

The Applewhite Reservoir was a project that the city had been discussing since the early 1970s.[31] It was expected to increase the water supply for the city by fifty thousand acre-feet. In June 1981, when the permit for the Applewhite project was under consideration by the

Texas Department of Water Resources and approval very much in doubt because of a perceived ambivalence of the city regarding the project, the San Antonio City Council passed Resolution No. 81-34-64 by a vote of 7 to 4, reaffirming support for the Applewhite project.[32] Nonetheless, public support for the project, which was not strong to begin with, was beginning to wane.

In the history of failed attempts by San Antonio to develop surface water supplies, one can see the tensions developing between the city and the downstream interests, particularly the Guadalupe-Blanco River Authority, that were dependent on springflow to ensure surface water availability.

At a political level, the City of San Antonio was being balkanized into factions of those who accepted the premise that the city needed to develop surface water supplies and those who did not accept the premise, either because the threat to urban water security from growth and development was not viewed as real or imminent or because of the ready availability of inexpensive Edwards water.

In 1981, in addressing the controversy on the council regarding the Applewhite Reservoir, Mayor Cisneros told the city council, "Now, this City has been rife with factionalism and strife on the question of surface water. Those who wanted Cibolo supported Cibolo and nothing else. Those who wanted Canyon supported Canyon and nothing else. . . . We know we need surface water and yet we cannot get a Council to put together the votes to go with a surface water program. It's pure and simple."[33]

As we shall see, the city, the downstream interests, and others continued to come up with surface water alternatives—this time in the context of a region-wide, consensus-based effort that also included aquifer management. When that attempt failed, the tension from the earlier attempts resurfaced, the skirmishes stopped, and the water war began in earnest.

The Regional Water Resources Plan

In 1982, the City Planning Commission formed an ad hoc committee to review water planning issues. Consistent with a report the commission released in 1979, the committee recommended a detailed study of water needs and sources on a regional basis. The study would be undertaken in concert with the Edwards Underground Water District.[34]

The Texas Legislature had created the Edwards Underground Water District in 1959. Five counties—Bexar, Medina, Uvalde, Comal, and Hays—were included in the district, with each county having three members on the district board. The legislature authorized the district "to conserve, preserve, protect and increase the recharge of and prevent pollution of the underground water." But it did not authorize the Edwards Underground Water District to restrict the rights of landowners to pump water from beneath their land.[35]

San Antonio mayor Henry Cisneros and Robert Hasslocher, chair of the board of directors of the Edwards Underground Water District, worked together in the development of the study recommended by the City Planning Commission.[36] In November 1983 the city and the district signed a memorandum of understanding to jointly study the long-range water needs of the region and the alternatives for satisfying those needs.[37]

A technical advisory team was created to oversee the preparation of the study by a consulting group, CH2M Hill. The completed study was sent to the Edwards Underground Water District and the San Antonio City Council by the Technical Advisory Committee on March 21, 1986.[38] The study was frank about the consequences of failing to act:

> The Edwards Aquifer is now the sole source of water for the City of San Antonio and the primary water source for Bexar, Uvalde, Medina, Comal and Hays Counties. Recharge water entering the aquifer is pumped by many users, and the "overflow" emerges from springs that provide a major portion of the water in the Comal, San Marcos and Guadalupe Rivers. If current practices are continued, this "overflow" will cease permanently after the turn of the century, and the springs will go dry during drought periods before that time. Aquifer water levels will begin to drop, declining by over 140 feet in San Antonio by the year 2040.[39]

The Implementation Advisory Task Force was promptly formed to develop consensus recommendations based on the study to be considered by the city and the Edwards Underground Water District. The task force submitted recommendations in December 1986.

Early in 1987, the City of San Antonio and Edwards Underground Water District convened the Joint Committee on Water Resources, consisting of five members of the San Antonio City Council, headed by Mayor Cisneros, and five members of the Edwards Underground

Water District Board, chaired by Robert Hasslocher, to develop a plan for implementing the recommendations of the task force.

In March 1987, the city and the district adopted a joint resolution describing the principles and policies agreed to up to that point.[40] The purpose of the joint resolution was to inform the legislature of the efforts and progress made in developing the plan.[41] The key policy in the resolution was that the aquifer should not be overdrafted during periods of average rainfall, to ensure natural flows at the Comal and San Marcos Springs. The resolution also called for "new laws" to provide for conjunctive management of surface and groundwater to allow optimal use of these resources.[42] In addition, the resolution recognized the need for a plan to manage regional drought emergencies and agreed that the Edwards Underground Water District would seek legislative authority to develop and implement a drought management plan.

The Edwards Underground Water District approved the joint resolution by a vote of 14 to 1.[43] As the city council considered the resolution, members expressed concern about giving the Edwards Underground Water District more authority without first restructuring the board for the district. The council members' concerns regarding this issue were alleviated when the general manager of the district, Tom Fox, said the board would be willing to discuss a restructuring. The city council then unanimously approved the joint resolution.[44]

In 1987, the Texas Legislature enacted House Bill 1942, authorizing the Edwards Underground Water District to develop and enforce a regional drought management plan by September 1988.[45] Pursuant to an agreement struck in Uvalde in the parking lot of the First State Bank, owned by former Texas governor Dolph Briscoe, the bill was amended in committee to increase the Bexar County representation on the board in 1989 to six members while keeping the representation of each of the other four counties to three members each.[46] As a quid pro quo, the amendment allowed 10 percent of the residents of a county in the district to petition for a referendum to determine whether that county should remain in the district. A referendum would be held if the directors of that county voted unanimously for the referendum. As we shall see, this opt-out provision would have fatal consequences for the efforts of the city and the Edwards Underground Water District.

In October 1987 the composition of the Joint Committee on Water Resources was expanded to include one member of the Edwards

Underground Water Districts board from each of the five counties in the district and one representative each from the San Antonio, Guadalupe-Blanco, and Nueces River Authorities. The restructured joint committee then turned to developing a plan for managing water resources between 1990 and 2040.

The joint committee met every Thursday for more than a year to develop the Regional Water Resources Plan.[47] Mayor Cisneros was masterful in facilitating the discussions of the Joint Committee.[48] He carefully recorded on charts the issues on which agreement had been reached and those on which agreement had not be reached, which were reserved for later discussion. He repeatedly returned to the issues on which agreement had been reached to confirm that everyone was still on board. On issues that had not been resolved, he alternatively led, mediated, and persuaded until agreement on an entire plan was reached.

The plan included both a strategy to regulate the use of the aquifer and a strategy to develop and pay for alternative water supplies for the region. The architects of the plan based it on their analysis of the average recharge for the period of record at that time: 608,000 acre-feet per year.[49] It set as a goal eventually limiting the pumping of the Edwards Aquifer to 75 percent of average annual recharge or roughly 450,000 acre-feet per year during average recharge conditions.

The plan called for the allocation of water based on historical use. Originally, the joint resolution stated that the allocation for irrigated agriculture would be two acre-feet per acre based upon the number of acres irrigated during the historical period.[50] But the Regional Water Resources Plan itself did not specify any allocation for the irrigators. Instead, it simply said that irrigators would be allowed to pump the annual amount they needed to grow crops on the number of acres used at any time during the historical record.[51] It did not specify how that amount would be determined.

The Regional Water Resources Plan recognized that, even under average rainfall conditions, the region would suffer a water deficit by 2010 unless new surface water were developed and that any serious drought would "hasten the onset of the crisis."[52] To address this impending crisis, the plan called for water savings through conservation and water reuse. The plan also called for the development of Apple-white Reservoir with "all due speed" and for the eventual construction of one reservoir at Cibolo and two at Cuero to protect the region from severe drought after the year 2000.[53] The completed projects were projected to add as much as 245,000 acre-feet to the water supplies of the region.[54]

The costs of the plan components would be met as follows:

- An ad valorem property tax levied by the Edwards Underground Water District would be used to fund implementation of the groundwater withdrawal policy and the conservation program.
- Sewer use charges would be used to fund the wastewater reuse program.
- Area-wide water purveyor rates, water availability charges (hook-up fees), and groundwater withdrawal fees during times of relative abundance would be used to fund surface water development.[55]

Despite an apparent consensus among the diverse membership of the joint committee, the Regional Water Resources Plan had created tremendous controversy.[56] The agricultural community in the western part of the region fiercely resisted any management of the aquifer because of the private property rights associated with the water and the protection of those rights afforded by the rule of capture. On one occasion, Robert Hasslocher rode with Mayor Cisneros to a public meeting in Uvalde in a city car driven by Ronnie Torres, a member of the San Antonio Police Department. As they neared Uvalde, Cisneros asked whether to expect a difficult meeting. Hasslocher told him that feelings were running very high and that things could get nasty. Torres asked the mayor what he wanted to do. Before Cisneros could answer, Hasslocher said, "Just keep the motor running."[57]

Speaking to a group of seventy-five people at that meeting, Cisneros said, "Frankly, what we've said here today is that everybody go ahead and pump as much as we can. You will pump and we will pump and someday our children will say how could we do this to them." Charles Griffin, a director of the Edwards Underground Water District, responded, "The citizens of Uvalde County will not accept allocations for agriculture." In a classic example of understatement, the meeting was described as "heated."[58]

On July 7, 1988, the joint committee voted 9 to 0 with two abstentions to approve the Regional Water Resources Plan. It was endorsed by the three river authorities.[59] Foreshadowing things to come, however, the two abstentions on the joint committee vote were directors on the

Edwards Underground Water District board from Medina and Uvalde Counties, and a petition was beginning to be circulated in Uvalde County for a referendum to withdraw from the Edwards Underground Water District.[60]

Perhaps to quell the growing opposition in Medina and Uvalde Counties, Mayor Cisneros and Chair Hasslocher told the citizens of the region,

> In developing this plan, special notice has been taken of the often competing viewpoints of the three principal segments of our regional economy: the San Antonio metropolitan center, the agricultural sector, and downstream/recreation interests. In the past, these interests have often been pitted against each other, promoting a "winner take all" approach to the resolution of conflict. In contrast, this plan has been designed to protect and accommodate each of these concerns. As such it has inevitably, and properly, led to compromise. In arriving at these compromises, every possible consideration has been afforded to the public interest, individual property and business rights, the environment, and the projected needs of the region. Compromise obviously implies mutual concessions. It also suggests—and this plan has been developed in that spirit— mutual gains and benefits. It is the intent of this plan that its burdens and benefits be fairly and rationally distributed among all the parties involved.[61]

On July 28, 1988, the day after Mayor Cisneros announced that he would not run for another term, the San Antonio City Council approved the Regional Water Resources Plan by a vote of 9 to 1.[62] Subsequently, the board of the Edwards Underground Water District approved the plan by a 9-to-6 vote, with the board members from Medina and Uvalde Counties voting against it.[63] In a seemingly inconsistent statement, Mayor Cisneros described the vote as "decisive" but predicted that Uvalde County might withdraw from the Edwards Underground Water District. Rene Aelvoet, the Medina County representative on the joint committee, said he opposed the plan but predicted Medina County would stay in the district because pulling out, he said, "would be a disaster."[64] The plan was now clearly in jeopardy.

The failure to anticipate the magnitude of the problems in the western counties probably was not a case of failing "to read the street." Rodney Reagan, a district board member, attended the joint committee meetings and had made his strong opposition known to the committee. His opposition should have been a red flag because it was widely understood that, because of his close business relationships with former governor Dolph Briscoe, a rancher and lifelong resident of Uvalde, Reagan usually spoke for him, at least unofficially, on water matters.[65] According to Mayor Nelson Wolff, "Briscoe may not be at the table but believe me, nothing happens in those western counties without his approval."[66]

Hasslocher has said that the perilous future of the plan came as no surprise even before the vote of the district board. According to Hasslocher, the success of the Regional Water Resource Plan was very important to Mayor Cisneros, who had faith in his ability to persuade the region of the need to go forward with it. Cisneros's ability to sell the western counties on the plan would have been facing a tough challenge under any circumstance.[67] However, promoting the plan was made more difficult by the untimely death of Leslie Pepper, the district representative from Uvalde County on the joint committee. Pepper was a consensus builder, both on the committee and in Uvalde County, and he generally supported the plan. According to Rodney Reagan, Pepper was a "fine, fine man."[68]

Even though the city and the district had approved the Regional Water Resource Plan, they still had to go to the legislature to implement significant parts of it. Led by Mayor Cisneros, representatives of the joint committee attempted to bring the western counties on board, even offering to try to accommodate some of agricultural interests' concerns. The farmers' concern, however, was one of principle— in their view, they owned the groundwater, and the plan unlawfully took their water away from them by limiting, contrary to the rule of capture, the amount of water that they could pump.[69]

As a result of the furor over the plan, the board members from Medina and Uvalde Counties asked for a referendum to allow those counties to secede from the Edwards Underground Water District, as they were allowed to do under House Bill 1942. With an eye on the referendum that was only days away, the Edwards Underground Water District board voted 8 to 6 not to send any plan to the legislature.[70] Nonetheless, on January 21, 1989, Uvalde and Medina Counties voted to secede from the district and to create their own single-county districts.[71] The vote was 2,181 to 846 for seceding in Medina County and 3,120 to 305 in Uvalde County.

The loss of these two counties undercut the regional scope of both the Regional Water Resource Plan and the Drought Management Plan that the Edwards Underground Water District had adopted in 1988. It also diminished the stature of the regional district in future discussions regarding the Edwards Issue.[72]

In January 1989 the City of San Antonio, the Edwards Underground Water District, the City of New Braunfels, the City of San Marcos, the San Antonio River Authority, the Guadalupe-Blanco River Authority, City Public Service of San Antonio, and the City of San Antonio Water Board established a coalition to seek legislation authorizing the Texas Water Commission to regulate water use in the aquifer. Weir Labatt, a member of the San Antonio City Council, served as chair. The proposed bill would have given the Texas Water Commission authority to regulate pumping from the Edwards Aquifer in the region, including pumping from wells in Medina and Uvalde Counties.[73]

The proposal of the coalition was opposed by Uvalde and Medina Counties and the Texas Farm Bureau.[74] The battle in the Texas Legislature was contentious. At one hearing before the House Natural Resources Committee, more than three hundred residents of Uvalde and Medina Counties voiced their strong opposition to the coalition bill.[75] There was a lack of anything even approaching consensus among the parties, so no legislation with respect to water allocation in the Edwards Aquifer was enacted in the 1989 session. Instead, in May 1989, Lieutenant Governor Bob Bullock and Speaker of the House Gib Lewis established the Special Committee on the Edwards Aquifer to investigate issues concerning groundwater and associated surface water management in the region, with the hope that it might assist in resolving the controversy surrounding any proposed management plan.

In the absence of legislative action in 1989, the coalition supporting the Regional Water Resource Plan rapidly dissolved. Nonetheless, despite the failure of the plan, it was extraordinary in scope, addressing both alternate water supplies and aquifer management. Moreover, it recognized the need to move away from the rule of capture if the aquifer was to be protected. Further, it would have been one of the first instances in Texas where groundwater and surface water would be managed as an interconnected system. Finally, it was the first attempt to develop a regional consensus approach regarding the use of the Edwards Aquifer.

The region, however, was now fragmented and trust was ebbing. With opposition to the Applewhite Reservoir growing, the prospects for a surface water project for the city of San Antonio had become increasingly remote. Likewise, the prospects for creating a regional authority to manage the aquifer had diminished. Thus, the incentive for the downstream interests to continue to work with the City of San Antonio no longer existed in any significant way. Likewise, the differing opinions about preserving the rule of capture created a wide gap between agricultural communities and the City of San Antonio.

While it is doubtful that anyone expected the status quo to prevail in these circumstances, few participants in the matter probably anticipated that change would result from eight critters almost too tiny to see with the naked eye, a river that runs underground, and a pond full of catfish. But water in Texas was still part of the wild, wild West, and things were about to get rowdy.

Events That Changed the Scope of the Edwards Issue

After the failure of the Regional Water Resource Plan, three events dramatically changed the course of the Edwards Issue. First, on June 15, 1989, the Guadalupe-Blanco River Authority issued a notice of intent to sue for violations of the Endangered Species Act.[76] The notice, required by the Endangered Species Act to be sent at least sixty days prior to filing a citizen suit, brought the federally listed species into the debate over the use of the aquifer. The strategy from the perspective of the Guadalupe-Blanco River Authority was quite simple: if it were possible to get the court to order management of the aquifer to protect the federally listed species, the downstream surface water rights holders would be assured additional springflow to contribute to the Guadalupe River, particularly during droughts. In addition, the notice also raised the specter of federal intervention, already an anathema in Texas, sparking renewed efforts to resolve the matter within the region.[77]

Second, the Guadalupe-Blanco River Authority filed suit in Hays County against two hundred defendants asking the court to declare the aquifer to be an underground river and, thus, a "water of the State."[78] If the aquifer received formal designation as an underground river, the Texas Water Commission would have jurisdiction to regulate it without having to obtain new authority from the legislature.[79] If successful, the effort to redefine the aquifer would effect an end run on the extremely powerful influence of irrigated agriculture interests in the Texas Legislature.

The third significant event took place in March 1991, when a soon-to-be infamous catfish farm began operations in southern Bexar County. The catfish farm was owned by Ron Pucek from Alvin, Texas, and Louis Blumberg, an investor from New York. Under the rule of capture, the catfish farm was free to take as much water from the aquifer as it could put to a "beneficial use." The catfish farm well was producing about 45 million gallons of water per day—enough water to support 250,000 people, or about one-fourth of the population of San Antonio at that time.[80] The situation strongly reinforced for the City of San Antonio the threat that the rule of capture posed to its own access to the Edwards Aquifer water. The *Houston Chronicle* observed, "After four decades, it took Pucek to get San Antonio to change directions so quickly—to say to its neighbors to the east and west, we'll limit our pumping and, thus, possibly our growth."[81]

As a result of these events, serious attempts were made to resolve the Edwards Issue. Unlike earlier efforts, there would now be three distinct factions involved: the City of San Antonio, the downstream interests, and the agricultural interests. Moreover, the role of the Guadalupe-Blanco River Authority changed, as it had both threatened and brought litigation to attempt to force the issue to be solved. The introduction of federally listed species into the issue focused the debate on aquifer management more than on obtaining alternate water supplies and made the involvement of environmental interests a real possibility. The specter of federal intervention spurred discussions. But, at the end of the day, there were just too many interests, too much baggage, and too few tools to achieve resolution.

THE GUADALUPE-BLANCO RIVER AUTHORITY
UNDERGROUND RIVER SUIT

The Guadalupe-Blanco River Authority suit led to discussions among many parties, including the municipalities of San Antonio, New Braunfels, and San Marcos, the Edwards Underground Water District, San Antonio River Authority, Nueces River Authority, and Guadalupe-Blanco River Authority in the fall of 1989.

On August 17, 1989, the Edwards Underground Water District and San Antonio River Authority requested the initial meeting to see if the

Guadalupe-Blanco River Authority suit could be resolved and if the filing of an Endangered Species Act lawsuit could be avoided.[82] The initial meeting on August 23, 1989, was largely devoted to staking out the positions of the various parties.[83] Subsequent meetings were held on August 29; September 15, 21, and 27; and October 2, 9, and 20, 1989.[84] They focused on the litigation, using a settlement of the litigation as a vehicle for resolving the Edwards Issue, and related procedural issues.

The meetings were closed to the public.[85] A *San Antonio Light* article, however, provides the flavor of the meetings: "They meet at the Edwards office . . . filling the parking lot with Porsches and BMWs of prosperous lawyers. At one recent meeting the city [of San Antonio] alone was counted to have six attorneys present."[86]

A one-on-one negotiation between the City of San Antonio and the Guadalupe-Blanco River Authority took place on October 6, 1989. Weir Labatt, chair of the City Council Water Task Force, reported back to San Antonio mayor Lila Cockrell.[87] He said that the Guadalupe-Blanco River Authority issued an ultimatum requiring that its position be accepted "immediately" or the talks would be broken off. The demands were that: (1) the city must agree to the regulation of groundwater withdrawals, (2) regulation must be accomplished through the GBRA lawsuit rather than legislation, and (3) regulation must be accomplished under a state water concept rather than a private water concept. Mayor Cockrell distributed the report to the meeting participants, along with her view that she was "personally shocked" at the position of the GBRA, particularly with the "attempt to force an ultimatum without the other participants at the table" and the declaration of the authority that a lawsuit under the Endangered Species Act would be filed "within a two week period."[88] Things were not going all that well.

The next full meeting, held three days later, was tense and did not accomplish much.[89] At the end of the meeting, John Specht, the general manager of the Guadalupe-Blanco River Authority, confirmed that the authority intended to file suit in two weeks if progress was not being made.

At a subsequent meeting, on October 20, 1989, state senator Cyndi Taylor Krier discussed the plans for the Special Committee on the Edwards Aquifer that had been created during the previous legislative session.[90] Buck Wynne, chair of the Texas Water Commission, reported that the commissioners had a plan that they hoped could prevent the filing of the Endangered Species Act lawsuit. He indicated that he would be concentrating on springflow and central Edwards Aquifer interest groups; Commissioner John Birdwell would be working with the western interests, and Commissioner Cliff Johnson would be working on other state interests. Birdwell would be responsible for putting the plan down on paper.

At this point, the focus of resolving the disputes shifted from the Guadalupe-Blanco River Authority lawsuit to these other forums.

SPECIAL COMMITTEE ON THE EDWARDS AQUIFER

Although the Texas Legislature did not enact relevant legislation in 1989, it did establish the Special Committee on the Edwards Aquifer to investigate issues concerning groundwater and associated surface water management in the region. Senator Cyndi Taylor Krier and Representative Terral Smith co-chaired the special committee. Over the course of the next nineteen months, the special committee held nine meetings, including seven at which testimony was taken.

The committee appointed the Technical Advisory Panel in 1989 to review and study scientific data regarding the Edwards Aquifer. The overriding conclusion of the panel was that "appropriate technical expertise and legal authority should be vested in a single management entity to allow conjunctive management of the total water resources of the Edwards aquifer, the Nueces, San Antonio, and Guadalupe Rivers, and associated bays and estuaries." The panel further found that, to maintain springflow at Comal Springs during a recurrence of the drought of record, annual withdrawals from the aquifer should not exceed 250,000 acre-feet.[91]

In August 1990 the Special Committee on the Edwards Aquifer convened key stakeholders in the dispute and asked them to consider using a mediator to help resolve the conflict. The stakeholders chose John Folk-Williams to conduct the mediation. He met with the parties individually and collectively from September 1990 through February 1991.[92] The parties included representatives from San Antonio/Bexar County, Uvalde County, Medina County, New Braunfels/Comal County, San Marcos/Hays County, the Guadalupe-Blanco River Authority, and downstream interests. The US Fish and Wildlife Service, Texas Parks and Wildlife Department, and Edwards Underground Water District participated only as observers, and the meetings were closed to the public and press. There were to be six day-long meetings that included all of the stakeholders, as well as numerous meetings with individual or small groups of stakeholders. It was agreed in advance that the mediation process would end on January 31, 1991.

The mediation reached an impasse in January because of an inability to resolve the question of who would pay for alternative water sources. The mediator then issued a series of interim proposals aimed at achieving the requirements of the Endangered Species Act. However, consensus remained out of reach. The primary areas of disagreement were: (1) the degree of regional authority that should be exerted, (2) the degree of regional versus local control, and (3) how much each party should contribute toward development of additional water supplies. Weir Labatt, one of the lead negotiators for Bexar County, explained that his group would agree to pumping limits if they were imposed by a regional authority but that Uvalde County officials would not accept a regional authority. Putting a finer point on Labatt's view, Rodney Reagan, an irrigator and associate of former governor Briscoe, said, "San Antonio isn't committed to anything but getting a handout. . . . We're willing to do our part, but we're not going to do it with San Antonio." Finally, John Folk-Williams admitted, "I don't see the parties I've been negotiating with changing their positions and coming up with a consensus bill."[93]

The special committee submitted its final report to the legislature on January 8, 1991. Absent consensus, the committee voted unanimously not to include any recommendations.[94] Bills were introduced in both the House and Senate but were assigned to a subcommittee and left pending.

JOHN BIRDWELL'S EFFORTS TO NEGOTIATE
A REGIONAL COMPROMISE

As Texas Water Commission chair Buck Wynne had announced at the meeting at the Edwards Underground Water District in October, Commissioner John Birdwell had begun a series of meetings with individual interests to negotiate a compromise on an Edwards allocation strategy. In November 1989 Birdwell circulated a draft memorandum of agreement regarding a possible resolution of the Edwards Issue.[95] The draft proposed that the management of the Edwards Aquifer would be handled by three local underground water districts: the West District, comprising Medina and Uvalde Counties; the Central District, comprising all of Bexar County; and the East District, comprising Hays and

Comal Counties. The available water in the Edwards Aquifer would be divided among the districts, with some being reserved for spring-flow protection. The three districts would be responsible for allocating water within their jurisdiction. Disputes between the districts would be resolved by the Texas Water Commission.

Unable to get consensus on this or any other long-term proposal, Birdwell reported to the Special Committee on the Edwards Aquifer on February 26, 1990, that the greatest hurdle to consensus was the rule of capture, but he warned that, if the aquifer was allowed to go unmanaged, "there will be very serious consequences."[96]

Facing the possibility of the springs drying up in the summer of 1990, Birdwell was able to forge a tentative agreement on a short-term emergency management plan.[97] Like the Edwards Underground Water District Drought Management Plan, Birdwell's plan identified specific measures that would be implemented at each drought stage to reduce demand on the aquifer. The Edwards Underground Water District would enforce the plan.[98] It would apply to southern Hays County and all of Bexar, Comal, Medina, and Uvalde Counties. Birdwell warned, "As late as it is, we're doing the most we can do to protect Comal Springs. That's not to say . . . it won't go dry."[99]

The Emergency Management Plan was formally accepted on July 10, 1990, at a meeting attended by representatives of San Antonio, New Braunfels, and San Marcos, of Bexar, Hays, Comal, Medina, and Uvalde Counties, by irrigators from Medina and Uvalde Counties, and by Bexar County development interests.[100] The plan would expire on December 31, 1990, so the intention was to try to get a long-term plan in place before December 31. On July 5, 1990, the City of San Antonio enacted an emergency action plan, as requested by the Texas Water Commission.[101] The Edwards Underground Water District Board of Directors enacted the plan on July 11, 1990.[102]

On July 3, 1990, Birdwell asked the US Fish and Wildlife Service to review and comment on the Emergency Action Plan. In response to Birdwell's request, Michael Spear, director of Region 2 of the US Fish and Wildlife Service, said that the plan "falls short in preserving flows in Comal Springs for the endangered fountain darter." Spear explained that "the more stringent water reduction measures in the plan . . . do not come into effect until the water level in J-17 well reaches 612 feet mean sea level, which is after Comal Springs cease flowing (approx. 619 feet mean sea level)." Spear also expressed concern because many of the reduction measures were not mandatory. He concluded, "[We] cannot emphasize too strongly that the interim plan has a long way to go before it meets the requirements of a long-term solution."[103]

Birdwell responded to Spear's letter on August 3, 1990. He told Spear that efforts "are under way to implement the plan and to develop a long-term solution to water management problems in the area." Notwithstanding Spear's comments, Birdwell opined that "I feel the Emergency Action Plan adequately addresses significant reduction of nonessential water uses." The long-term solution was never negotiated by Birdwell. The urgency for the long-term plan may have been lost because, as Birdwell explained to Spear, the region had received "significant rainfall" and the "water levels in the J-17 index well have risen to near pre-drought level and spring flows have increased as well."[104] Birdwell died on August 6, 1991, without having made any significant additional progress on a long-term plan.

Rejection of the Applewhite Project

After the San Antonio City Council initially approved the construction of the Applewhite Reservoir, design work and permitting began. The City Water Board received the state permit for the project from the Texas Water Commission in 1982.[105] The US Army Corps of Engineers began processing the permit application to discharge dredge and fill material as required by section 404 of the Clean Water Act. It completed a draft environmental impact statement for issuance of the permit, but the final environmental impact statement and issuance of the permit awaited a formal statement from the city that it intended to proceed with the project.[106] In 1988 the city authorized the actual construction of the Applewhite Reservoir by a vote of 8 to 3.[107] Construction began soon after a section 404 permit was received from the ACOE on August 28, 1989. However, opposition to the project did not go away.

The leaders of the opposition to the Applewhite Reservoir included Kirk and Carol Patterson, who would later be very active in the Edwards Aquifer Recovery Implementation Program. The Pattersons had been involved in water issues for more than twenty years. They opposed the construction of reservoirs and instead advocated constructing additional recharge structures and wells that would augment springflow at Comal and San Marcos Springs.[108]

In early 1991, the city received a petition with enough signatures to force an election on continued construction of the Applewhite Reservoir. There were questions, however, about the legal status of the petition because it sought to force the abandonment of a project on which money had already been spent.[109]

After unanimously rejecting an ordinance to abandon the project, the San Antonio City Council voted 7 to 2 to have it placed on the ballot of a citywide election to be held on May 4, 1991. Voters defeated the proposition by a narrow margin, 63,258 to 59,833. The city had already spent $28 million on the Applewhite project and would have to spend almost $12 million more to abandon it.[110]

2 : JOHN HALL AND THE EDWARDS UNDERGROUND RIVER

If I have seen a little further it is by standing on the shoulders of Giants.
— Isaac Newton to Robert Hooke (1676)

ll of the historical efforts to resolve the Edwards Issue are important to the ultimate success of the Edwards Aquifer Recovery Implementation Program (EARIP). However, one effort stands out because of how close it came to succeeding and because it had a direct impact on subsequent legislation. That effort was made in 1991–92 by John Hall, who had recently become chair of the Texas Water Commission. Because of the importance of this effort to subsequent events, it is discussed separately, and in detail, in this chapter.

In November 1990 Ann Richards, a Democrat, was elected governor of Texas, an increasingly Republican, conservative state. She promised a "New Texas" and a more environmentally friendly approach by state agencies.[1]

In May 1991 Governor Richards appointed John Hall to the Texas Water Commission, and, in June, when Buck Wynne stepped down as chair, she selected Hall to head the commission.[2] One of Hall's major responsibilities was to head the Environmental Agencies Transition Committee as it worked to merge the Texas Water Commission, Air Control Board, and the environmental programs of the Department of Health into the Texas Natural Resource Conservation Commission by September 1, 1993.

The six-foot-five Hall was the first African American to head the Texas Water Commission. Raised in Washington-on-the-Brazos, he graduated from Sam Houston State University and obtained a master's degree from the Lyndon B. Johnson School of Public Affairs at the University of Texas at Austin. He had worked at the US Department of Housing and Urban Development, as a staff assistant in the White House Office of Intergovernmental Affairs during the Carter administration, as a special deputy to US senator Lloyd Bentsen, and as senior deputy commissioner for Commissioner Garry Mauro in the Texas

General Land Office. Prior to his appointment to head the Texas Water Commission, Hall was director of the Lower Colorado River Authority Conservation and Environmental Division. He was well known as a workaholic and a problem solver.

From the start, Hall made it clear that he did not plan to be a passive member of the commission.[3] Spurred to action after the Sierra Club filed suit in 1991 against the Fish and Wildlife Service (FWS) for violations of the Endangered Species Act in the Edwards region, John Hall picked up the mantle of Commissioner Birdwell's efforts, telling a reporter, "The one thing he said to me prior to his death is . . . try to solve the Edwards issue."[4] In September 1991 Hall told stakeholders in the region that if they did not come up with a plan to manage the aquifer, he would ask the Texas Water Commission to do so on February 5, 1992.[5]

On September 13, 1991, Hall requested an expedited legal opinion from Dan Morales, the state attorney general, regarding the continuing validity of an attorney general opinion from 1941.[6] That 1941 opinion held that the predecessor of section 28.011 of the Texas Water Code, which authorized the Board of Water Engineers [the predecessor agency to the Texas Water Commission] to regulate privately owned wells, was an unconstitutional delegation of authority.[7] On November 4, 1991, Attorney General Morales overruled the earlier 1941 opinion and found that neither the current section 28.011 nor its predecessor was an unconstitutional delegation of power. In other words, the commission had *constitutional* authority to regulate privately owned wells; Morales's opinion, however, did not define the scope of the authority granted under section 28.011.[8] Nonetheless, it was widely viewed that his opinion opened the way for the Texas Water Commission to attempt to regulate the use of the Edwards Aquifer.[9]

Within days of the issuance of the attorney general's opinion, the mayors of San Antonio and San Marcos, with the support of John Hall, requested that Bruce Todd, mayor of Austin, and an Austin attorney, Tom Forbes, mediate the negotiations among the stakeholders to come up with a plan for managing the aquifer.[10] The negotiators began meeting in late November 1991.

In January 1992 the City of San Antonio and Bexar County came up with a proposal that Weir Labatt, the lead negotiator for the city, described as "hot as a habanero pepper." It included an offer to reduce withdrawals from the Edwards Aquifer in exchange for water from

Canyon Lake.[11] The proposal also involved paying farmers in Medina and Uvalde Counties not to irrigate crops during drought—in other words, a dry-year option. It also called for all users of the aquifer to help fund the dry-year option program and for irrigators to put meters on their wells. Agriculture representatives said the plan to pay irrigators not to pump might be acceptable, if the price was right, but that they would not agree to install meters on their wells. Curtis Lytle, president of the Uvalde County Water Conservation Association, stated, "When you look at a farmer who thinks he has a free right of capture, he doesn't want to put a meter on his well."[12]

Later, after some of the heat had apparently gone out of the proposal, a narrower five-point plan agreed to by the negotiators was presented to the commission on February 4. It called for: (1) a voluntary program to pay farmers in Medina and Uvalde Counties not to irrigate, (2) a public fund to help farmers switch to water-conserving irrigation systems, (3) emergency plans for cutting municipal water use in times of drought, (4) new rules to outlaw water waste, and (5) further negotiations toward a long-term water plan to be mediated by the commission. The Guadalupe-Blanco River Authority and New Braunfels and San Marcos objected to one aspect of the plan—failure to ensure that the Comal Springs would not go dry. In response, Labatt characterized their objections as a "kamikaze approach."[13]

At the commission meeting on February 5, John Hall announced that the Texas Water Commission was taking over efforts to design a management plan for the aquifer. He said the commission would publish the plan in early March if a settlement could not be reached. Hall further said that in two weeks the commission would publish a "very detailed" concept paper that outlined what the management plan would include.[14]

On February 18, 1992, the Texas Water Commission issued the concept paper. It consisted of an interim plan and a comprehensive long-term plan. The interim plan was intended to maintain flows levels at the J-17 index well at 632 feet mean sea level at least 80 percent of the time, "as determined by hydrologic simulations using the 1959 to 1989 period-of-record"; the benchmark data thus did not include any from the drought of record. The plan assumed that the 632-foot water level at the J-17 index well equated to a springflow of approximately 100 cubic feet per second at Comal Springs. The Texas Water Commission explained, "It should also be emphasized that the proposed spring flow maintenance criteria [are] an interim objective that should be replaced by a higher standard in a long-range water management plan for the region."[15]

The key elements of the interim plan included

- aggressively implementing water conservation and water reuse programs to reduce water use by 25 percent (i.e., a goal of reducing annual pumping to 450,000 acre-feet);
- setting up an emergency water conservation plan that would go into effect when the aquifer drops to certain levels;
- looking into the feasibility of springflow augmentation and enhancement strategies; and
- acquiring alternative water supplies, a particular goal for the City of San Antonio.[16]

The interim plan developed two options for emergency conservation plans: withdrawal reductions or a dry-year option program.

The concept paper also proposed developing a comprehensive long-range water management plan for the region. It stated that the "essential feature of a comprehensive plan is that it must provide for a higher degree of protection for aquifer levels and spring flow than that provided under the interim plan." The intent was to establish a blue ribbon task force to recommend a long-term plan by January 1, 1995, to be "substantially implemented" by 2002.[17]

Hall set final negotiations on the concept plan for March 10, 11, and 12, but he was not optimistic, saying, "I think all of the parties have convinced themselves that their positions will prevail in court."[18] When events proved his pessimism to have been well founded, on April 2, 1992, the commissioners sent the stakeholders a plan and gave them until April 14 to agree to it or the commission would impose the controls on its own.[19] The key elements of the "take-it-or leave-it" plan closely resembled the interim plan in the concept paper and included

- an interim springflow criterion of one hundred cubic feet per second at Comal Springs at least 80 percent of the time except during a severe drought such as the drought of record;
- aggressive water conservation and reuse programs;
- a drought management plan;
- commitment to effective local or regional enforcement of the plan with oversight by the Texas Water Commission;

- funding for studies on artificial springflow augmentation; and
- support for and participation in a process leading to the development of a long-term plan by January 1, 1995.[20]

One difference between the plan and the concept paper was that the plan chose the dry-year option (referred to as the Irrigation Water Conservation Program) coupled with municipal, industrial, and aquacultural withdrawal reductions as the emergency conservation measure. The measure included two significant provisions.

- If the water level in the J-17 index well on January 1 was at or below 649 feet mean sea level, 30 percent of irrigated land in Bexar, Medina, and Uvalde Counties would be withdrawn from irrigation and overall municipal, industrial, and aquacultural use would be reduced by 15 percent.
- If the water level was at or below 632 feet mean sea level on January 1, 50 percent of irrigated acreage would be withheld from irrigation and withdrawals by municipal, industrial, and aquacultural users would be reduced by 30 percent.[21]

Water users in Bexar, Medina, and Uvalde Counties would pay two-thirds of the cost of the Irrigation Water Conservation Program and the downstream users would pay one-third.

No agreement was reached on the "take-it-or leave-it" plan the Texas Water Commission proposed. Irrigators in the western part of the Edwards region rejected the plan outright. While leaving the door open slightly for future discussion, the City of San Antonio also rejected the plan, appearing to prefer instead to fight to protect the traditional water supply from state and federal control.[22]

While Hall was waiting for a response to his "take-it-or-leave-it" plan, Michael J. Spear, director of US Fish and Wildlife Service Region 2, met with Hall and submitted comments on the plan. Spear characterized the concept plan as "moving the process in the right direction." He encouraged the Texas Water Commission to obtain an incidental take permit, but he cautioned that the Fish and Wildlife Service could not approve an incidental take permit that would cause "jeopardy." He said that FWS had not determined the specific flow rate at which jeopardy occurs but that clearly jeopardy would have occurred when the springs ceased flowing. Spear explained that once "the Service further refines its opinion on the jeopardy level (*i.e.*, where above 0 cubic feet per second jeopardy occurs), all activities must ensure that the Springs are maintained at or above that level."[23]

Spear also pointed out that the Texas Water Commission model produced "overly optimistic results" and that the Fish and Wildlife Service would have to "assign a large margin of error to the actual results." On behalf of the FWS he concluded, "We applaud your repeated emphasis that the interim plan is only for a short-term period, and that the Commission intends to produce a 'comprehensive long range water management plan' which 'provide(s) for a higher degree of protection for aquifer levels and spring flow than provided under an interim plan.'"[24]

An attachment to the Spear letter contained more extensive comments. In them the Fish and Wildlife Service indicated that it was "of great concern" that 20 percent of the time the levels in the J-17 index well would still be below 632 feet when the drought of record was excluded from the model. Further, the FWS also found of "great concern" that, from the modeling data prepared by Texas Water Commission, it appeared that Comal Springs would cease flowing completely for one and one-half years during the time period from 1959 through 1989—a period that did not include the drought of record. This, the FWS said, would jeopardize the continued existence of the species.[25]

On April 11, 1992, the Texas Water Commission issued a resolution urging the Fish and Wildlife Service to consider the public health, safety, and welfare and the economic well-being of the Edwards region in establishing springflow goals at Comal Springs. The resolution requested that the FWS adopt one hundred cubic feet per second at least 80 percent of the time as the interim springflow goal at Comal Springs.[26]

On April 15, 1992, the Texas Water Commission took over the regulation of the Edwards Aquifer and issued proposed regulations for management of it. The commission asserted that it had jurisdiction because the aquifer was not groundwater but an underground river.[27] The proposed regulations lacked the specificity of the concept paper or the "take-it-or-leave-it" proposal, leaving the commission with significant discretion with respect to management strategies.

This action of the commission was not well received.[28] San Antonio mayor Nelson Wolff was surprised by it, saying, "I think they pulled a complete surprise on us. This is a totally different approach than what I was anticipating."[29] The Sierra Club and Texas Farm Bureau strongly opposed the plan.[30]

The City of San Antonio did not agree with the commission's determination that the aquifer was an underground river. Indeed, in May 1992, the city sued the Texas Water Commission over that designation.[31] Nonetheless, the city promptly began negotiations with the Texas Water Commission on the regulations that would be used to prepare legislation creating an agency to manage the aquifer.[32] On April 23, 1992, local radio and television stations broadcast John Hall's encounter with the San Antonio City Council as he tried, with limited success, to provide assurances that the commission would accommodate the council members' concerns when the final rules were made.[33] At a joint meeting of the San Antonio Water System Board of Trustees and the San Antonio City Council on April 29, the San Antonio Water System was directed to prepare comments on the proposed regulations.[34] Concurrently with drafting the comments, the San Antonio Water System continued its negotiations with John Hall.

On May 30, Hall announced that, although the commission intended to go forward with the final regulations, it would delay their implementation until after the legislature met in 1993 because of the "strong sentiment" in the legislature for creating a water management plan for the Edwards Aquifer.[35] Hall's announcement pleased Mayor Wolff. The delay in the effective date of the new rules separated the issue of the underground river concept, to which the city strongly objected, from the need to manage the aquifer, which the city supported.

On June 16, the San Antonio Water System Board of Trustees authorized the staff to send the comments on the proposed regulations to the city council. The next day, Cliff Morton, developer and chair of the San Antonio Water System Board of Trustees; Joe Aceves, San Antonio Water System president; Russell Johnson, an attorney for the water system; and USAA chair Robert McDermott reached a tentative compromise with Hall on recommended regulations.[36] According to the *Dallas Morning News*, "Mr. Hall said Wednesday's agreement 'absolutely' could provide the basis for aquifer legislation in January." On June 18, the city council informally expressed approval of the recommendations and comments. "After the briefing," the *San Antonio Express-News* reported, "[Morton] confirmed Water Commission Chairman John Hall had reacted with enthusiasm Wednesday to the proposals, indicating the commission and city would have a deal on the proposed management scheme if council approves the document."[37]

The San Antonio Water System Board of Trustees formally approved the comments on June 23. On June 25, 1992, as the city council considered formal approval, Morton reiterated, "Hall is in agreement with specifics of the proposal." The city council unanimously approved the recommended comments of the water system board of trustees.[38]

The comments were in the form of a twenty-one-page document and attachments, including a marked-up copy of the proposed regulations. The Aquifer Management Goals that framed the core of the comments included

- preventing long-term mining of the aquifer by ensuring that average annual discharge does not exceed average annual recharge;
- providing for regional water uses by establishing the firm yield of the aquifer at not less than 450,000 acre-feet per year in an effort to protect springflow by maintaining 100 cubic feet per second flows at Comal Springs 80 percent of the time and preserving some natural flow at San Marcos Springs;
- providing for management of the aquifer that is based upon objective and specific criteria and not subject to broad administrative discretion;
- allowing increased pumping to the extent that yield from the aquifer can be increased; providing reasonable access to excess water in the Edwards Aquifer over and above that required to supply pumping requirements and minimal environmental needs at Comal and San Marcos Springs;
- providing for implementation of a market for pumping rights from the Edwards Aquifer in order to encourage highest and best use of aquifer water;
- resolving the Endangered Species Act problem; and
- creating equitable cost-sharing to achieve regional goals and acquire additional supplies.[39]

Hall elaborated on the details of the agreement that had been reached. "What we have told the City of San Antonio," he said, "is that the firm yield will be 450,000 acre-feet[,] then it will go to 400,000 acre-feet in 15 years." Hall also explained that "on top of the firm yield (concept) you would have to put in a drought management plan focusing on San Marcos Springs."[40] Morton confirmed the details that Hall presented.

Soon after the compromise was reached, the Texas Water Development Board released a report that, among other things, modeled the impacts of the compromise on springflow during the drought of record. The model showed that, with the dry-year option offered by the Texas Water Commission, the Comal Springs would have no flow for twenty-five months and flow at one hundred cubic feet per second or greater 74 percent of the time during a repeat of the drought of record.[41]

On July 6, the Texas Water Commission prepared a document providing its "current views" regarding the water management regulations.[42] The commission's views were consistent with understandings that had been reached with the City of San Antonio. According to the document, all wells, except for exempt domestic and livestock wells, would be metered. Overall withdrawals would initially be limited to 450,000 acre-feet per year. Within fifteen years, water withdrawals would be reduced to 400,000 acre-feet per year. The fifteen-year delay in reducing the cap to 400,000 acre-feet was to allow water utilities an opportunity to move to alternative water supplies.[43] An additional 88,000 acre-feet of water would be allocated but would be available only when the water level at the J-17 index well was above 666 feet mean sea level.

The dry-year option, and the costs associated with it, had been dropped.[44] If the aquifer levels at the J-17 index well fell below 619 feet mean sea level, water use would be reduced to 350,000 acre-feet. The regulations also required the City of San Antonio to implement strategies to "further reduce stress on the aquifer and springs." These strategies included the possibility of diverting some rights to Edwards water from the Guadalupe River downstream of Comal and San Marcos Springs. Individual rights to use water from the aquifer would be quantified and transferable to provide the basis for a "market-based water transfer system." It was reported that the deal would result in the San Antonio Water System and others getting their average historical allocation of water.[45]

The commission asserted that the regulations "will provide as much protection as is humanly possible given the fact that a repeat of the drought-of-record is a natural phenomenon over which human beings have no control" and that the likelihood of a recurrence was "remote." Hall told reporters, "My view has always been that you don't always need the firm yield pegged at the drought of record."[46]

The Texas Water Commission now claimed that modeling results showed that the compromise would assure "a minimum continuous flow of 100 cubic feet per second at Comal Springs at all times under hydrological conditions that existed from 1958–1990," that is, excluding the drought of record. Steve Cullinan, the Fish and Wildlife Service Region 2 hydrologist, had noted in an earlier meeting with the Texas Water Commission that, to achieve this continuous minimum flow, the model had to make the assumption that the aquifer was full when the drought of record ended. According to Cullinan, that approach erred "on the side of water users."[47]

Hall met in Hondo with fifty Medina County irrigators on July 6 to answer questions and hear comments on proposed regulations.[48] The next day he and five staff members flew to Albuquerque to present the current views of the commission regarding the water management plan to Michael Spear and discuss the next steps that the Texas Water Commission would take.[49] Spear told reporters, "What John Hall is doing is to develop a plan that takes into account the needs of the people of Texas and the requirements of the Endangered Species Act." Spear declined to comment to the press on the details of the compromise plan but said the Fish and Wildlife Service was "going to have to respond to the plan as a whole."[50]

The compromise plan was rejected by agricultural interests, the Sierra Club, and the Guadalupe-Blanco River Authority. The agricultural community generally continued to oppose any management plan that would limit its ability to pump from the aquifer. Hall, however, had been meeting with irrigators to try to find solutions that would bring them on board with the compromise plan. The meetings, particularly in Uvalde County, were not always friendly. The *Uvalde Leader-News* challenged John Hall and John Specht to "climb into the same tube and run the Edwards River."[51]

On May 19, 1992, representatives of the Medina County Water Protection and Conservation Association met with Hall at his office in Austin to discuss the proposed rules.[52] They suggested to Hall that an allocation of two acre-feet of water per acre of historically cultivated cropland might be tolerated, at least in Medina County. Subsequently, they told Hall in a letter that a poll showed that 90 percent of their members "felt that two acre-feet of water was sufficient."[53]

Reinforcing this suggestion, the Medina County Underground Water Conservation District adopted rules that set an irrigation limit of two acre-feet per year per irrigated acre, with certain exceptions.[54] Hall said that he also had one-on-one meetings with agricultural interests, including a meeting with former governor Briscoe in which the two-acre-foot allocation was discussed as a possible basis for consensus.[55]

Stuart Henry, the attorney for the Sierra Club, said, "We're not going to agree to any management scheme that allows Comal Springs to dry up. I think we can all agree that this plan will not only dry up Comal Springs, but also San Marcos Springs."[56] The Guadalupe-Blanco River Authority, which had espoused the notion that the Edwards Aquifer was an underground river, rejected the compromise because "you don't just simply ignore the drought of record. You can't rationalize it away by saying it occurs every 200 or 300 years."[57]

On August 19, 1992, the US Fish and Wildlife Service responded to the water management plan prepared by the Texas Water Commission. Spear began by acknowledging that the plan was "a major and positive step forward by the State of Texas." He opined that if certain modifications were made, the plan could increase protection and assurances of flows at San Marcos and Comal Springs and "provide a sound basis for resolving endangered species issues." He explained that the FWS believed that "there is a high probability of uninterrupted flow at San Marcos and Comal Springs if the proposed plan is implemented subject to our recommended changes."[58]

Spear pointed out that, even with full implementation of the plan, there was the possibility that some "take" of listed species might occur. To address this issue, he suggested that the State of Texas, or an appropriate regional management agency, apply for an incidental take permit for a term of twenty years. Spear then stated, "Based on current data, the following provisions would be required as part of the HCP [habitat conservation plan]." Spear's letter outlined the required provisions. Although dressed up as "recommended changes" or required provisions to obtain the incidental take permit, the provisions were in fact virtually identical to what had been proposed after discussions with the City of San Antonio, what had been discussed with Spear on July 7, and what would appear in the final rule about a week later.[59]

On the day that Spear wrote to John Hall, Spear explained to the press, "We don't believe we can save endangered species from all occurrences, but I don't believe fish would have survived a drought as severe as the one in the '50s anyway."[60] Judge Lucius D. Bunton, however, found that "the Comal Springs would not have dried up in the drought of record but for human withdrawals."[61] Moreover, modeling demonstrated that, at the Comal Springs during a repeat of the drought of record, the lowest flows that would have occurred without any pumping would have been slightly below three hundred cubic feet per second—well above the flows that would cause either "take" or "jeopardy."[62]

The Texas Water Commission presented the proposed final rule on August 26, 1992, and set September 9 as the date for a meeting to decide on the adoption of the final rule. John Hall explained at the August meeting that "it is hoped that the lawmakers will use the commission plan as a framework to build on."[63]

After the August 26 meeting, San Antonio mayor Nelson Wolff told a news conference in San Antonio, "We can live with these rules. We've come a long way." He said that the Texas Water Commission took into account concerns expressed by San Antonio after the first rules were proposed in April. "The city can," he said, "walk arm in arm with the Texas Water Commission to the Legislature."[64]

At the hearing on the adoption of the final rule, San Antonio, New Braunfels, and San Marcos supported the proposal. Vocal opposition came from agricultural interests that characterized Hall's actions as robbing "landowners of property rights" and implied Hall was a "self-serving Bolshevik." Billy Clayton, former Texas House Speaker turned lobbyist, called the rules "un-American and un-Texan." Nonetheless, the Texas Water Commission unanimously adopted the proposed rule.[65]

In the preamble to the final rule, the Texas Water Commission acknowledged the pending *Sierra Club v. Babbitt* lawsuit over violations of the Endangered Species Act and asserted, "The water management plan contained in these rules is intended, among other things, to provide a basis for a resolution by the state of the issues raised in that lawsuit. This plan allows for the necessary planning and preparation, including time to develop alternative sources of water supply."[66]

As had been agreed with the City of San Antonio, the rules required that, when the elevations in the J-17 index well fell below 666 feet, the total water pumped would be restricted to 450,000 acre-feet. Within fifteen years, this water use limit would fall to 400,000 acre-feet. If the aquifer levels at the J-17 index well fell below 625 feet mean sea level, water use would be reduced to 350,000 acre-feet. Initial stages of the reduction were to be implemented when the water levels in the J-17 index well fell to 649 feet mean sea level. When the levels in the J-17 index well fell to 640 feet mean sea level, the Texas Water Commission would consult with the US Fish and Wildlife Service and Texas Parks and Wildlife Department regarding any actions to be taken in response to the potential emergency. The commission left open the possibility of modifying the pumping reduction and providing "additional protection for aquatic and wildlife habitat, if necessary."

All non-exempt wells were required to have a metering device installed. Permits for withdrawals were to be based on historical use. To the extent the water was available for appropriation, each existing user would receive an amount equivalent to the "maximum actual beneficial use of water without waste" during any one of the calendar years beginning January 1, 1982, through April 15, 1992. If an existing user had operated a well for three or more years during the historical period, that user would receive the average amount withdrawn for beneficial use, without waste, during the historical period. A two-acre-foot allocation for agriculture was not included in the rule.

Each applicant would have to submit a drought management plan setting out the measures used to achieve the 350,000-acre-foot withdrawal limitation. In addition, each existing user authorized for 1,500 acre-feet or more of water per year would have to prepare a water management plan. As predicate for a long-term strategy, that plan would have to contain, among other things, a study identifying feasible alternative sources of water supply, the reuse of water, and the steps and time schedule for the implementation of the water plan.

The Texas Water Commission delayed implementation of the rule until June 1, 1993, to allow the legislature to come up with a solution of its own. In anticipation of possible legislative action, the rules allowed the commission to delegate its authority to another jurisdiction having the authority to implement the regional water management plan.[67]

As soon as the Texas Water Commission asserted jurisdiction over the Edwards Aquifer in April, agricultural interests, acting through the Texas Farm Bureau and other irrigators, filed suit in state district court in Austin seeking an injunction to stop the Texas Water Commission actions. Two days after the final rules were adopted, the Austin district court acted, invalidating the designation of Edwards Aquifer as an underground river and blocking the implementation of the final rules.[68] Commission chair Hall said that his agency was likely to appeal the ruling.[69] In announcing the plans for the appeal, Hall said, "Farmers' opposition to the reasonable (water management) plan we have put forth is a virtual invitation for federal marshals to come to Texas and regulate water supplies with the compassion of the Internal Revenue Service and the efficiency of the Postal Service."[70]

The battle over John Hall's attempt to assert jurisdiction over the Edwards Aquifer did not end when the district court invalidated the rules.[71] Texas agriculture commissioner Rick Perry accused Hall and the Texas Water Commission of conspiring with federal authorities to try to take control of the Edwards Aquifer. He said, "Now we find actions indicating that the threatened federal intervention was at least partly the commission's own creation. The commission told the Fish and Wildlife Service what to direct the commission to do[,] creating a false hammer to force through their own management plan. It would be reprehensible for a state official to secretly conspire to undermine the sovereignty of the state and invite federal control of our water supply in order to promote their own agenda." Hall characterized Perry's comments as "ridiculous" and "absurd." He explained that if "Rick Perry would devote a fraction of the energy, imagination and fanatical determination he has spent in trying to wreck the progress we've made, progress that is finally being made on a serious problem, which is toward solving the Edwards problem, that problem would be solved today."[72]

Hall further claimed that Spear's August 19 letter demonstrated that, through negotiations, he was able to have the Fish and Wildlife Service back off from its demand for continuous flows at the springs.[73] One newspaper reported that "the wildlife service's endorsement is a 'big deal' because the federal agency this year had urged that annual pumpage be cut to 200,000 acre-feet. In March, the Service said the Commission's plans were going in the right direction but inadequate."[74]

Alisa Shull, branch chief in the Austin field office of the Ecological Service (part of the Fish and Wildlife Service) and the person who had a major role in drafting the August 19 letter, said that there was no intention to signal in that letter that continuous minimum flows would not be required to obtain an incidental take permit.[75] Indeed, subsequently, Spear testified at the trial in the Sierra Club case that, to obtain an incidental take permit, the Texas Water Commission would have to demonstrate that the plan "will not take flows below zero."[76] Spear said that he did not "negotiate" with Hall regarding what any habitat conservation plan might have to contain.[77] In his discussions with Hall, Spear believed that Hall's major objectives were to be sure that the Fish and Wildlife Service was serious in its professed willingness to take over the management of the aquifer and to determine what would have to be included in an agreement that would allow the management of the aquifer to remain in Texas.

Spear also indicated that the August letter was simply the beginning of the discussions of a possible habitat conservation plan and that substantive discussions would have to await the submission of an actual plan. He explained that, as he stated in his March 26, 1992, letter, to obtain an incidental take permit the Texas Water Commission would have to ensure that the pumping did not cause jeopardy. However, he said that the 350,000-acre-foot requirement for the drought management plan ultimately may have been an acceptable interim target until long-term measures in the plan could be implemented.

Consistent with Spear's view that the 350,000-acre-foot requirement would be simply an interim measure, the preamble to the regulations promulgated by the Texas Water Commission recognized that the regulations were designed to allow "the necessary planning and preparation, including time[,] to develop alternative sources of water supply."[78] That the compromise was intended only as an interim measure is also supported by the plan filed by the Texas Water Commission in *Sierra Club v. Babbitt* just a short five months later that contained short-, intermediate-, and long-term measures to avoid jeopardy. The 350,000-acre-foot withdrawal plan was an element of the short-term measures in that plan.

Because it represents such a sea change from the position of the Fish and Wildlife Service in Spear's March letter, Spear probably intended the letter of August 1992 only to support Hall's efforts to get a regulatory authority in place. One goal of the City of San Antonio was ensuring that any plan would resolve the Endangered Species Act issue. According to water system officials, "Obviously, the management plan adopted for the Aquifer must provide the City and other users assurance that they can use the Aquifer under the plan without interference or regulation under the Endangered Species Act."[79] Indeed, at the trial in the Sierra Club case, Spear conceded that the purpose of his August 19 letter was "to begin to give . . . the people of Texas a sense of confidence that this was not an intractable problem."[80]

Regardless, John Hall deserves credit for attempting to resolve the most vexing problem—the lack of any agency with the authority to regulate the aquifer and to stave off the imminent trial in Judge Bunton's court. Hall did not appear to have been interested in expanding the jurisdiction of the Texas Water Commission or blazing new frontiers in the question of what constituted an underground river. Everything indicates that he and the commission would have been content to have the legislature establish a regional agency to regulate the aquifer. He was indeed, to repeat, a man well known as a problem solver.

Like the Regional Water Resource Plan, the plan drawn up by the Texas Water Commission came tantalizingly close to resolving the Edwards Issue, only to fail largely due to the opposition of agricultural interests. Looking back, Hall said that including the two-acre-foot allocation in the rule may have been the key to reaching a consensus.[81] Luana Buckner, who was heavily involved in the debate in 1992 on behalf of Medina County aquifer users, said she did not think including the two-acre-foot allocation in the final rule would have made a difference; the sentiment for the rule of capture was just too strong, particularly in Uvalde County.[82]

Even if you could not ride a tube down the "Edwards River," the efforts of the Texas Water Commission provided the framework for subsequent legislation that would be needed to address the decision of the court in the Sierra Club case.

3 : JUDGE LUCIUS BUNTON AND
SIERRA CLUB V. BABBITT

> I speak for the trees, for the trees have no tongues.
> — Dr. Seuss, *The Lorax* (1971)

On April 12, 1990, while the Edwards region was still in severe drought, the Sierra Club issued a notice of intent to sue with respect to violations of the Endangered Species Act. On May 19, 1991, within days of the failure of the Applewhite project and with the Texas Legislature showing no inclination to act during the 1991 session, the Sierra Club filed suit in the US District Court for the Western District of Texas against the US Fish and Wildlife Service under the Endangered Species Act for failing to protect the federally listed species in the Comal and San Marcos Springs.[1] The case was assigned to Judge Lucius Bunton in Midland, Texas.[2]

Judge Bunton grew up in Marfa in Presidio County, Texas. He was appointed to the bench in 1979 by President Carter and gained a reputation as a hard-driving, no-nonsense judge who was unafraid to make difficult decisions.[3] He had an interesting, dry sense of humor and a great deal of impatience with long-winded lawyers. According to an Austin newspaper article, "Bunton had even been known to use a squirt gun on lawyers who were testy or too long-winded." In a now legendary *San Antonio Express-News* photograph, Judge Bunton posed, barefoot and in his robes, while appearing to walk on water.[4]

The Sierra Club made two basic allegations regarding violations of section 9 of the Endangered Species Act. It alleged that the Fish and Wildlife Service was responsible for the take of listed species by: (1) failing to impose pumping restrictions to maintain necessary springflows and (2) failing to develop and disseminate information regarding the springflows necessary to protect the species. After the federal government asserted that it had no authority to impose pumping restrictions, the Sierra Club amended its complaint to strike its claim that the Endangered Species Act required the FWS to regulate pumping from the Edwards Aquifer.[5]

Negotiations continued on legislation that could be introduced in the 1993 legislative session.[6] Meanwhile, the court ordered a four-day non-jury trial to begin on November 16, 1992. The trial ended promptly on November 19, 1992. True to his reputation, Judge Bunton wore a yellow hard hat into the courtroom on the last day of trial. Emblazoned on the hard hat was a bolt of lightning that he said "stands for lightning fast decision."[7]

Following the trial, the court ruled in favor of the Sierra Club on February 1, 1993.[8] The judgment set out two basic requirements: (1) the Fish and Wildlife Service had to make formal determinations regarding the minimum flows necessary to avoid "take" and "jeopardy" and (2) the Texas Water Commission had to submit a plan to ensure that the springflow determinations would not fall below the rates established by the FWS. The Texas Water Commission actually asked the court to be assigned the latter task.[9]

In what was the most significant part of the judgment, the court stated that it would allow plaintiff and plaintiff-intervenors to seek appropriate relief after May 31, 1993, when the legislative session was scheduled to end, "*if the State of Texas does not have in effect at such time . . .* a regulatory system pursuant to which withdrawals from the Edwards Aquifer can and will be limited to whatever extent may be required to avoid unlawful takings of listed species, any appreciable reduction in the likelihood of survival and recovery of listed species in the wild, and any appreciable diminution of the value of critical habitat for the survival and recovery of the species, even in a repeat of the drought of record."[10] In short, Judge Bunton made it clear that he expected the Texas Legislature, then in session, to act immediately to protect the species or the court would do so.

The "Take" and "Jeopardy" Determinations

The decision of the court repeatedly emphasized the importance of continuous minimum springflows in protecting the listed species: "The endangered or threatened species living either at or downstream of the Comal and San Marcos Springs or in the Edwards rely on adequate and continuous natural flows of fresh water through the Edwards and exiting from the natural spring openings as an environment for their survival." Judge Bunton equated those minimum flows with the jeopardy levels: "At a minimum, the objective requires pumping controls to avoid jeopardy to the species by maintaining aquifer levels which assure a minimum spring flow at Comal Springs." The court specifically found limiting "pumping to an average of 200,000 acre-feet per year would provide some minimal continuous Comal springflows." The court rejected the contention that the firm yield of the Edwards Aquifer was 350,000 acre-feet per year: "pumping 350,000 acre-feet per year throughout a repeat of the drought of the 1950's will cause the Edwards to drop to levels far below the historic low of 612.51 feet mean sea level, dry up Comal Springs for years and San Marcos Springs for substantial periods of time."[11]

Judge Bunton found that the Fish and Wildlife Service had not identified the necessary minimum flows to be maintained to avoid take, jeopardy, and adverse modification of critical habitat for the listed species at Comal and San Marcos Springs.[12] He ordered the FWS to make these determinations within forty-five days. The court stated that the FWS "may at any time and from time to time modify any of its minimum springflow or Edwards Aquifer level determinations, based on available information and in the exercise of its best professional judgment."[13]

Judge Bunton established "minimum springflow findings" to serve as interim springflow findings until the Fish and Wildlife Service made the relevant determinations. He set the jeopardy level at the Comal Springs for the fountain darter at "some (as yet) undefined springflow or range of springflows greater than zero." He emphatically stated that allowing "the springs to cease flowing for *any* period of time, even during drought conditions, would pose an unacceptable risk to the continued existence of the Fountain Darter."[14]

The Fish and Wildlife Service made the determinations required by the court.[15] These determinations are summarized in the table. The response, however, was highly qualified. The service explained that because the "take" evaluation was conducted with far fewer data than are normally available, it was forced to base the determination on "best professional judgment" and that the determinations were conservative. It further explained that, as more information became available, the numbers it was providing might "change to more accurately reflect that best available scientific and commercial information."[16]

With respect to "jeopardy," the Fish and Wildlife Service reiterated concern regarding the "significant gaps in knowledge." It explained that these gaps resulted in a "conservative approach" regarding the flow estimates. It found that flow levels at Comal Springs could be reduced to sixty cubic feet per second for short time periods during cer-

SUMMARY OF THE US FISH AND WILDLIFE SERVICE DETERMINATION OF
MINIMUM SPRINGFLOWS (CUBIC FEET PER SECOND), 1993

Species	Take	Jeopardy	Adverse modification
Fountain darter in Comal	200	150	100
Fountain darter in San Marcos	100	100	100
San Marcos gambusia	100	100	60
San Marcos salamander	60	60	60
Texas blind salamander	50	50	N/A
Damage and destruction			
Texas wild-rice	100	100	100

tain times of the year without jeopardizing the continued existence of the fountain darter if a "very effective" program to control the giant rams-horn snail was in place and if there was the ability to control the timing and duration of low springflows.[17]

The Fish and Wildlife Service also found that short-term reductions in flow levels below one hundred cubic feet per second might avoid jeopardy for Texas wild-rice if: (1) exotic species (e.g., nutria) could be effectively controlled, (2) an aquifer management plan was implemented to control timing and duration of lower flows, and (3) the distribution of the species was improved throughout its historic range. However, it did not specify what flow levels might be acceptable if those conditions were satisfied.

The Texas Water Commission Plan

The Texas Water Commission submitted its management plan on March 1, 1993, as directed by the court. The commission stated that the plan would "maintain spring flow at Comal Springs, even in a recurrence of the drought of record, following its full implementation."[18]

The Texas Water Commission relied in its recommendations on the findings of the court that the droughts of 1984, 1989, and 1990 were "once in a decade" droughts.[19] It also indicated that it was "the probable repeat of *these* droughts, rather than the highly unlikely repeat of the 1950's drought, which represents the most immediate threat to the species."[20] Accordingly, it was the view of the Texas Water Commission that continued reliance on a 350,000-acre-foot annual rate of pumping "*during periodic drought* is absolutely necessary until additional water supplies are developed." The interim 350,000-acre-foot reduction during an episodic drought was not based on the needs of the species but rather on the Texas Water Commission's view that "an immediate reduction of pumping below that amount likely would create chaos for the region's population, unacceptable health and public safety risks[,] as well as an unprecedented economic crisis." The commission also stated that "significant additional water supplies must be brought on line over the next 30 years, both to protect the endangered species and to promote public health and safety." It found that because the drought of record was a two-hundred- to three-hundred-year event, it was "unlikely to recur during the next 30 years."[21]

Consistent with the above-stated views, the Texas Water Commission divided the recommendations into short-term (1993 to 2008), intermediate (2008 to 2023), and long-term (later than 2023) categories. The objective of the short-term recommendations was to provide continuous flow at Comal Springs during the reasonably anticipated conditions, that is, periodic droughts, and continuous flows at San Marcos Springs. The recommendations for the short-term period included

1. creating legislatively a local/regional management entity;
2. reducing annual pumping to 450,000 acre-feet;
3. developing an equitable system for allocating the water similar to the way surface water is allocated in the State;
4. having the managing entity apply for an Incidental Take Permit to allow takings "until enough additional water supplies can be developed to reduce aquifer withdrawals and to promote continuous springflow at all times";
5. launching or accelerating immediately planning efforts to allow the development of additional water supplies and other measures; and
6. implementing a "highly effective" Emergency Drought Management Plan that will reduce withdrawals to 350,000 acre-feet when water levels at the J-17 index well drop below 649 feet mean sea level. The 350,000 acre-feet reductions must be obtained by the time J-17 reaches 625 feet mean sea level.

The Emergency Drought Management Plan required consultation with the Fish and Wildlife Service when water levels at the J-17 index well fell to 649 feet mean sea level "to determine additional plans that could be implemented."[22]

The Texas Water Commission recommended that, during the intermediate phase, the region would continue the short-term measures but make additional movement away from total reliance on pumping and begin the transition to alternative supplies. To assist in achieving this recommendation, the commission recommended reducing the allowable reductions to 400,000 acre-feet by December 31, 2008.

After 2023, the plan required compliance with the "then-current" jeopardy determinations. The delay was recommended in light of the fact that it would take thirty years to complete various water-related projects. It stated that, by 2023, the aquifer pumping would be reduced to 200,000 to 225,000 acre-feet during dry periods by developing 480,000 acre-feet of additional water supplies.

4 : SENATE BILL 1477 AND THE CREATION
OF THE EDWARDS AQUIFER AUTHORITY

The next session of the Texas Legislature offers the last chance for
adoption of an adequate state plan before the "blunt axes" of Federal
intervention have to be dropped.
— *Sierra Club v. Babbitt*, "Amended Findings," para. 196.

Even before Judge Bunton ruled in the *Sierra Club v. Babbitt* case, plans were being made to introduce an aquifer management bill in the 2003 session of the Texas Legislature. Representative Robert Puente said he expected to sponsor legislation based on the Texas Water Commission's rules.[1] The City of San Antonio also was planning a legislative strategy to pursue.[2] In December, city officials met with Bexar County lawmakers, including Representative Robert Puente, to discuss that strategy.[3]

All sides hired lobbyists for the session. The San Antonio Water System even hired a political consultant to coordinate the seven lobbyists retained by the city. The San Antonio Chamber of Commerce formed a political action committee. The agricultural interests in Uvalde County and the Texas Farm Bureau retained former House Speaker Billy Clayton to lead their efforts in the session. Representative Leticia Van de Putte observed, "This is probably the 'lobbyist full-employment act of 1993.'"[4] Between the 1993 legislative session, the Sierra Club case, and the underground river issue, the luxury car dealers must have been doing quite well.

After the court issued a decision in the Sierra Club case on February 1, 1993, the activity in the legislature developed a sense of urgency because the court required that the state take action by May 31, 1993, to avoid possible federal intervention.

House Bill 1792
As promised, Representative Robert Puente, along with Representative Libby Linebarger, from Hays County, introduced House Bill 1792, which largely tracked the proposal of John Hall.[5] A companion bill, Senate Bill 1320, was introduced by Senators Gregory Luna,

Frank Madla, and Jeff Wentworth. Like the Texas Water Commission's underground river rules, House Bill 1792 called for withdrawals from the aquifer to be limited to 450,000 acre-feet per year until January 1, 2008, when the withdrawal cap would be reduced to 400,000 acre-feet. House Bill 1792 allowed additional withdrawals of up to 88,000 acre-feet, to be authorized on an interruptible basis through the issuance of a term permit when the water level at the J-17 index well was equal to or greater than 665 feet mean sea level.

The bill replaced the Edwards Underground Water District with a new regional authority to manage the aquifer: the Edwards Aquifer Water Resource Management Authority. This new authority was to have a nine-member board with two directors appointed by the City of San Antonio and one director each appointed by Bexar, Medina, and Uvalde Counties and by San Marcos and New Braunfels. One member would be appointed alternately from Kinney and Atascosa Counties. One director would be jointly appointed by Comal, Guadalupe, and Hays Counties. According to the bill, this authority would be subject to supervision by the Texas Water Commission.

House Bill 1792 directed the newly created authority to prepare a demand management plan for approval by the Texas Water Commission. Similar to the Texas Water Commission plan submitted to the court, the first phase of the demand management plan would be triggered when the water level at the J-17 index well was at 649 feet mean sea level; permitted withdrawals would have to be reduced to 350,000 acre-feet when the water level at the J-17 index well was at or below 625 feet mean sea level.

All non-exempt withdrawals would require a permit based on the maximum beneficial use during any calendar year in the historical period. If the total amount of water qualifying for a permit exceeded the withdrawal cap, the authority had to adjust the amount permitted to the water available, except that any existing user that had operated a well for three years would receive a permit for not less than the average water withdrawn during the historical period.

Aquifer users would pay management fees based on permitted rights. Special fees would be assessed against permitted aquifer users to pay for any permit reductions required to reduce the permit cap from 450,000 to 400,000 acre-feet. Consumptive and nonconsumptive water rights holders in the Guadalupe River Basin also would pay special fees needed to buy down the permits from 450,000 to 400,000 acre-feet. The special fees were to be apportioned equally between the aquifer users and downstream water rights holders.

Similar to the compromise reached by the Texas Water Commission and the City of San Antonio, House Bill 1792 would have allowed any permitted aquifer user to withdraw a portion of the water allotted to it from a diversion point on the Guadalupe River and that right would be senior to all other surface water rights in the basin.

House Bill 1792 drew strong opposition from the agricultural interests and the representatives of largely agricultural districts. Despite the efforts of Representative Puente, Representative David Counts of Knox City, chair of the House Natural Resources Committee, would not allow the bill out of his committee.

Representative Counts had been appointed to the chair by the newly elected House Speaker, Pete Laney, who was from Hale Center, an agricultural community in the Texas Panhandle.[6] The chair of the Senate Natural Resources Committee was Bill Sims, from San Angelo, a city with a strong agricultural base. Senator Sims had filed his own bill, Senate Bill 1370, that would have created an eighteen-county regional management authority but would not have authorized the agency to impose withdrawal caps. Obviously, agricultural interests were going to have an important role in putting together a response to Judge Bunton. The crux of the issue was going to be whether any response that could garner enough support could be completed by May 31.

Senate Bill 1477

During the session, while much of the attention was focused on House Bill 1792, Senator Ken Armbrister from Victoria, at the request of Lieutenant Governor Bob Bullock, had been meeting with the different interest groups in an attempt to forge an agreement. On April 19, 1993, the Senate Natural Resources Committee appointed him as a subcommittee of one to nail down the agreement. Armbrister met with various interest groups in what was described as "marathon bargaining sessions."[7] On April 27, those sessions bore fruit in the form of a compromise that appeared to have broad support.[8] Armbrister, however, admitted that agriculture did not "wholeheartedly" support the proposed legislation. However, Rodney Reagan, president of the Uvalde County Underground Water Conservation Association, was a little more direct: "This is absolutely a violation of people's constitutional rights to own property."[9]

On May 5, 1993, Senator Armbrister, along with Senators Gonzalo Barrientos, Jeff Wentworth, Judith Zaffirini, and Frank Madla, introduced Senate Bill 1477. This bill embodied much of the basic framework of House Bill 1792 but also reflected the compromises that had been reached in Senator Armbrister's meetings with the stakeholders. A committee substitute was quickly reported out of the Senate Natural Resources Committee on May 7 by a vote of 8 to 3. The negative votes had been cast by senators from rural areas who believed the bill did not go far enough to protect agricultural interests. Committee chair Bill Sims, from San Angelo, said, "It's still going to take their water away. They are going to have to pay to use their own water, and the people of San Antonio are not going to have to pay any more for it."[10]

The Senate passed the bill by voice vote on May 11, 1993. However, it still had to go to the House, where irrigators from Uvalde County and the Texas Farm Bureau had already vowed to defeat the measure.[11] The clock was ticking, and, as Robert Puente explained to me, as the legislative session progresses, the procedural issues can become as great an obstacle to passage of a bill as the substantive issues.[12]

The sponsor of Senate Bill 1477 in the House was Representative Ron Lewis, from Mauriceville, Texas. Although Representative Puente supported the measure, he had declined to sponsor the compromise legislation: "If I file a bill from San Antonio that has anything to do with water, it will get immediate scrutiny, immediate attention, immediate opposition to it no matter what it is."[13]

The Senate bill was amended extensively by the House Natural Resources Committee to reflect the views of the agricultural and private property interests. The amended bill was passed out of the committee on May 17 and was passed by the House on May 24.[14]

On May 27, not unexpectedly, the Senate rejected the amendments, and a conference committee was appointed. Prior to the conference committee meeting, Bruce Babbitt, secretary of the US Department of the Interior, sent a letter to the governor and other state officials expressing support for the Senate bill and criticizing the House version as one that would not meet Judge Bunton's requirements.[15] In conference, agreement was reached on a bill that contained most of the major positions in the version of the bill that was passed by the Senate.

The conference committee report was adopted on May 30, 1993, and the final bill was signed in the House and Senate on May 31. Governor

Ann Richards signed the bill on June 11, 1993, at a ceremony attended by Secretary Babbitt.[16]

Senate Bill 1477 created the Edwards Aquifer Authority.[17] The authority would have a nine-member board of appointed directors. The board would consist of three residents of Bexar County; one resident of Comal County or the city of New Braunfels; one resident of Hays County; one resident of Medina County appointed by the governing body of the Medina County Underground Water Conservation District; one resident of Uvalde County appointed by the governing body of the Uvalde Underground Water Conservation District; one person appointed in rotation from Atascosa, Medina, and Uvalde Counties; and one member appointed by the South Central Texas Water Advisory Committee.[18]

Senate Bill 1477 included three principal provisions regarding how the Edwards Aquifer was to be managed. First, it prohibited, with certain limited exceptions, withdrawing water from the aquifer without a permit from the Edwards Aquifer Authority. It also capped the amount of water that could be permitted but established guaranteed statutory minimum amounts that each qualified permittee would receive as part of the permit. Second, it required measures to be implemented that would ensure continuous minimum springflows to protect the listed species. Third, Senate Bill 1477 required the Edwards Aquifer Authority to prepare and coordinate implementation of a critical period management plan for periods of drought.

In addition, as an accommodation to agricultural interests, Senate Bill 1477 required all non-exempt wells to be metered, but the cost of the metering was to be paid by the new Edwards Aquifer Authority. The bill also established that withdrawal reductions in the Uvalde pool would be based on the J-27 index well. Finally, it based the fees that could be charged to an irrigator on the amount of water withdrawn at 20 percent of the fee charged to municipal and industrial users. By contrast, the fees for municipal and industrial users were to be based on the full amount of water that they were authorized to withdraw under their permits.

Senate Bill 1477 also provided that, unless the legislature voted to extend the terms of the Guadalupe-Blanco River Authority directors, the terms of all members of the board would expire on September 1, 1995.[19] This provision was apparently triggered by the actions of John Specht, general manager of the Guadalupe-Blanco River Authority.[20] Specht allegedly provided misleading information to the legislature and had a very heated confrontation with Senator Armbrister.[21] He was placed on administrative leave, and he subsequently retired from the authority. The legislature extended the tenure of the Guadalupe-Blanco River Authority board in 1995, and the provision was repealed.[22]

Four principal provisions of the act would have significant impact on subsequent events. For that reason we will now delve more deeply into the specifics of those four provisions: statutory minimums, withdrawal caps, continuous minimum springflows, and "critical period management" withdrawal reductions.

STATUTORY MINIMUMS

Senate Bill 1477 required the Edwards Aquifer Authority to issue permits with minimum pumping rights based on historic use and guaranteed specific withdrawal rights for qualifying users. Existing users could apply for an initial regular permit by filing a declaration of historical use from June 1, 1972, through May 31, 1993.[23] To the extent water was available, the authority was to issue permits based on an amount of water equal to the user's maximum beneficial use during any one calendar year of the historical period. The legislature set specific "statutory minimums" that the Edwards Aquifer Authority was to use in issuing permits: "An existing irrigation user shall receive a permit for not less than two acre-feet a year for each acre of land the user actually irrigated in any one calendar year during the historical period. An existing user who has operated a well for three or more years during the historical period shall receive a permit for at least the average amount of water withdrawn annually during the historical period."[24] The two acre-feet per irrigated acre allocated to irrigators was what the Medina County Underground Water Conservation District had placed in its rules and what some irrigators indicated they might accept in the Texas Water Commission's rules that were invalidated in September 1992.

WITHDRAWAL CAPS

Senate Bill 1477 directed the Edwards Aquifer Authority to limit the permitted withdrawals to 450,000 acre-feet per year. It further required the Edwards Aquifer Authority to prepare and implement a plan for reducing the maximum annual volume of water authorized to be withdrawn under regular permits to 400,000 acre-feet per year beginning January 1, 2008.[25] The plan had to be enforceable and include measures to promote water conservation and reuse, to retire water rights, and to achieve the necessary reduction levels. If, through studies and implementation of water management strategies, the authority determined that additional supplies were available, it could, in consultation with appropriate state and federal agencies, raise the withdrawal caps.[26]

To meet the withdrawal caps, the legislature directed the Edwards Aquifer Authority to make proportional adjustments to the amount of water authorized for withdrawal under the permits to meet the amount available. Each existing user, however, would be guaranteed its statutory minimum withdrawal amount.[27]

A conflict could and in fact did arise when the statutory minimum exceeded the withdrawal cap. In anticipation of just such a conflict, the Texas Legislature required that the cost of reducing withdrawals or retiring permits to get to the 450,000-acre-foot cap was to be borne solely by the pumpers. The cost of retiring the water rights to get from 450,000 to 400,000 acre-feet was to be borne equally by aquifer users and downstream water rights holders.[28]

Historically, the caps were intended to serve two purposes: (1) preventing mining of the aquifer by allowing withdrawals to exceed the average annual recharge and (2) encouraging the development of alternative water supplies. Judge Bunton's decision did not specifically address withdrawal caps. The 450,000-acre-foot cap was chosen in the Regional Water Resource Plan because it was 75 percent of the annual average recharge at that time. The concept of reducing the cap to 400,000 acre-feet in fifteen years was developed by John Hall and intended to force primarily the City of San Antonio to decrease reliance on the aquifer. The fifteen-year delay of the effective date was to give the city an incentive to begin developing non-Edwards water supplies promptly.

CONTINUOUS MINIMUM SPRINGFLOWS

With respect to continuous minimum flows, Senate Bill 1477 directed the Edwards Aquifer Authority, by June 1, 1994, to "implement and enforce water management practices, procedures, and methods to ensure, by December 31, 2012, that the continuous minimum springflows of the Comal Springs and the San Marcos Springs are maintained to protect the endangered and threatened species to the extent required by federal law." To satisfy this requirement, the Edwards Aquifer Authority was directed to require: (1) phased reductions in the amount of water that may be used or withdrawn by existing users or categories of other users or (2) implementation of alternative management practices, procedures, and methods.[29]

The statute called for the Edwards Aquifer Authority to begin to put together and implement a strategy for ensuring continuous minimum flows within nine months of the effective date of the act but did not require that they be fully effective until December 31, 2012. Allowing the Edwards Aquifer Authority until 2013 to fully comply with this requirement seems inconsistent with the importance Judge Bunton attached to such flows. However, Judge Bunton contemplated a two-step process. The ultimate solution would be the development of alternative water supplies—a process that obviously would take time. Until that was done, the court contemplated that an incidental take permit would be obtained pursuant to section 10(a) of the Endangered Species Act: "The ESA provides mechanisms to allow the State of Texas substantial time to reduce withdrawals from the Edwards in an orderly and non-disruptive manner. One of those mechanisms is a § 10(a) incidental take permit. The Federal Defendants are willing to grant the State a § 10(a) permit if, but only if, an adequate State Plan for pumping controls is adopted and its implementation reasonably assured. . . . The sooner Texas adopts an adequate plan and obtains a § 10(a) permit, the better."[30]

The need to ensure continuous minimum flows was the central theme of Judge Bunton's decision. His findings at trial made clear that withdrawals from the aquifer during drought would have to be limited to 200,000 acre-feet to ensure continuous flows from the Comal Springs. This finding echoed the conclusions of the work of the Technical Advisory Panel for the legislature's Special Committee on the Edwards Aquifer.[31] It is also reflected in the Fish and Wildlife Service's determination that the requisite minimum flow at Comal Springs was 150 cubic feet per second to avoid jeopardy.

Thus, at that time, it was clear what needed to be achieved to comply with federal law, absent a convincing case being made to the contrary. What the Edwards Aquifer Authority needed to supply were the measures to achieve compliance, and they were to begin putting those measures in place immediately.

Senate Bill 1477 required the Edwards Aquifer Authority to prepare and implement a critical period management plan before September 1, 1995.[32] It directed that the plan must: (1) distinguish between discretionary and nondiscretionary use; (2) require reductions of all discretionary use to the maximum extent feasible; (3) require utility pricing, to the maximum extent feasible, to limit discretionary use by the customers of water utilities; and (4) require reduction of nondiscretionary use by permitted or contractual users, to the extent further reductions were necessary, in the reverse order of the following water use preferences:

(a)   Municipal, domestic, and livestock
(b)   Industrial and crop irrigation
(c)   Residential landscape irrigation
(d)   Recreational and pleasure
(e)   Other uses authorized by law

The statute did not specify any triggers, amount of reductions, or a floor on withdrawal reductions.

The EAA and the Voting Rights Act

In the 1990s, under section 5 of the Voting Rights Act of 1965, states with a past history of discriminating against minority voters had to submit any change affecting voters or elections to the US Department of Justice for preclearance. After enactment of Senate Bill 1477, John Hannah, the Texas secretary of state, submitted the legislation for preclearance. The Mexican American Legal Defense and Education Fund opposed the preclearance of the Edwards Aquifer Authority Act. On November 19, 1993, the Department of Justice notified the State of Texas that the decision of the legislature to shift from having an elected board for the Edwards Underground Water District to having an appointed board violated the federal Voting Rights Act. The Department of Justice explained that "at this time, none of the bodies responsible for making the appointments have a Hispanic majority among the selecting officials, and only the appointing bodies within Bexar County have any substantial Hispanic representation. Thus, it appears that Hispanic voters will have considerably less influence over the selection of members of the governing body of the Edwards Aquifer . . . than they currently have under the direct-election system for the water district."[33]

Unless the determination from the Department of Justice could be overturned, the legislature would have to address the issue and run the risk of reopening the debate for other amendments.[34] Governor Ann Richards rejected the possibility of calling a special session, stating that "a special session is not going to solve it."[35] Thus, notwithstanding Judge Bunton's direction that the state must put a regulatory system in effect by May 31, 1993, it appeared likely that the judge would have to wait until at least the 1995 legislative session for Texas to have that accomplished.

5 : SHARPENING THE "BLUNT AXE" OF FEDERAL INTERVENTION

The Court will not act if it is clear that the Court lacks any authority. But, if no one else will solve the problems in time, the Court will resolve any close questions or disputes over authority in favor of action to prevent irreversible harm, unless and until the Fifth Circuit rules otherwise.

— *Sierra Club v. Babbitt*, "Order on the Sierra Club's Second Motion for Additional Relief" (March 6, 1995)

When the Department of Justice decided that the Edwards Aquifer Authority Act violated the Voting Rights Act, Judge Bunton found himself in an awkward position. His initial order made clear that he intended to allow the plaintiff and plaintiff-intervenors an opportunity to seek additional relief if the state did not have a regulatory system "in effect" by May 31, 2003. The state appeared to have established this system with the enactment of Senate Bill 1477. But, the decision of the Justice Department placed the viability of the act in doubt. Judge Bunton reacted cautiously at first: "I've never wanted to take control of the aquifer, but I may have to, if something else doesn't get done on it. . . . I'll just have to tread water for awhile, maybe appoint a monitor to oversee the thing in case the situation gets bad. That was my choice to begin with—to give the state a chance to handle the matter—and I am still inclined that way. I think it is a state matter and it ought to be handled by the state."[1] However, the prolonged delay that the Voting Right Act issue introduced played an important role in many of the court's subsequent actions in the case.

With the Department of Justice decision on the Voting Rights Act issue looming and the prospect of a severe drought in the summer of 1994, the Sierra Club filed a motion on November 12, 1993, seeking to have the court appoint a monitor. As Judge Bunton indicated he would do, he granted the motion.[2] After affording the parties an opportunity to agree on a monitor, the court appointed Dr. Joe G. Moore Jr. to serve as the court monitor. The court found that even though the Texas Legislature had passed Senate Bill 1477, there was a need to appoint a monitor because there was "no plan in effect by any Federal[,] State[,] or local government entity that adequately protects against violations of the ESA [Endangered Species Act] caused by unregulated pumping from the Edwards Aquifer."[3]

The court expected the monitor to collect information regarding the use and status of the Edwards Aquifer, analyze plans to reduce withdrawals from the aquifer, monitor efforts to conserve water, and advise the court on the necessity and implementation of remedial actions. In his order, Judge Bunton "strongly" urged the City of San Antonio "to take all actions necessary so that the City will be able to supply to its citizens and other water customers the substantial amounts of water currently available from sources other than the Edwards Aquifer at the earliest possible date."[4] Judge Bunton was clearly signaling that he was prepared to take over management of the aquifer if the drought worsened and proper protections not in place.

Subsequently, the Sierra Club requested the court's permission to file an amended complaint that would add to the case new claims and new defendants, including the Department of Defense and other federal agencies, the City of San Antonio, and the Texas Natural Resource Conservation Commission.[5] In the proposed amended complaint, the Sierra Club sought extensive injunctive relief, including requiring federal agencies, such as the Department of Defense and Department of Agriculture, to begin consultation with the Fish and Wildlife Service on activities that could affect listed species. In addition, the amended complaint asked the court to declare an emergency regarding the Edwards Aquifer and to instruct the court monitor to prepare an emergency withdrawal reduction plan to avoid "jeopardy" even during a repeat of the drought of record. It also sought an order directing the Texas Natural Resource Conservation Commission to enforce the emergency withdrawal reduction plan after it had been approved by the court.

On May 5, 1994, Judge Bunton denied the relief requested by Sierra Club. He explained that the Sierra Club motion sought to "promote an entirely new and different lawsuit." He said that if the Sierra Club wanted to litigate new claims or seek relief against new parties, it would have "to file a wholly new lawsuit." If the Sierra Club wanted additional relief, Judge Bunton advised the plaintiff to delete "all new defendants and all new causes of action" and submit "the resulting document as a motion for further relief."[6]

Quickly following up on this advice, the Sierra Club filed a motion for additional relief without any new parties or new claims.[7] The relief sought was limited to an order declaring an emergency, directing the court monitor to prepare an emergency withdrawal plan, and directing the Fish and Wildlife Service to publish a recovery plan on or before August 1, 1994.

Judge Bunton denied the request for an order declaring an emergency but granted the Sierra Club motion with respect to the emergency withdrawal reduction plan and the recovery plan. He directed that the emergency withdrawal reduction plan should be adequate to prevent jeopardy at all times, beginning that summer, even in a repeat of the drought of record. He also warned that "any future remedial relief ordered by this Court . . . will almost certainly include court-ordered restrictions on pumping from the Aquifer."[8]

Trying to Take a Second Bite of the Apple

The Voting Rights Act issue presented a very serious problem for the court, particularly because there was potential for the region to move into another severe drought. The court's cautious reaction to the Voting Rights Act issue, however, was dealt a blow when an attempt by the City of San Antonio to resurrect the Applewhite project was again rejected by the voters of San Antonio.

The efforts to build the Applewhite Reservoir did not end with the vote in 1991. In November 1993 Mayor Nelson Wolff appointed a twenty-six-member citizens' committee, known as the 2050 Water Resource Committee, to recommend to the San Antonio City Council a water resource plan that would satisfy the water needs of the city through 2050.[9] The motivation for establishing the committee was the imminent expiration of the permits for the Applewhite project as well as the need for a water management plan precipitated by the ruling in *Sierra Club v. Babbitt*. Weir Labatt chaired the committee, and it prepared the SAWS/2050 Committee Water Resources Plan. It consisted of four components: (1) construction of a retooled Applewhite Reservoir, (2) acquisition of Edwards Aquifer water rights from irrigators and industrial users, (3) reuse of treated water from the wastewater treatment plants the city operated, and (4) enhancement of recharge into the aquifer.[10]

On May 19, 1994, the city council unanimously passed a resolution approving the plan, and it then approved by a vote of 9 to 2 the construction of the Applewhite project as part of the 2050 Water Resource Plan.[11] But, by unanimous vote, the council also approved holding a second city-wide vote on the Applewhite project.[12]

Parties involved in the Edwards Issue from outside the city got involved in the debate regarding the upcoming election. On June 16, the Guadalupe-Blanco River Authority issued a lukewarm endorsement of the Applewhite project.[13] In June, the Fish and Wildlife Service called a summit of sixty-nine federal agencies to consider whether, in light of the lack of a plan for managing the aquifer, the agencies needed to consult under ESA section 7(a)(2) with respect to their programs' impacts on the Edwards Aquifer listed species. Implicit in the action of the FWS was the possibility of losing funding for these programs. Moreover, some viewed the summit as an attempt to encourage support for the Applewhite project.[14]

On August 8, 1994, days before the Applewhite vote, the Sierra Club "blasted" the Applewhite project and said that San Antonio should instead go to surface water from other basins. In a motion to the court, the Sierra Club said the project "badly fails feasibility and/or cost-benefits tests and, as a result, places both endangered species and humans dependent on the Edwards at unnecessary severe and prolonged risk of emergency (rationing) or failure of water supplies."[15] Judge Bunton said he discerned in the Sierra Club motion "an invitation to the court to make a political statement" and "the court disapproves of those motives."[16]

On August 13, 1994, the citizens of San Antonio again rejected the Applewhite project, this time by a 7,100-vote margin.[17] Because the SAWS/2050 Committee Water Resources Plan centered on the timely completion of the Applewhite Reservoir, the vote marked the demise of the entire plan. The city council directed the San Antonio Water System to start disposing of the property within the Applewhite project site.

Kirk and Carol Patterson were again among the leaders of the opponents of the Applewhite project. They continued to aggressively advocate using recharge structures and augmentation to supplement springflow rather than reservoirs, despite serious doubts about the overall feasibility of that approach.[18] Indeed, Judge Bunton characterized springflow augmentation by saying, "No es bueno."[19] Nonetheless, for a second time, the Pattersons were instrumental in defeating the Applewhite project.

On September 25, 1994, after the residents of San Antonio had rejected the Applewhite project for the second time, Judge Bunton ordered the formation of a panel, chaired by the court monitor, to draft a regional water management/habitat conservation plan to obtain an incidental take permit.[20] The court instructed the monitor to establish the panel but directed that representatives from the City of San Antonio, the Uvalde County Underground Water Conservation District, the Medina County Underground Water Conservation District, the Edwards Underground Water District, the San Antonio River Authority, and the Guadalupe-Blanco River Authority, at a minimum, should participate on the panel. The panel held numerous public meetings throughout the region. These meetings included opportunities for the public to address the panel. On June 23, 1995, the court monitor submitted a draft habitat conservation plan to the court as required by Judge Bunton's order.[21]

The Axe Starts to Fall

All of the pieces were in place to make 1995 the decisive point in the Sierra Club lawsuit. The legislature would be in session, and addressing the Voting Rights Act issue would be a high priority. The Applewhite project was dead. Recharge had been below average and pumping higher than average the preceding two years, so a severe drought was a possibility, which would again raise the issue of federal intervention.[22] Judge Bunton was growing increasingly frustrated with the lack of a regulatory mechanism to protect the species and appeared poised to order additional relief if he could not persuade the state to take some action.[23]

However, Judge Bunton had to confront the reality that he had entered final judgment only against the Fish and Wildlife Service and then only with respect to the very limited issue of the failure of the FWS to develop and issue information regarding the minimum springflows needed to protect the listed species. Thus, there might be limits on the judge's ability to protect the listed species, at least in the context of the lawsuit before him. Moreover, the irrigators in Medina County who were unhappy with Senate Bill 1477 and still resolute in their support of the rule of capture continued to have the potential to affect the process.

With the 1995 legislative session set to begin, the Sierra Club filed a new motion on December 21, 1994, seeking additional relief from the court to ensure that measures were in place to protect the listed species if the drought continued. The motion also asked the court to have the Emergency Withdrawal Reduction Plan updated and amended.

On March 6, 1995, the court granted the Sierra Club motion and instructed the court monitor to update the Emergency Withdrawal Reduction Plan and to amend it to include a "specific enforceable concept of discretionary use and proposed irrigation use trigger level(s)."[24] Judge Bunton used his March 6 order to make it clear that he intended "to do whatever is necessary to keep the Comal and San Marcos Springs flowing." He strongly suggested that he would order the Texas Natural Resource Conservation Commission, the successor to the Texas Water Commission, to implement the Emergency Withdrawal Reduction Plan. Judge Bunton also asked the secretary of the interior and the US Fish and Wildlife Service to report, in detail, with respect to the US Department of Agriculture, on "the extent to which federal taxpayer dollars are subsidizing the pumping that causes this crisis." In the order, the court also scheduled an evidentiary hearing for May 19 to determine whether to require the implementation of the Emergency Withdrawal Reduction Plan.[25]

On April 10, 1995, the Sierra Club filed another motion seeking leave to amend the complaint it had filed four years earlier to add the Texas Natural Resource Conservation Commission to the lawsuit and to request an order that the commission implement a withdrawal reduction plan. This time, Judge Bunton allowed the Sierra Club to amend its complaint.[26] The State of Texas and defendant-intervenors representing agricultural interests immediately asked the US Court of Appeals for the Fifth Circuit to set aside Judge Bunton's order.[27]

On May 19, 1995, Judge Bunton held the evidentiary hearing concerning the authority of the court to impose pumping limits, the current status of the aquifer, and the economic effects of the court monitor's Revised Emergency Withdrawal Reduction Plan. At the close of the hearing, Judge Bunton named a five-member lawyers' panel and gave the members until June 1 to develop a compromise withdrawal reduction plan.[28] The compromise plan was submitted to the court on June 1.

Meanwhile, on May 29, 1995, after an extremely contentious debate and with the outcome in doubt until the last minute, the Texas Legislature enacted House Bill 3189, which was intended to resolve the Voting Rights Act issue.[29] Authored by Representative Robert Puente and sponsored in the upper chamber by Senator Ken Armbrister, House Bill 3189 enlarged the Edwards Aquifer Authority board and changed it from an appointed to an elected board.[30] It called for electing fifteen members of the board from single-member districts, with Bexar County getting seven members, the western counties getting four members, and the eastern counties getting four members. Two nonvoting directors would be appointed—one member to represent the South Central Texas Water Advisory Committee and one member to represent Medina and Uvalde Counties. The legislature appointed a temporary board until the election for regular members could be held. The changes would go into effect on August 28, 1995.

On June 14, 1995, buoyed by the legislative action and much-needed rainfall near the end of May, Judge Bunton announced that, "although convinced of its jurisdiction to do so," he would not order "that the Texas Natural Resource Conservation Commission implement Edwards Aquifer emergency withdrawal reductions." Instead, he decided to wait to see the effectiveness of the "voluntary responses to the lawyer's panel's proposed restrictions." Judge Bunton concluded by warning that if the panel's plan did not maintain Comal springflow at 150 cubic feet per second, the court would "have no other alternative but to implement its own emergency withdrawal."[31]

Five days later, the Fifth Circuit Court of Appeals set aside Judge Bunton's order to add the Texas Natural Resource Conservation Commission as a defendant on procedural grounds.[32]

In early August, the Department of Justice approved the new selection method for the Edwards Aquifer Authority Board of Directors as set forth in House Bill 3189.[33] It appeared that the authority would at last start to function. However, before the temporary board could be seated, the Medina County Underground Conservation District, on August 23, 1995, facially challenged the constitutionality of Senate Bill 1477, alleging that the legislation took away a vested property right in groundwater.[34] This strategically timed suit further delayed the Edwards Aquifer Authority's ability to manage the aquifer or respond to the ongoing drought.[35]

The case was heard by state district judge Mickey Pennington, elected from a district that included Medina, Real, and Uvalde Counties. He promptly issued a temporary restraining order and injunction that enjoined the Edwards Aquifer Authority from managing the aquifer.[36] On October 28, 1995, Judge Pennington ruled in favor of the plaintiffs and enjoined the implementation of the enabling act of the Edwards Aquifer Authority.[37] The state, however, was successful in obtaining a direct appeal to the Texas Supreme Court, thus considerably shortening the time before a decision would be obtained.

While waiting on the state court's decision, Judge Bunton must have let his frustration with the delay in getting a regulatory system in place and his concern about the ongoing drought get the best of him. "This court grows weary of this four-year suit in which nothing has been done," he said. "The buck stops here. This court will implement a plan by Jan. 1, 1996, that is regulated directly by this court or by a federal agency designated by this court."[38]

On October 18, the US Court of Appeals for the Fifth Circuit ordered Judge Bunton to cease all proceedings in the Sierra Club suit, including the work of the court monitor, and remanded the case to the district court to hold a hearing to consider, among other things, whether the disputes regarding the Edwards Aquifer Authority compelled federal courts to abstain from further consideration of the case and whether the Fifth Circuit would continue to have jurisdiction to hear the appeal.[39] The Fifth Circuit emphatically stated, "One thing is clear. It is time for this litigation to end."[40]

Judge Bunton conducted the hearing on October 20, 1995, and issued an order and findings and conclusions of law responding to the October 18 order from the Fifth Circuit.[41] He found that "in view of the threat facing the Edwards-dependent species," there was no reason to abstain from further consideration of the case in deference to ongoing state proceedings.[42] It was to no avail.

On February 14, 1996, the US Fish and Wildlife Service finished the recovery plan the district court had previously ordered.[43] At that point, the Fifth Circuit ordered Judge Bunton to dismiss the lawsuit. The court of appeals found that the Sierra Club had sought only limited relief related to the "biological requirements of the species" and that "all the relief sought, that could be awarded, has been obtained through the Recovery Plan." The Fifth Circuit explained that "if the Sierra Club wants additional relief then it must file a new action. No amount of post-judgment paper generation can convert a judgment ordering federal defendants to create and disseminate information into a judgment enjoining Texas to restrict pumping from the Edwards." Judge Bunton had found the limits of his authority.[44]

Looking ahead, Russ Johnson, attorney for the San Antonio Water System, said, "I think it's a good decision and a correct one. But it sets the stage for Round Two."[45]

As directed, Judge Bunton dismissed the suit against the Fish and Wildlife Service.

Round Two and *Sierra Club v. City of San Antonio*

With the court lacking any remaining jurisdiction over the original suit, on June 10, 1996, the Sierra Club filed suit in the Western District of Texas against the City of San Antonio, Bexar Metropolitan Water District, Department of Defense, irrigators in Bexar, Atascosa, Medina, Uvalde, Kinney, Hays, and Comal Counties, and numerous other individuals, corporations, and municipalities. The suit alleged that the defendants had violated section 9 of the Endangered Species Act by causing springflows to fall below the take and jeopardy levels set by the US Fish and Wildlife Service.

On June 28, 1996, the Texas Supreme Court rejected the plaintiffs' claim in the *Barshop v. Medina County Underground Conservation District* case.[46] With the lawsuits finished for the time being, the Edwards Aquifer Authority temporary board of directors began meeting in July 1996. At that time, the region was still in a severe drought. Since late May 1996, flows at the San Marcos and Comal Springs had fallen below "jeopardy" levels identified by the Fish and Wildlife Service. However, as Judge Bunton would later note, the Edwards Aquifer Authority had twice "failed to recognize the current emergency in votes it had taken."[47]

On August 1, 1996, Judge Bunton appointed Todd Votteler as special master and ordered him to develop a new Emergency Withdrawal Reduction Plan within ten days. When the special master delivered the new plan on August 23, 1996, the court dropped the blunt axe of federal intervention.

At that point, the plaintiffs filed a motion seeking a preliminary injunction against the aquifer users. The court granted the plaintiffs' motion. Before setting out his order, Judge Bunton stated that it was not the intention of the court to "frustrate or impede" the attempts of the Edwards Aquifer Authority to produce and enforce a critical management plan. He explained, however, that the court could not ignore a federal statute designed to protect the endangered species "merely because the EAA has a great learning curve to overcome before it is ready to manage the Aquifer." Until the Edwards Aquifer Authority was ready, "it is the duty of this Court to follow Congress' directive that the endangered species and their critical habitat must be protected."[48]

The court found that "an emergency presently exists and takes of endangered species are occurring" and that "without a fundamental change in the value the region places on fresh water, a major effort to conserve and reuse Aquifer water, and implemented plans to import supplemental supplies of water, the region's quality of life and economic future [are] imperiled."[49]

The court incorporated by reference the 1996 Emergency Withdrawal Reduction Plan, which provided for comprehensive regulation of pumping from the aquifer, but it did not immediately impose the requirements of that plan. Instead, Judge Bunton ordered specific limitations on pumping based on springflows. These reductions were taken from the plan prepared by the lawyers' panel in June 1995. The court allowed the parties to determine how to meet those reductions. With respect to municipalities, the order was to remain in effect until the defendants demonstrated that the Edwards Aquifer Authority was enforcing a critical management plan that would preserve endangered species in their natural habitat.

On August 26, 1996, the City of San Antonio appealed the order to the US Court of Appeals for the Fifth Circuit and asked the Fifth Circuit to stay Judge Bunton's preliminary injunction. On September 10, 1996, the Fifth Circuit granted the requested stay.

Before the Fifth Circuit ruled in 1997, the Edwards Aquifer Authority had issued a critical period management plan and an interim critical period management rule. On April 30, 1997, after briefing and oral argument, the Fifth Circuit reversed the district court decision and vacated the injunction.[50] The court vacated the injunction because the plaintiff could not establish a substantial likelihood of success on the merits in light of the abstention doctrine enunciated in *Burford v. Sun Oil Co.* This doctrine directs a court to abstain from hearing a case as a matter of comity to allow the state to resolve the issue. The Sierra Club request for rehearing and rehearing *en banc* was denied on June 20, 1997. Subsequently, the Supreme Court of the United States also denied the Sierra Club petition for a writ of certiorari.

The City of San Antonio case then languished. Judge Bunton retired from the bench in May 2000, and the case was transferred to Judge Sam Sparks in Austin.[51] There had been no significant developments in the case after the Fifth Circuit ruled in 1997. At the request of the state and the City of San Antonio, Judge Sparks dismissed the case without opposition. The Sierra Club attorney said, "There's nothing to prevent us from cranking another suit. The EAA is pretty consistently not doing anything. I don't look for the EAA to adopt any drought management plan until they absolutely have to, and it's going to be on an emergency basis. Heaven forbid that one would plan for drought in a semi-arid region."[52]

Judge Bunton died on January 18, 2001.[53] Todd Votteler, who had worked for Judge Bunton for more than six years, said, "Meeting Judge Bunton was a true milestone in my life. Frankly, I was in awe of him."[54]

Without Judge Bunton and the *Sierra Club v. Babbitt* lawsuit, a regulatory authority might never have been created to manage the Edwards Aquifer—or at least might not have been created until many more years had passed. Without the threat of the "blunt axes of federal intervention," the strong opposition of the agricultural interests probably would have presented too formidable an obstacle to the passage of a bill such as Representative Puente's House Bill 1792 in 1993. Like John Hall, Judge Bunton was pragmatic, which can have positive or negative connotations depending on one's perspective. True to his word, the judge pushed his authority to the limits, and perhaps beyond. The Fifth Circuit then overruled him. At the end of the day, however, he had coerced the creation of the key to resolving the Edwards Issue—a regulatory system to manage withdrawals from the aquifer. Now it was up to the newly created Edwards Aquifer Authority to fulfill the responsibilities with which it was charged.

6 : ATTEMPTS BY THE EDWARDS AQUIFER AUTHORITY TO TACKLE THE EDWARDS ISSUE

"Politics stops at the water's edge."
— US Senator Arthur Vandenberg (ca. 1947)

The Edwards Aquifer Authority had an elected board that was created largely to address the Edwards Issue. While issuing permits to meet the withdrawal caps was important to preventing sustained mining of the aquifer and lessening dependence on the aquifer, it was not an element of Judge Bunton's decision. The primary regulatory issue with respect to protecting the species was how to come up with a strategy for achieving continuous minimum springflows. It was not going to be an easy task because the composition of the board reflected the interests that had divided the region for years. The question was whether the members of the board elected from districts intended to reflect the various interests could put their differences aside and carry out the tasks that Senate Bill 1477 mandated to protect the listed species in the two spring systems.

Protecting Listed Species by Ensuring
Continuous Minimum Springflows

As the year 2000 approached, the Edwards Aquifer Authority still had not put in place the continuous minimum springflow measures that Senate Bill 1477 required it to implement within nine months creation of the authority. It was under pressure for failure to address this requirement.

In 1998 the Edwards Aquifer Authority received notices of intent to sue from the Sierra Club, Environmental Defense Fund, and National Wildlife Federation regarding alleged violations of section 9 of the Endangered Species Act as a result of failure to take action.[1] In 2000 the US Fish and Wildlife Service also threatened to bring suit against the Edwards Aquifer Authority: "As we have communicated to you previously, your current drought management plan provides reductions in aquifer water use that we believe are not sufficient to adequately protect flows to avoid take or jeopardizing the continued existence of listed species. This inadequate regulation of aquifer pumping has likely resulted in illegal take of listed species. Unless EAA takes further actions to reduce pumping to essential uses, the Service will consider enforcement action against your agency for non-compliance with the ESA."[2]

To address the continuous minimum springflow requirement, the Edwards Aquifer Authority chose to start the process of applying for an incidental take permit that would require the preparation of a habitat conservation plan (HCP).[3] Almost two and one-half years after the authority board was seated, in December 1998, it approved the preparation of the habitat conservation plan intended to support a fifty-year incidental take permit. Early in the process, the Fish and Wildlife Service told the authority that "unforeseen conditions would be those conditions worse than existing drought of record conditions. Existing drought of record conditions would be those conditions to be foreseen under the proposed 50-year term of the permit."[4]

With this direction and after developing several sets of alternatives, the Edwards Aquifer Authority in late 2002 prepared a draft of the habitat conservation plan/environmental impact statement addressing five alternative pumping scenarios. Despite the clear direction of the Fish and Wildlife Service, the alternatives included withdrawal reduction floors of 340,000 and 350,000 acre-feet. The authority, however, did not evaluate the effects of these alternatives on springflow during a repeat of the drought of record.

In response, the Fish and Wildlife Service asked for modeling of the different withdrawal caps with various critical period management reduction regimens over the period of the drought of record.[5] The FWS reminded the Edwards Aquifer Authority that the "HCP should plan for those conditions that are foreseeable in the life of the permit." The Edwards Aquifer Authority agreed to the additional model runs and incorporated them in the subsequent draft of the habitat conservation plan/environmental impact statement.[6]

In 2003 Greg Ellis, general manager of the Edwards Aquifer Authority, told the House Natural Resources Committee that the 340,000-acre-foot floor for withdrawal restrictions would not protect the federally listed species during a repeat of the drought of record. It was selected, he stated, solely based on the belief held by the authority that the figure was the lowest to which withdrawals could be reduced and not threaten public safety.[7] While he did not explain to the committee the basis for that belief, the Edwards Aquifer Authority had previously told the Fish and Wildlife Service that "340,000 ac-ft was used as a 'placeholder' in the State Water Planning and it's what the cities have been using to plan around. Cities say: if I am going to measure human health and safety item by item then okay, in order to keep firefighting we need a pressurized system, so we have to pump what we pump now." The Edwards Aquifer Authority, however, conceded that, in fact, it had "had a very difficult time getting the municipalities to supply them with a human health and safety number."[8]

The Edwards Aquifer Authority prepared another draft of the habitat conservation plan/environmental impact statement in 2004. This draft had four alternatives. The preferred alternative included withdrawal caps of 450,000 acre-feet and, beginning in 2008, 400,000 acre-feet, as required by Senate Bill 1477. It had a critical period management withdrawal floor of 340,000 acre-feet. With the 450,000-acre-foot cap, simulations showed that Comal Springs would cease to flow (i.e., zero cubic feet per second) for 1,400 days, about ten times the number of days of zero flow during the actual drought of record. The flows at Comal Springs would have been below 60 cubic feet per second for 5,802 days and below 150 cubic feet per second (the jeopardy level established by the Fish and Wildlife Service) for 9,978 days. Even excluding the drought of record from the analysis, zero flow would occur for approximately 100 days and flows below 60 cubic feet per second would have occurred for 1,434 days and, below 150 cubic feet per second, for 7,276 days.[9]

When the 400,000-acre-foot cap kicked in, the modeling, including the drought of record, predicted 1,236 days at zero flow, 3,097 days below 60 cubic feet per second, and approximately 8,263 days below 150 cubic feet per second. Even excluding the drought of record from the analysis, zero flow would occur for approximately 50 days and flows below 60 cubic feet per second would have occurred for 788 days and, below 150 cubic feet per second, for 5,583 days. In short, as long as the withdrawal reduction floor was 340,000 acre-feet, springflows at Comal Springs would cease and extended periods of time would occur during which springflows would be below 60 cubic feet per second. This was true whether or not the drought of record was included in the analysis.

Under these conditions, the draft habitat conservation plan avoided deeper critical period management withdrawal reductions by relying on artificial means to ensure the survival of threatened and endangered species: "During [periods of very low flows] off-site refugia and captive propagation may be necessary to ensure the continued survival of the species."[10] The use of refugia entails removing the species from their natural habitat during very severe drought and placing them in aquaria, troughs, or other similar structures and trying to preserve them until the drought abates and they can be reintroduced into the wild.

The Edwards Aquifer Authority released this draft of the habitat conservation plan/environmental impact statement for public comment in September 2004. Twenty comments were received. Those of the downstream interests and environmental community were generally negative. Most focused on the failure of the preferred alternative to ensure continuous minimal springflow.[11] One representative of an environmental group commented, "There is no way that the EAA can truthfully assert that the action it has taken thus far in implementing its enabling statute will avoid jeopardy to threatened and endangered species. Therefore the EAA should not move forward with its draft HCP until it has carried out its statutory obligations in a way that will achieve [continuous minimum flows]."[12]

The San Antonio Water System was supportive of the Edwards Aquifer Authority's draft plan but, nonetheless, concluded, "We feel that the current draft has significant economic, scientific and legal shortcomings that should be addressed prior to EAA board approval."[13]

Undaunted by the majority of the comments it received, the Edwards Aquifer Authority made few of the suggested changes.[14] Instead, the staff took the extraordinary step of removing all mention of withdrawal caps and all of the information pertaining to the environmental impact statement (EIS) and submitting what remained of the draft to the board for approval to send the draft to the Fish and Wildlife Service.[15] The authority's board approved sending the much-abbreviated draft plan to the Fish and Wildlife Service by a 10-to-4 vote on March 8, 2005.[16] It was submitted to the FWS on March 11, 2005.[17]

The board's decision to submit the draft was greeted with disapproval in large part because pumping limits were not part of the plan and because the withdrawal limits during drought would not ensure continuous minimum springflows. Jerry James, who had become one of the nonvoting members of the Edwards Aquifer Authority Board of Directors, said that the authority should have done more work on the plan before submitting it: "We, along with several other entities, urged them not to (approve the plan). The document they produced, we hadn't had time to review it and we have serious concerns about the way the document was put together as far as actually protecting the species. But they decided they had spent enough time and would submit the application as is."[18]

At the board meeting, many members of the public and some directors believed that the authority had not provided enough time for public review.[19] David Chardavoyne, chief executive officer of the San Antonio Water System, voiced this view: "This draft is being rushed out of the door prior to review by us and others."[20]

The Fish and Wildlife Service did not take any action on the draft submitted. Bob Pine, supervisor of the Austin field office, and Carrie Thompson, also from that office, met with Robert Potts, Rick Illgner, and Bob Hall from the Edwards Aquifer Authority on November 16, 2005, to discuss the draft habitat conservation plan. The FWS made it clear at that meeting that it "would not be able to review their HCP when [the Edwards Aquifer Authority's] management plan was in flux"—a process that Potts told them could take a year and a half to resolve. The FWS explained that aquifer management was the core of the habitat conservation plan. The FWS would have to have "some level of assurance that the plan we evaluate can and will be implemented. Changing rules were a moving target and did not provide a 'plan' that could be evaluated." According to the FWS, Potts seemed "somewhat surprised by this statement, but seemed to understand."[21]

In her summary of the meeting, Thompson noted that the draft submitted "did not contain any of the EIS, nor did it contain essential information regarding pumping caps for aquifer management."[22] She said that the authority staff explained that it was "stripped down so that the Board would vote to release it to start review." She concluded that the "Edwards Aquifer Authority never made any progress . . . as to making firm decisions on the pumping caps, drought management information core to the HCP. The FWS never considered this a true submission as a draft. . . . This document sat on a shelf awaiting additional materials from Edwards Aquifer Authority which never came."[23]

After spending five years and approximately $3 million, the Edwards Aquifer Authority had developed a preferred alternative with a 340,000-acre-foot floor that would not ensure the continuous flows that were so central to the federal court determination in *Sierra Club v. Babbitt* and required by Senate Bill 1477, or that Michael Spear had testified had to be achieved to obtain an incidental take permit.

Indeed, in 1998 the Fish and Wildlife Service had told the Edwards Aquifer Authority what it believed the withdrawal limits would have to be to ensure the continuous minimum springflows required by federal law: "A determination should be made regarding what withdrawal levels would be needed to be limited to in order to assure the goal in S.B. 1477. . . . It appears to us, based on a review of available information (including TWDB [Texas Water Development Board] model runs), that that level is probably somewhere between 200,000 and 250,000 acre-feet."[24]

Moreover, the Biological Advisory Team, established by the Edwards Aquifer Authority, told the authority that the draft plan did not meet the continuous minimum flow requirement: "Biological goals as stated in the EA/HCP do not comply with the Edwards Authority Act 1.14(h), which states the EAA must ensure 'the continuous minimum springflows of the Comal Springs and San Marcos Springs are maintained' for the protection of listed species."[25]

The objective of the Edwards Aquifer Authority in submitting the abbreviated draft of the habitat conservation plan apparently was to negotiate an agreement with the Fish and Wildlife Service to reduce the jeopardy number to a withdrawal floor acceptable to the authority board and to allow the use of refugia and captive propagation to provide the remaining protection needed. According the board, "Through the process of negotiating the HCP it should become evident that there is no necessity for designating firm springflow numbers to define threats to survival in the wild." Instead, it was "hoped" that "a more reliable and holistically developed set of criteria will emerge."[26]

For an incidental take permit to be issued, however, the actions covered by the permit could not jeopardize the listed species "in the wild"; taking them out of the wild and placing them in aquaria until adequate flows were reestablished would not satisfy the "in the wild" requirement.[27] Moreover, the captive propagation policy of the FWS made clear that controlled propagation could not be "a substitute for addressing factors responsible for an endangered or threatened species' decline."[28] In other words, the refugia could be used as a safety net only to protect the species if the assumption regarding the effectiveness of the measures to avoid jeopardy proved not to be valid—it could not be one of the measures used to avoid jeopardy. Thus, the reliance of the

Edwards Aquifer Authority on refugia and captive propagation probably would not have produced a legally defensible habitat conservation plan even if Potts had been able to sell it to the FWS.

Regardless, the overarching problem with the strategy of the Edwards Aquifer Authority for obtaining an incidental take permit was that the habitat conservation plan without the withdrawal caps provided no adequate basis for the Fish and Wildlife Service to begin the evaluation. Habitat conservation plans are voluntary. The FWS approves or disapproves "complete applications" submitted by applicants. It does not tell an applicant what will constitute an approvable plan before it receives a complete application based on what the applicant is willing to commit to implementing. The strategy, apparently based on the authority board's inability to reach agreement on what it was willing to commit to, simply was not enough even to get the authority a ticket to the game.

Attempts to Implement the Required Withdrawal Caps

The Edwards Aquifer Authority began processing applications for initial regular permits in 1996. In 2000 the authority issued a rule requiring a proportional adjustment of all permits if the 450,000-acre-foot cap was exceeded, as well as compensation for affected pumpers for the difference between the statutory minimum at the fair market value for the water.[29]

By 2003 the Edwards Aquifer Authority had approved more acre-feet of permitted rights than allowed by the 450,000-acre-foot withdrawal cap. Because some of the permits would not be effective until January 1, 2004, the Edwards Aquifer Authority was not yet in violation of the cap.

The cost of the compensation would have been substantial. At a hearing of the House Natural Resources Committee in 2003, both Mike Beldon, chair of the Edwards Aquifer Authority board, and Greg Ellis, general manager of the authority, testified that the price obtained in a recent water sale was $2,000 per acre-foot. At that price, they testified, a buy-down would cost at least $400 million (presumably including debt service).[30]

The board initially decided in 2003 to ask the legislature for a three-year extension of the period in which it was to achieve compliance with the cap. Board members changed their minds, however, and decided to "toss the problem to the Legislature without a recommendation." Beldon, the board chair, summarized the problem: "The Legislature gave us an unworkable piece of legislation in 1993. The Legislature needs to solve it. It's just that simple."[31]

Later in the 2003 legislative session the Edwards Aquifer Authority Board of Directors reconsidered again and asked the legislature to raise the cap to 550,000 acre-feet.[32] The proposed legislation also called for cutting pumping to 350,000 acre-feet in severe drought. The legislation, House Bill 3586, was introduced by Representative Robert Puente. A similar bill, Senate Bill 1914, was introduced in the Senate by Senator Jeff Wentworth. Not surprisingly, the bills encountered significant opposition.

After a hearing on the House bill that went well into the evening, Representative Puente introduced a committee substitute that would extend the deadline for the aquifer authority to comply with the 450,000-acre-foot cap until January 1, 2008, and extend the time to achieve compliance with the 400,000-acre-foot cap until January 1, 2010. The bill also included a provision setting the critical period management withdrawal floor at 350,000 acre-feet. The bill was reported favorably out of the House Natural Resources Committee. Senate Bill 1914 also was passed out of the Senate Natural Resources Committee. Neither bill, however, received a floor vote. Representative Puente explained, "There were too many hoops to jump through to get that cap lifted."[33]

By November 1, 2003, the Edwards Aquifer Authority had approved initial regular permits for 502,517 acre-feet. Having not received any relief from the legislature, the Edwards Aquifer Authority had to implement rules to limit withdrawals to 450,000 acre-feet, including compensating affected pumpers, or come up with an alternative solution by January 1, 2004.[34]

Because of the high cost of compensation, the Edwards Aquifer Authority abandoned the compensation rule in December 2003 in favor of a bifurcated permitting structure to reduce the permitted withdrawals to 450,000 acre-feet.[35] Under the bifurcated permitting structure, the Edwards Aquifer Authority would reduce the total amount of every permitted withdrawal proportionally to bring the authorized amount to 450,000 acre-feet.[36] The proportionally reduced withdrawal amounts were designated "senior" or "uninterruptible" rights. The amount of reduction for each permit between the proportionally reduced amount and the statutory minimum was designated a "junior" or "interruptible" right that could not be used if the levels in the J-17 and J-27 index wells fell below a critical period management trigger. To allow the legislature ample time to weigh in on the problem before the 400,000-acre-foot cap was triggered, the Edwards Aquifer Authority set the rule to expire on December 31, 2007.

On February 12, 2004, the oversight group created by Senate Bill 1477 to protect downstream interests—the South Central Texas Water Advisory Committee—requested the Edwards Aquifer Authority to reconsider the bifurcated permit rule because it was prejudicial to downstream interests.[37] On May 11, 2004, the Edwards Aquifer Authority's board rejected the request. On June 3, 2004, the South Central Texas Water Advisory Committee requested that the Texas Commission on Environmental Quality review the bifurcated permit rule.[38]

Despite a contrary recommendation by the executive director of the Texas Commission on Environmental Quality, on January 11, 2006, the commission unanimously found in favor of the South Central Texas Water Advisory Committee and recommended that the Edwards Aquifer Authority reconsider the bifurcated permitting rules as a means to limit permits to 450,000 acre-feet per year and to minimize the measurable impact on downstream surface water rights holders and other downstream interests.[39]

On March 16, 2006, Representative Harvey Hilderbran, co-chair of the Edwards Aquifer Legislative Oversight Committee, requested a legal opinion on the Edwards Aquifer Authority bifurcated permit rule from Greg Abbott, the attorney general of Texas.[40] Rather than waiting for that opinion, on July 11, 2006, the Edwards Aquifer Authority adopted temporary rules to implement the bifurcated permit rules adopted in 2003. The temporary rules would have expired on December 31, 2007.

Critical Period Management Withdrawals

In 1996 the Edwards Aquifer Authority adopted the critical period management plan.[41] Subsequently, it promulgated interim critical period rules on January 28, 1997.[42] These rules established different triggers for: (1) Bexar County and portions of Comal, Hays, Caldwell, and Guadalupe Counties; (2) Medina County and the portion of Atascosa County within the authority; and (3) Uvalde County.

The reductions were based on a usage amount consisting of the average monthly total groundwater usage for November and December 1995 and January 1996. The maximum allowable pumping for each stage was determined by multiplying the base usage by a reduction multiplier. The reduction multiplier was as follows: stage I, 1.8; stage II, 1.6; stage III, 1.4; and stage IV, either 1.2, 1.3, or 1.4, as subsequently determined by the aquifer authority. The pumpers had to file monthly usage reports for compliance purposes.

In 1998 Living Waters Artesian Springs, Ltd. (the notorious catfish farm), filed suit in district court in Travis County challenging the permitting and regional drought rules of the Edwards Aquifer Authority and alleging that the rules did not comply with the Texas Administrative Procedures Act.[43] The court issued a temporary restraining order blocking implementation of the drought rules, as well as rules implementing the filing and processing of permits.[44] Subsequently, the court found in favor of the plaintiff and invalidated the permit rules.[45] The authority did not appeal that judgment but instead repealed the invalidated and proposed rules to rectify the problems that caused them to be invalidated.[46]

On May 9, 2000, the authority adopted new emergency critical period management rules.[47] On November 22, 2002, the Edwards Aquifer Authority Board of Directors adopted demand management/ critical period management rules. The rules established four reduction stages: 10, 15, 20, and 30 percent, respectively. At each stage all permittees were to collect water usage data on a weekly basis and report the data to the authority on a monthly basis for compliance purposes.

Thus, going into the 2005 legislative session, the Edwards Aquifer Authority believed, notwithstanding the challenge from the South Central Texas Water Advisory Committee, it had solved at least part of the withdrawal cap issue—getting the cap to 450,000 acre-feet. It had gotten a critical period management plan in place and promulgated withdrawal limits consistent with that plan. But it had not fulfilled the mandate to implement measures to ensure continuous minimum flows, and any illusion it may have harbored that the draft habitat conservation plan it had prepared would someday satisfy that requirement was just that—an illusion.

The Legislative Session for 2005
In the seventy-ninth session of the Texas Legislature, convened in 2005, Senator Ken Armbrister introduced Senate Bill 3. Along with contentious issues such as environmental flows, article 5 of Senate Bill 3

addressed the Edwards Aquifer withdrawal caps. The centerpiece of that article was increasing the withdrawal cap to 480,000 acre-feet and striking the 400,000-acre-feet withdrawal cap reduction scheduled for January 1, 2008. The critical period management reductions were triggered by specific springflow levels at the Comal and San Marcos Springs, and the reductions were based on a ninety-day budget submitted by the permit holder. There was no specified withdrawal floor, but the maximum allowable pumping would have been 60 percent of the budgeted amount in the San Antonio pool and 70 percent in the Uvalde pool.

The Senate Natural Resources Committee staff held discussions with stakeholders on April 7, 8, and 12. On April 12, a proposal was made by the Edwards Aquifer Authority and the San Antonio Water System that would have raised the cap to the sum of all regular permits issued or for which an application had been filed by January 1, 2005, thus, avoiding the need for to buy-down the permits. The proposal set the floor on critical period management reductions at 340,000 acre-feet. After January 1, 2012, the floor would be 320,000 acre-feet, and after 2020 the floor would be dropped to 288,000 acre-feet.

On April 18, 2005, the Guadalupe Basin Coalition, led by the City of Victoria, accepted the proposal.[48] The proposal was reported out of the Senate Natural Resources Committee as a committee substitute on April 26, 2005. The Senate passed Senate Bill 3 on April 29, 2005.

Representative Robert Puente sponsored the bill in the House. It was voted out 6 to 3 by the House Natural Resources Committee in the waning days of the session. With respect to the Edwards Aquifer, it was very similar to the Senate committee substitute except that it did not address the critical period management floor in 2020. However, it was not voted on by the House and died when the session ended. Puente explained, "It was one of those things where I think you have to have a drought and a budget surplus to pass a bill like that. It was very good legislation. It had lots of support, but there wasn't the urgency to do it."[49]

In the two special sessions in 2005, Senator Armbrister and Representative Puente reintroduced as Senate Bill 24 and House Bill 41, respectively, just the elements of Senate Bill 3 that affected the Edwards Aquifer. The bills were essentially identical.

These bills would have: (1) set the pumping cap at the sum of all regular permits issued or for which an application had been filed and

(2) adopted critical period management reductions with a floor of 340,000 acre-feet. After January 1, 2012, the critical period management reductions could not exceed 320,000 acre-feet unless adjusted through a multistage, scientifically based stakeholder process. After 2020, the maximum withdrawals could be set at what were deemed appropriate levels through that stakeholder process.

In provisions that foreshadowed what would be used in setting up the EARIP, the bills established the Edwards Aquifer Stakeholder Committee, which consisted of fifteen members—five municipal permit holders, two irrigation permit holders, three industrial permit holders and four downstream water rights holders in the Guadalupe Basin, and one public interest representative related to in-stream flows into the bays and estuaries and the Edwards Aquifer Authority. The stakeholders would have appointed a seven-member expert science team that would utilize a collaborative process designed to achieve consensus on recommendations regarding withdrawal reduction levels and stages for critical period management.

While neither bill was passed in the special sessions in 2005, they are nonetheless important because they largely presage many of the elements of Senate Bill 3 of the 2007 legislative session and because they framed the debate leading up to the 2007 session.

Between the Sessions

After the conclusion of the 2005 legislative session, prospects looked good for raising the withdrawal cap. The bills addressing the withdrawal cap had been better received in the legislature in 2005 than they had in 2003. There was at least qualified support for changing the withdrawal caps by the downstream interests, although they still harbored very serious reservations regarding the withdrawal floors specified in Senate Bill 24 and House Bill 41. The strongest opposition to raising the cap came from the environmental community, including the Sierra Club:

The EAA—with the support of SAWS and many San Antonio officials—has apparently decided to pursue legislation in this session of the Texas Legislature to raise the pumping cap to the permitted amount of 549,000 acre-feet per year *without* any finding that doing so is scientifically valid. Indeed the fact that the EAA Board is seeking this legislative "fix" rather than taking such action in the manner authorized in its enabling law is a tacit admission that such a cap increase is *not* scientifically justified.

The EAA has dismissed the alternatives to raising the cap—apparently on the assumption that proportional reduction of permits across-the-board is too politically volatile and that acquisition of specific permits would be too costly. In truth, however, EAA has produced no in-depth analysis of these two alternatives to allow the public to have a frank and open discussion on these options.[50]

While on the surface things looked favorable for compromise, beneath the surface there was renewed rancor between two of the key players: the San Antonio Water System and the Guadalupe-Blanco River Authority. On May 10, 2001, the San Antonio Water System and the San Antonio River Authority had entered into an agreement with the Guadalupe-Blanco River Authority for delivery of approximately 70,000 acre-feet of water per year (the Lower Guadalupe Supply Project).[51] The contract provided a seven-year reservation period in which to determine the feasibility of the project. The diversion for the surface water was to be located below the confluence of the Guadalupe and San Antonio Rivers, near Tivoli, Texas. In 2003 an additional 24,500 acre-feet of groundwater from the Gulf Coast Aquifer in Goliad and Refugio Counties was added to the project, which the San Antonio River Authority managed.

This fifty-year water supply contract provided 90 percent of the water from the project to the San Antonio Water System. The remaining 10 percent was to be available to communities in the jurisdictional area of the San Antonio River Authority. The amount of water that the Guadalupe-Blanco River Authority committed to deliver to San Antonio from the Guadalupe River would have been reduced gradually over the life of the project.[52]

In 2004 the project began to unravel.[53] Finally, in 2005, the San Antonio Water System withdrew from the Lower Guadalupe Water Supply Project.[54] At the same time, the San Antonio Water System announced plans to continue to acquire additional Edwards Aquifer supplies "as insurance against state or federal legislative changes."[55] Bill West, general manager of the Guadalupe-Blanco River Authority, responded, "It looks like (SAWS is) going back to its old ways of relying on the Edwards."[56]

The Guadalupe-Blanco River Authority wanted a large water project such as the Lower Guadalupe Supply Project and needed a partner such as the San Antonio Water System to ensure the feasibility of the project. With the apparent inevitability of the withdrawal cap being raised from 450,000 to 500,000 acre-feet, lowering the withdrawal floor would have forced the San Antonio Water System to look for alternative water supply projects in addition to providing additional protection for the species and enhanced surface water supplies during drought. It was in this context that the Guadalupe-Blanco River Authority took the lead in finding a compromise solution that addressed both the pumping cap and the withdrawal floor. It was aided in its efforts by an unanticipated ally: the US Fish and Wildlife Service.

The Fish and Wildlife Service had had success with an informal strategy known as a "recovery implementation program." A recovery implementation program is a voluntary, multistakeholder initiative developed by the FWS to balance water use and development with the needs of federally listed species.[57] These programs typically involved federal agencies that operated dams on major rivers, such as the Bureau of Recreation and/or the US Army Corps of Engineers, as well as federal agencies and states dependent on the water from these facilities.

The most recent success of the Fish and Wildlife Service with a recovery implementation program had been the Middle Rio Grande Recovery Implementation Program. The leader of that effort for the FWS was Dr. Joy Nicholopoulos, state director for New Mexico. The Texas state director for the FWS, Renne Lohoefener, was scheduled to leave that job for the assistant regional director's post in the southwest region. Dr. Nicholopoulos had been selected as his replacement.

On December 14, 2005, with the prospect of an increase in the withdrawal cap looming, Dr. Todd Votteler met with Dale Hall, the director of the Fish and Wildlife Service in Washington, DC.[58] Hall had previously been the director for Region 2 and was very familiar with Edwards Aquifer issues. Although recovery implementation programs were not discussed, Votteler did discuss the status of the Edwards and upcoming issues in the Texas Legislature and the region.

On January 7, 2006, Bill West, general manager of the Guadalupe-Blanco River Authority, met with Lohoefener in Phoenix, Arizona, at a National Water Resources Association leadership conference.[59] Lohoefener suggested that the region should consider using a recovery implementation program to address the water/Endangered Species

Act conflict. West was immediately enthusiastic about the prospects of using a recovery implementation program for the Edwards Aquifer. West and Votteler promptly began meeting with officials high up in the state agencies involved with Edwards issues.[60] Later, they had a series of meetings with key legislators and stakeholders.[61]

On February 3, 2006, Bill West and Todd Votteler met with Joy Nicholopoulos in Austin to discuss the recovery implementation process. Following up on the groundwork being laid by the Guadalupe-Blanco River Authority, Nicholopoulos met with Kathleen White, chair of the Texas Commission on Environmental Quality, on March 22, 2006. She reported back to West and Votteler:

> I met with Chairman White yesterday and we discussed a comparative agrmt/some sort of recovery implementation program for the Edwards Aquifer. We discussed the Federal "connection" to bring all the stakeholders together and decided against a section 7 (regulatory under the ESA) nexus. The unfinished HCP seems a much better instrument (that involves a voluntary section 10 permit under the ESA). We also discussed various roles for stakeholders and agreed that the FWS shouldn't be the stimulus, and perhaps TPWD would be a better center piece for such a group. Chairman White was going to visit with Bob Cook. I will also visit with him to see about getting this effort off the ground.[62]

Subsequently, on June 28, 2006, Joy Nicholopoulos and Anna Munoz met with Bob Cook, executive director of the Texas Parks and Wildlife Department, and asked the department to take the lead on the recovery implementation program (RIP). To encourage the department to take the lead, Nicholopoulos told Cook that "we were very successful in obtaining Federal funds for the RIP participants to implement recovery actions for listed aquatic species (up to ~$11 million appropriated annually since 2002) in NM, and I am confident we could generate similar Congressional interest in TX."[63] On July 18, 2006, Nicholopoulos told Votteler, "I have met with TPWD and I am waiting for their response (proposal for an EA RIP with TPWD lead/coordination). I will let you know when I get some news."[64] While interested in the program, the department subsequently declined to lead it.[65]

Nicholopoulos also began an outreach program to the stakeholders to try to encourage their participation in a recovery implementation program. Much of her approach centered on the past success of other recovery implementation programs. She emphasized the ability of those programs to attract federal funding not only for the process itself but also for the implementation of the plan. Although she was careful not to promise such funding, it was a strong selling point and may have created unrealistic expectations.

On August 2, 2006, the Edwards Aquifer Authority staff met with the US Fish and Wildlife Service to discuss with Nicholopoulos the Edwards Aquifer Authority's draft habitat conservation plan. "The new Administrator is interested in using a new method to finish the HCP that begins with a Recovery Implementation Program." The authority explained, "Having the Service take charge of the process will result in a more aggressive completion schedule. A regular meeting will be established once the process for completing the HCP is outlined."[66] Subsequently, on October 10, 2006, Nicholopoulos gave a presentation to the Edwards Aquifer Authority Board of Directors. She said that the information developed in the habitat conservation plan drafting process could give the recovery implementation program "a leg up" in the development of its own habitat conservation plan. At the conclusion of that presentation, Nicholopoulos said that if the EARIP came together she would talk to the secretary and see if she could "get it on the fast track to get [the funding] authorized."[67]

Preparing for the Legislature

After a discussion at the annual workshop of the Edwards Aquifer Authority board, the group approved a four-point legislative agenda on September 12, 2006. The agenda included: (1) setting the withdrawal cap at 549,000 acre-feet and eliminating the 400,000-acre-foot cap required to be implemented in 2008; (2) having the critical period management reductions set by the legislature, with a limit on withdrawals to an annual rate of 340,000 acre-feet per year; (3) ensuring that, if any reductions were required, downstream interests would pay 50 percent of the cost while Edwards Aquifer Authority permit holders would pay the other 50 percent; and (4) allowing the Edwards Aquifer Authority to build recharge structures and issue bonds.[68] This agenda was essentially a reprise of what was included in House Bill 3586 in 2003 and House Bill 41 in 2005.

Robert Potts, general manager of the Edwards Aquifer Authority, was instrumental in garnering support for the legislative agenda in the San Antonio area. Those efforts began in the fall of 2006 when he arranged a meeting with Mayor Phil Hardberger and Larry Zinn, the mayor's chief of staff.[69] Doug Miller, chair of the aquifer authority board, also participated in the meeting, during which Potts briefed members on the need for legislation to raise the withdrawal cap.

As a result of that meeting, Mayor Hardberger hosted a meeting in the late fall. The attendees included the chief executive officers and chairs of the Edwards Aquifer Authority, San Antonio Water System, and San Antonio River Authority, as well as Bexar County judge Nelson Wolff, the Greater San Antonio Chamber of Commerce, and others. Senators Wentworth and Van de Putte and Representative Puente attended the meeting, which Mayor Hardberger and Judge Wolff chaired. The parties agreed to get behind one bill to address the issue of raising the withdrawal cap. Senator Wentworth and Representative Puente agreed to sponsor the legislation. The city and county officials committed their legislative teams to work on the issue. Potts remained active in the legislative process, particularly in keeping the city and county apprised of activities in the legislature.

On September 22, 2006, a joint meeting of the House and Senate Natural Resources Committees was held in San Antonio.[70] Both Robert Potts and Bill West testified at the meeting. Potts testified generally on the four points in the legislative agenda of the Edwards Aquifer Authority, but he focused on the need to raise the cap.

West testified that the 549,000-acre-foot cap with a 340,000-acre-foot floor, as outlined in the Edwards Aquifer legislative agenda, would not work. He said that testimony in *Sierra Club v. Babbitt* suggested that, during a repeat of the drought of record, pumping of 200,000 acre-feet was necessary to maintain continuous springflows. He explained that the 340,000-acre-foot cap was not based on science but came from the Regional L Water Plan of 2002.[71] He said it was intended to be a placeholder in the plan, not a measure of the firm yield of the aquifer. He conceded that in times of average or above average flows a pumping cap of 549,000 acre-feet might be reasonable. He proposed, however, that the issue of the floor should be addressed with the Fish and Wildlife Service through a recovery implementation program that included the development of a habitat conservation plan.[72] An increase in the cap in average or above average rainfall conditions coupled with a recovery implementation program, he said, was the way forward in the 2007 legislative session. This approach, he explained, would leave to the FWS the ultimate decision as to what was needed to protect the species.

On October 5, 2006, the Joint Legislative Committee on the Oversight of the Edwards Aquifer met.[73] In large part, the meeting was a reprise of the testimony in San Antonio. Two important points emerged, however. First, the co-chair of the committee, Representative Harvey Hilderbran, suggested that a regional solution would be needed if any legislation was to go forward in 2007, and he asked each of the representatives of the downstream interests when he could expect a paper setting out their interests for the upcoming session. Second, to a varying degree, the various downstream interests all suggested that they might not oppose the San Antonio Water System's position on the pumping cap if the proposed 340,000-acre-foot floor were lowered. Bill West again expressed his support for the recovery implementation program strategy discussed by the US Fish and Wildlife Service. He pointed out that the FWS had discussed the potential for federal funding not only to support the process but also to pay for implementation of the plan.

On November 9, 2006, the Guadalupe Basin Coalition released a resolution setting out its agenda for the upcoming legislative session.[74] The resolution was highly critical of the legislative agenda of the Edwards Aquifer Authority. It stated, however, that it would not oppose increasing the cap in the 2007 session so long as the legislation: (1) included a five-stage critical period management reduction plan based on springflows at Comal and San Marcos Springs or the J-17 index well and proposed total withdrawal reductions for each stage in each pool (stage V reductions were 40 percent in the San Antonio pool and 30 percent in the Uvalde pool); (2) created a task force, consisting of the presiding officers of the Edwards Aquifer Authority, Guadalupe-Blanco River Authority, Texas Parks and Wildlife Department, San Antonio Water System, Texas Water Development Board, and Texas Commission on Environmental Quality, that would be empowered to decrease further pumping during stages and IV and V for up to a month; (3) required the state, through the Texas Commission on Environmental Quality, Texas Parks and Wildlife Department, Texas Department of Agriculture, and Texas Water Development Board, to participate with other stakeholders in a recovery implementation process to achieve consensus on a management plan to conserve the spring ecosystems and the listed species, with approval of the planned process by the US Fish and Wildlife Service by January 1, 2012; and (4) did not require surface water permit holders to contribute to any needed buy-down.

On November 15, 2006, Nicholopoulos gave a presentation on recovery implementation programs to the board of the Guadalupe-Blanco River Authority.[75] Afterwards, the board voted to support the Guadalupe Basin Coalition's resolution that it would not oppose an increased pumping cap if a recovery implementation program was used to address the withdrawal reduction floor. According to the Guadalupe-Blanco River Authority, the "Recovery Implementation Program process had already been presented to the Edwards Aquifer Authority, SAWS and other groups[,] with positive responses."[76] According to Calvin Finch, from the San Antonio Water System, "The fact that all of us are supporting it indicates that we're all ready to do some compromising. We probably should have done this a long time ago."[77]

Other reports suggested that a full meeting of the minds had not occurred:

> San Antonio Water System and EAA officials say they are encouraged by a resolution passed by the Guadalupe Basin Coalition—endorsed by the GBRA board—that supports raising the pumping cap to 549,000 acre-feet during times of plenty with certain conditions. San Antonio area officials interpret the resolution to also voice support of a 349,000 acre-feet limit during severe drought. West, who believes the science shows a limit of 200,000 acre-feet is needed to protect spring flows during tough times, says the resolution actually supports a cooperative process involving all stakeholders to determine the pumping allowed during severe drought.[78]

Thus, as the 2007 session of the Texas Legislature approached, the pieces seemed to be there for a compromise that would on one hand raise the cap on withdrawals from the Edwards Aquifer and on the other hand establish a process for resolving the continuous minimum flow issue that involved the US Fish and Wildlife Service. However, unless those pieces could be made to fall into place, no legislation would be likely to result, and the region could face unaffordable costs to buy down permits and a possible return to federal court.

The Eightieth Session of the Texas Legislature

During the early stages of the new legislative session that began in 2007, there were three significant events that probably influenced the ultimate outcome. First, on January 9, the first day of the session, Texas attorney general Greg Abbott issued an opinion concluding the

Edwards Aquifer Authority did not have the statutory authority to reduce the withdrawal rights of permit holders or issue interruptible "junior" withdrawal rights below the statutory minimum.[79] Unless the legislature fixed the problem, the Edwards users and downstream interests would have to buy back some of the water rights to make up the difference.[80] The cost of an acre-foot of Edwards water had risen to more than $5,000 per acre-foot. The cost to buy down permits to 450,000 acre-feet and retiring permits to get to 400,000 acre-feet was estimated to be $750 million.[81] The cost to downstream surface water users responsible for one-half of the cost of retiring permits to get from 450,000 to 400,000 acre-feet would have been $125 million. Thus, both the pumpers and the downstream interests had an incentive to have the cap raised.

Second, on February 12, 2007, the Texas Water Development Board issued a modeling report requested by Representative Patrick Rose.[82] Using a groundwater availability model, the Texas Water Development Board compared the effects of having (1) the cap at 450,000 and 400,000 acre-feet with the existing critical period management reduction rules having a floor of 340,000 acre-feet and (2) a cap of 549,000 acre-feet with the critical period management reductions having a floor at 340,000 acre-feet. The model runs showed that, under all of the cap scenarios, Comal Springs would stop flowing for between twenty-five and thirty months with a 340,000-acre-foot critical period management floor. Representative Puente responded to these model results in light of the 340,000-acre-foot pumping floor in his bill by saying, "Water experts suggested the lower level as adequate for a severe drought[,] but . . . Wednesday's computer model raises questions about that number." Senator Hegar concurred, saying, "That would be a disaster. That spring flow is vital. . . . Everybody can share some pain and have backup reserves," but "they won't last 30 months."[83]

Third, in November 2006, Glenn Hegar was elected to the Senate. His district included Victoria and other parts of the Guadalupe River Basin. The Guadalupe Basin Coalition, led by Jerry James and Gary Middleton, worked with Senator Hegar to secure his involvement with the Edwards legislation in the 2007 session. His office would serve as the driving force for bringing about the compromise. As he told the Guadalupe Basin Coalition on February 21, 2007, "If anything is going to happen, I need to be driving the train. There will be no bill unless it is a good bill."[84]

There were really two competing bills in the legislature with respect to the Edwards Aquifer, with one largely reflecting the views of the San Antonio area and the other, the views of the Guadalupe Basin Coalition and the Guadalupe-Blanco River Authority. On February 9, 2007, Representatives Robert Puente, Joaquín Castro, José Menéndez, and David Liebowitz filed House Bill 1292. It was identical to Senate Bill 24 and House Bill 41 from the 2005 session and was the vehicle supported by the San Antonio Water System, City of San Antonio, Greater San Antonio Chamber of Commerce, Bexar County, and the Edwards Aquifer Authority.[85] Senator Jeff Wentworth filed a companion bill, Senate Bill 659, on February 15, 2007.[86]

On March 8, 2007, Senator Hegar introduced Senate Bill 1341.[87] On March 9, 2007, Representative Geanie Morrison introduced the counterpart bill in the House (House Bill 3848). The Guadalupe-Blanco River Authority and the Guadalupe Basin Coalition endorsed Senate Bill 1341: "This endorsement is in support of using the Recovery Implementation Program process for the Edwards Aquifer, instead of simply allowing more pumping from the aquifer regardless of the consequences. The process would bring together federal, state and local stakeholders to develop a science-based plan that protects springflows and the surface water rights of all who depend on the Edwards Aquifer. The legislation would also postpone certain key deadlines in the Edwards Aquifer Authority Act to provide time for the stakeholder process to work."[88] What ensued after the bills were introduced clearly fit the analogy so aptly used to describe the legislative process: "making sausage."

The House Natural Resources Committee took comments on House Bill 1292 on March 21, 2007, but the bill was left pending in the committee. Representative Puente introduced a committee substitute for House Bill 1292 in the House Natural Resources Committee, which he chaired. It was reported out unanimously on April 11, 2007. The Senate Committee on Natural Resources considered Senate Bill 659, the companion to House Bill 1292, on April 10, 2007. That bill, too, was left pending in the committee.

The legislature focused instead on Senate Bill 1341, on which Senator Hegar had been having success in forging a compromise. The growing consensus in the legislature mirrored the growing consensus elsewhere among the stakeholders. In early March, Phil Hardberger, mayor of San Antonio, requested a meeting with representatives of Victoria at the San Antonio Water System on March 19, 2007.[89] The meeting was attended by Mayor Hardberger, Bexar County judge Nelson Wolff, Victoria mayor Will Armstrong, Victoria County judge Dan Pozzi, Victoria city manager Charles Windwehen, and Jerry James, director of environmental services, as well as Robert Potts and Doug Miller, general manager and board chair, respectively, of the Edwards Aquifer Authority, and Alex Briseño, who chaired the San Antonio Water System Board of Trustees. It was reported that "Victoria and San Antonio officials were talking, rather than shooting at each other, when they recently met. And they didn't even need to break out the booze to lubricate the discussion. The two cities are working together on water legislation that would better address the needs of both in regulating the use of the Edwards aquifer."[90] The meeting had the salutary effect of establishing a direct line of communication between the City of Victoria and the San Antonio Water System at a critical point in the negotiations.[91]

On April 26, 2007, after numerous meetings with stakeholders and input from Nicholopoulos, Senator Hegar stated, according to a newspaper report, "We're as close (to consensus) as we've been. At least everybody agrees on certain issues and agrees to disagree over minor issues."[92] At the meeting of the Senate Natural Resources Committee, Senator Hegar introduced a committee substitute that reflected those discussions.

The following provisions in Committee Substitute 1341 are relevant to subsequent negotiations and for the most part are included in the final bill, with some minor and clarifying changes. These provisions

- required all authorizations and rights to make a withdrawal under this act to be limited to recognize the extent of the hydro-geologic connection and interaction between surface water and groundwater;
- set the withdrawal cap at 572,000 acre-feet and did away with the buy-down provisions in Senate Bill 1477;
- maintained the requirement that the Edwards Aquifer Authority ensure that, not later than December 31, 2012, the continuous minimum springflows of the Comal Springs and the San Marcos Springs be maintained to protect endangered and threatened species but also indicated that the flows must also "achieve other purposes provided by Subsection (a) of this section and Section 1.26 of this article";

- established a statutory critical management program;
- limited stage IV withdrawals under the critical period management program to 340,000 acre-feet until January 1, 2013, at which time withdrawal limits in stage IV could go to 320,000 acre-feet unless a greater reduction was necessary to protect the federally listed species;
- allowed the authority to own, finance, design, construct, operate, and maintain recharge dams but excluded projects designed to recirculate water at Comal or San Marcos Springs;
- directed the Edwards Aquifer Authority and four state agencies to "develop a recovery implementation program through a facilitated, consensus-based" stakeholder process;
- required the stakeholders to use their "best efforts" to enter into a memorandum of agreement with the US Fish and Wildlife Service by December 31, 2007, and an implementing agreement with the FWS to develop a program document by December 31, 2009;
- directed the Edwards Aquifer Authority, the state agencies, and other stakeholders to jointly prepare a "program document that may be in the form of a habitat conservation plan used in the issuance of an incidental take permit";
- required that the program document provide, among other things, "recommendations for withdrawal adjustments based on a combination of spring discharge rates of the San Marcos and Comal springs and levels at the J-17 and J-27 index wells during critical periods to ensure that federally listed, threatened, and endangered species associated with the Aquifer will be protected at all times, including throughout a repeat of the drought of record";
- required that the plan be executed by each agency not later than September 1, 2012, and take effect by December 31, 2012;
- required the creation of a steering committee to oversee and assist in the development of the plan;
- identified the initial composition of the steering committee as including nineteen members representing environmental, water authority and purveyor, industrial, municipal, public utility, state agency, and agricultural interests related to the Edwards Aquifer and allowed additional members to be added by majority vote of the steering committee;

- required the steering committee to appoint an Edwards Aquifer area expert science subcommittee not later than December 31, 2007, and established specific tasks for the expert science committee and deadlines for completion of those tasks; and
- directed Texas A&M University to provide administrative support for the program, including hiring a program manager.

On April 27, 2007, Senators Wentworth, Van de Putte, and Carlos Uresti, representing the San Antonio area, announced that they were co-signing as sponsors of Senator Hegar's committee substitute.[93] Representative Puente announced that he intended to amend his bill to reflect the changes in the committee substitute bill.[94]

The Senate Natural Resources Committee reported out the committee substitute to Senate Bill 1341 by a vote of 9 to 0 on May 1, 2007. A few clarifying amendments and two substantive amendments were made on the Senate floor. With respect to the substantive amendments, Senator Uresti amended the bill to allow irrigators to finish out a crop before critical period management withdrawal reductions applied. Senator Kip Averitt amended the substitute to require the Edwards Aquifer Authority, San Antonio Water System, Guadalupe-Blanco River Authority, San Antonio River Authority, and Bexar County to each contribute $500,000 to fund the initial stages of the recovery implementation program process until federal, state, or other funds became available. The amended committee substitute was passed unanimously by the Senate on May 4, 2007.

On May 7, 2007, Senate Bill 1341 was received by the House and referred to the House Committee on Natural Resources. The next day, Representative Puente, chair of the House Natural Resources Committee, introduced to his committee a substitute version of the bill passed by the Senate. The substitute House version differed in only a few ways from what was passed by the Senate, but one of those differences was significant. The House substitute version reduced the initial makeup of the steering committee to only thirteen members. Further, those thirteen members did not include an environmental interest or specify the Guadalupe-Blanco River Authority as a member of the steering committee. On May 14, 2013, the House Natural Resources Committee reported out the substitute. However, it was not voted on in the House.

Senator Hegar reacted to Puente's changes in the substitute by saying that "we need to work all of this out or no bill."[95] A compromise was reached with Representative Puente to largely track the amended version of the bill that the Senate had passed. The compromise on the initial composition of the steering committee included "7 downstream interests, 7 San Antonio interests, 4 government agencies, and two pumper interests."[96] The twenty-first member of the steering committee was left to Senator Hegar to decide. He included a representative of the environmental interests. In addition, the compromise deleted Senator Averitt's amendment requiring certain specified stakeholders to fund the initial work of the recovery implementation program.

On May 22, 2007, at the request of Representative Puente, Representative Morrison introduced the compromise version of the House committee substitute for House Bill 1341 as an amendment (amendment 79) to Senate Bill 3 that had passed the Senate in March and was then being considered by the House. On May 23, 2007, the House passed the Senate bill with Representative Morrison's amendment, but it still had to go back to the Senate.

On May 24, 2007, the Senate failed to concur, and the two versions of the bill were sent to a conference committee. The failure to obtain concurrence was not significantly related to provisions regarding the Edwards Aquifer. Indeed, the conference committee made only minor changes to the Edwards portion of Senate Bill 3.

However, on May 28, 2007, with the clock running out for the session, Representative Stephen Frost, from Atlanta in northeastern Texas, during the debate on the conference report in the House, raised a point of order on an issue unrelated to the Edwards Aquifer. Because it was late in the session, this procedural issue could have killed the entire bill. Representative Puente, however, promptly worked with Frost to resolve the procedural issue so that the report could be voted on.[97]

Both the Senate and the House approved the conference report on May 28, 2007, and it was signed by Governor Rick Perry on June 16, 2007. In his prepared remarks at the signing in San Antonio, the governor said, "South Texans can be proud as well that local representative Robert Puente helped avert a $750 million price tag by raising the pumping cap in the Edwards Aquifer."[98]

Senate Bill 3 Provisions Pertinent to the EARIP

The legislature directed the Edwards Aquifer Authority and four state agencies to "cooperatively develop a recovery implementation program" through a facilitated, consensus-based stakeholder process.

Senate Bill 3 further directed the Edwards Aquifer Authority and other state agencies to participate in the EARIP and to jointly prepare, along with other stakeholders, a "program document that may be in the form of a habitat conservation plan used in the issuance of an incidental take permit."[99] It required that the program document provide, among other things, "recommendations for withdrawal adjustments based on a combination of spring discharge rates of the San Marcos and Comal springs and levels at the J-17 and J-27 index wells during critical periods to ensure that federally listed, threatened, and endangered species associated with the Aquifer will be protected at all times, including throughout a repeat of the drought of record." In addition, Senate Bill 3 required that the plan take effect by December 31, 2012.[100]

Senate Bill 3 called for the creation of a steering committee to oversee and assist in the development of the EARIP. The bill specifically identified twenty-one members of the steering committee, and they represented environmental, water authority and purveyor, industrial, municipal, public utility, state agency, and agricultural interests related to the Edwards Aquifer. However, the legislation allowed the steering committee to add members or change the composition of the committee.[101]

Senate Bill 3 set out deadlines by which the EARIP had to accomplish certain specific tasks:

- Create a steering committee by September 30, 2007.
- Hire a program manager by October 31, 2007.
- Enter into a memorandum of agreement by December 31, 2007.
- Appoint an expert science subcommittee by December 31, 2007.
- The Science Subcommittee must submit to the steering committee and stakeholders initial recommendations on issues identified in Senate Bill 3 by December 31, 2008
- Enter into an implementing agreement to develop a program document by December 31, 2009.[102]

PART II

THE EDWARDS AQUIFER RECOVERY
IMPLEMENTATION PROGRAM

At a time when dysfunction marks the upper levels of American government and politics, the Edwards region found a way to compromise and meet the needs of a hugely diverse set of interests.
— San Antonio Express-News Editorial Board, "Aquifer Plan a Major Success," December 29, 2011

This section of the book does not contain an exhaustive description of all of the many issues that the EARIP had to address. Instead, it focuses on the issues most important to the successful completion of the Senate Bill 3 mandates. Chapter 7 chronicles the organization of the EARIP and the procedures the stakeholders elected to follow in their decision making. Then, chapter 8 addresses the critical substantive issues of what minimum flows were needed and how those flows would be achieved. That chapter also describes how the EARIP went about making decisions. Chapter 9 tackles the thorny question of how the cost of implementing the habitat conservation plan would be allocated. Finally, chapter 10 attempts to provide some insight into why the EARIP was able to reach consensus where other efforts had failed.

7 : ORGANIZING THE PROGRAM

Had I been present at the creation, I would have given some useful hints
for the better ordering of the universe.
— Alphonso X "the Wise" of Castile (1221–84)

For fifty years, the competing interests in the Edwards region had tried to resolve their differences. Some efforts came close to succeeding, but all had ultimately failed. Over time, with each ensuing failure, the various interests in the region lost confidence in each other and in their collective ability to solve the problems. Entering into the EARIP process, the stakeholders had their doubts that this process would succeed where similar attempts to find a solution had failed. However, all understood that failure was likely to result in intervention by the federal court or the Texas Legislature, thus removing control of the aquifer from the region. It was now up to the EARIP to find a way to make it work.

Although far from simple, the task facing the EARIP was still somewhat simpler than that which confronted those who undertook earlier efforts to resolve the dispute. Irrigated agriculture, which was a major stumbling block to consensus in the early 1990s, had two representatives on the steering committee, but they no longer had strong positions to advance. The use of the Edwards Aquifer had been managed for more than a decade; the rule of capture was no longer in place. The statutory minimum amount of water for irrigated agriculture guaranteed the irrigators two acre-feet of water per acre planted during the historical period. This guarantee gave irrigators adequate water for their crops and in many instances provided a surplus that could be leased or sold—thus creating a water market.[1] Irrigators had to install meters on their wells, but, unlike for municipal and industrial pumpers, the costs of purchasing, installing, and maintaining the meters had to be paid by the Edwards Aquifer Authority.[2] In 2001 the legislature had capped the aquifer management fees for irrigated agriculture at two dollars per acre-foot of water pumped.[3] Finally, with respect to critical period management withdrawal reductions, Senate Bill 3 allowed irrigators to finish out the crop that was in the ground when the reduction was triggered.[4] Thus, irrigated agriculture's agenda in the EARIP was generally more in defending what it had obtained rather than advancing any particular position of its own.

Moreover, the number of issues requiring resolution by the EARIP had been narrowed. The legislature had just set the withdrawal caps and established the critical period management withdrawal reductions. Thus, the principal problems that the EARIP needed to resolve were the issues related to the mandated continuous minimum flows—what minimum flows were required, how those flows could be achieved, and how the cost of achieving those flows would be funded.

Resolution of these issues was still a daunting task. The Edwards Aquifer Authority had failed to achieve consensus on them. However, the EARIP had specific directions with respect to what the solution needed to accomplish—the solution had to be effective *even during a repeat of the drought of record.* Any plan to be approved by the US Fish and Wildlife Service would have to meet the requirements for the issuance of an incidental take permit, and the decision to approve such a permit would have to avoid jeopardy—that is, not appreciably reduce the likelihood of the survival and recovery of all listed species affected by the decision.[5]

Getting Started

While the legislature was considering Senate Bill 3, the initial voluntary meetings of the recovery implementation program were occurring. The US Fish and Wildlife Service held the first meeting of the proposed EARIP on February 16, 2007, at the Aquarena Center in San Marcos.[6] The meeting was led by Dr. Joy Nicholopoulos. Dr. Tarla Rai Peterson, from Texas A&M University, discussed the role the university would play in the EARIP process. She announced that Texas A&M would coordinate/facilitate the collaborative process and serve as a liaison with technical experts, local stakeholders, and governmental agencies. The other presentations scheduled by the FWS focused on other recovery implementation programs and the use of collaborative learning in the EARIP.

The subsequent meetings in 2007 focused on three basic issues: (1) collaborative learning, (2) the memorandum of agreement with the US Fish and Wildlife Service, and (3) the composition of the steering committee and its relationship to the other stakeholder participants.[7]

COLLABORATIVE LEARNING

The initial meeting of the EARIP included two presentations and accompanying exercises on "collaborative learning," led by Steve Daniels and Gregg Walker, from Utah State University and Oregon State University, respectively. Collaborative learning is "an approach appropriate for natural resource, environmental, and community decision-making situations with the following features: multiple parties, deeply held values, cultural differences, multiple issues, scientific and technical uncertainty, and legal and jurisdictional constraints. It emphasizes activities that encourage systems thinking, joint learning, open communication, constructive conflict management, and a focus on appropriate change."[8] The presentations were followed by workshops, held on February 28 and March 1, 2007, that focused on how to use collaborative learning. Daniels and Walker gave presentations, including an introduction to the "collaborative learning process," as well as specific aspects of that process, such as "rich picturing" and "situation mapping," and the application of situation mapping to the Edwards Aquifer.[9] At a subsequent EARIP meeting on April 5, 2007, held at the San Antonio Water System offices, the participants were each asked to submit statements of their views of the goals and purposes of the EARIP.[10]

I assumed the position of EARIP manager in December 2007, and at that point the role of Texas A&M in the EARIP meetings diminished. The EARIP did not really follow through on any of these group-learning exercises, at least in a formal, structured context. I do not recall ever discussing the goals and purposes statements or incorporating them in the decision-making process. The stakeholders were a very experienced group that had been living with the issues for years. They were anxious to get on with the substantive work and were concerned that these exercises had focused too much on the process and not enough on the substantive issues. Many of the participants believe that the credit for holding the EARIP together prior to a program manager coming on board goes to Anna Munoz, a graduate student under Dr. Peterson, who, because of her experience with the Middle Rio Grande Recovery Implementation Program, was able to focus on the substantive issues facing the EARIP.

Devoting a session or two to reviewing respectful communication styles probably was useful in establishing ground rules for thoughtful exchanges of conflicting perspectives. To do more than that would have interfered with the resolution of the substantive issues and created an obstacle in meeting the Senate Bill 3 deadlines. Most participants I contacted agree with this conclusion.[11]

At the close of each of the collaborative learning workshops, a draft memorandum of agreement (MOA) was distributed to the stakeholders for discussion at the next EARIP meeting. The initial draft was prepared by the Fish and Wildlife Service and was simply a marked-up copy of agreements used by other recovery implementation programs, adapted for the specifics of the EARIP and allowing for a habitat conservation plan to be part of that program.[12] Many of the details were left open for future discussion and resolution.

At the EARIP meeting on July 12, 2007, a committee was formed to work on the memorandum of agreement.[13] The committee met all day on a weekly basis in the cafeteria at the San Antonio Water System offices. At the EARIP meeting on September 6, 2007, it distributed a revised draft of the memorandum of agreement.[14] The revised draft focused on the structure, governance, and obligations of the EARIP under Senate Bill 3 and, to a lesser extent, on the specific obligations it had as a recovery implementation program. The language in the Fish and Wildlife Service draft regarding its authority to create such programs and the references to a cooperative agreement were stricken.[15] The revised draft of the memorandum of agreement included an express assurance that the non–steering committee members' interests would be recognized and protected: "The Steering Committee will develop procedures consistent with the MOA to ensure the Program includes, but is not limited to, the following procedural elements: an open process, advance notice of meetings and proposed actions, opportunity for stakeholder participation, open communication, and consensus-based decision-making."[16]

The committee chair reported that the two most difficult issues the committee faced in preparing the revised draft were providing additional representation on the steering committee and developing a decision-making process. To address concerns about the adequacy of representation on the steering committee, the memorandum of agreement committee recommended adding five new interest groups to the steering committee and identified the specific groups that should be added in the draft memorandum of agreement.[17] Two primary considerations informed the committee's recommendations: addressing the specific membership deficiencies previously identified by stakeholders and avoiding significant changes in the overall balance of interests represented on the steering committee, as set out in Senate Bill 3.

To address the decision-making process, the drafters made a distinction between significant decisions and routine decisions. The significant decisions required consensus. The memorandum of agreement established a 75 percent supermajority vote to allow the process to move forward in the event that consensus could not be reached. Routine decisions were to be made by majority vote.

The final version of the memorandum of agreement was circulated for execution on December 13, 2007, and, after execution by the requisite parties, went into effect on January 10, 2008.[18] The agreement had not changed significantly from the September draft. Ultimately, thirty-nine stakeholders, including all of the steering committee members, executed the memorandum of agreement.[19]

Beyond what it produced and the difficult issues it tackled, this committee was very important to the ultimate success of the EARIP process. The work that committee members did came at the very beginning of the process and tested whether the concepts of openness and transparency established in Senate Bill 3 could actually work among a group of hardened, grizzled veterans of the Edwards Issue. The members of that committee showed that it could work and, thus, set the tone for future collaboration and decision making.

The committee operated on the principle that all ideas would be discussed and that everyone got to be heard.[20] The committee members openly and candidly discussed the consequences of their decisions. This approach appears to have started restoring the bonds of trust in the region and humanized the process. As Colette Barron expressed it, "We broke bread together."[21] The future held many heated debates, but, for the most part, the discourse was civil, respectful, and productive.

To fully appreciate the importance of this committee's work, one only has to ask what kind of future the EARIP would have had if, at the start, it had been unable to agree even on the shape of the table.

Composition of the Steering Committee

Senate Bill 3 established the initial composition of the steering committee. The twenty-one-member committee was the result of a compromise achieved between Senator Hegar and Representative Puente.

According to Senator Hegar, "I was trying to get groups with funding to get the process running. Involvement by state agencies shows the federal government that the state is committed and interested. I also had to consider how to get this passed through the legislature and make sure that it is balanced. I tried to fashion it in a manner where one group or another doesn't have all of the say."[22] Not everyone agreed with the composition of the steering committee established by the legislature. George Rice, of Aquifer Guardians in Urban Areas, commented, "From the environmental point of view, the process is unfair due to steering committee composition. I am willing to spend time to make this a fair process, but for me as it stands, it is not a fair process."[23]

Senate Bill 3, however, allowed the steering committee to add members or change the composition of the committee.[24] The memorandum of agreement recommended that five additional specific interest groups be added "at the earliest opportunity." The recommended interests represented included: (1) a representative of a holder of an Edwards Aquifer Authority initial regular permit issued to a small municipality (population under fifty thousand) located east of San Antonio; (2) a representative of Edwards Aquifer region municipal ratepayers/general public; (3) a representative of Guadalupe River Basin municipal ratepayers/general public; (4) a representative of a conservation organization; and (5) a representative of the Nueces River Authority.[25]

At the EARIP meeting on February 14, 2008, Calvin Finch of the San Antonio Water System distributed heart-shaped boxes of Valentine's Day candy to each of the stakeholders. The group then discussed the possibility of expanding the steering committee, perhaps unaware that the process had been just a little more humanized and the loss of trust in the region ever so slightly diminished.[26] The steering committee agreed by consensus to ask for nominations of specific individuals or entities for each of the four categorical interest groups recommended in the memorandum of agreement and to ask the Nueces River Authority to identify its representative before for the next meeting. At that time, the steering committee would decide to accept all, some, or none of the five proposed additional members.

At the next meeting, I reported that nominations had been received for three of the four interest groups recommended by the memorandum of agreement but that no nominations were received for the position of representative for the Guadalupe River Basin municipal ratepayers/general public.[27] The Nueces River Authority had identified Con Mims, general manager of the authority, to serve as representative for that group. After extended discussion, it was agreed to add to the steering committee the three interest groups for which nominations had been received, as well as the Nueces River Authority. The entities representing those interest groups were the City of Garden Ridge, Regional Clean Air & Water, and the San Marcos River Foundation. The final position was filled by the Guadalupe Basin Coalition at the next meeting, held on April 10.[28]

The steering committee thus had twenty-six members, and the issue of the composition of the committee never came up again in any significant way. The steering committee members and the representatives of the organizations that were members are detailed in appendix 1.

The second difficult issue that confronted the drafters of the memorandum of agreement was how to turn this historically adversarial group into a consensus-based, decision-making body.

The memorandum of agreement recognized that not all decisions of the steering committee had the same degree of significance. It therefore categorized decisions into two tiers. Tier 1 decisions were the more significant ones (e.g., adopting or amending the program document). Tier 1 decisions would be decided by consensus. Tier 2 decisions would be decided by majority vote.[29]

The steering committee defined consensus as the absence of any objection: "The goal of the Steering Committee is to achieve consensus-based decisionmaking. Consensus is reached when no Member of the Steering Committee is opposed to a proposal. It is understood and accepted that in order to achieve a consensus on the Steering Committee, each Member will be open to pursuing 'win-win' alternatives and to considering variations on the proposal that he or she might initially prefer. In its deliberations, the Steering Committee shall seek to exhaust every reasonable and practicable effort to reach consensus."[30] Acquiescence rather than actual agreement made decision making easier. A steering committee representative did not have to go on record as actively supporting a particular decision. Even with this useful semantic difference, everyone realized that, given the gulf between the stakeholders on many issues, consensus could prove very elusive.

Accordingly, for tier 1 decisions, if the steering committee did not initially achieve consensus, an "issues team" would be appointed. An issues team would include members with different perspectives on the specific proposal and could include stakeholders as well as steering committee members. The issues team would further explore and/or reformulate the proposal to see if consensus could be achieved. However, if the issues team, after making diligent efforts, was unable to achieve consensus, the steering committee could resolve the issue through a 75 percent supermajority vote.[31]

Other procedural devices also assisted in achieving consensus. The steering committee expressly provided that abstention by a steering committee member would not count as a negative vote.[32] This provision was helpful because it allowed persons who held strong opinions and found themselves in a very small minority not to be forced to delay the process by objecting to a proposal for which there was no possibility of a compromise. Abstention was used many times during the EARIP decision-making process.

Also assisting the EARIP in avoiding impasse was an early understanding that a decision on any particular issue was not final until the entire deal was complete. The steering committee members were thus free to engage in "what ifs" without fear of being locked in to one component of a deal until everything was on the table and the value of the entire package could be assessed. To support this, the EARIP agreed not to record the negotiations, and the minutes documented only the final decisions rather the discussions leading up to those decisions.

Finally, the EARIP used dozens of small work groups and subcommittees to examine and make recommendations regarding specific issues before they were brought to the steering committee for decision. The use of these groups proved very effective in narrowing the issues and, thus, facilitating resolution of complex or contentious issues.

The issues team process served the EARIP well. It allowed discussions to be held off-line so as not to let any one issue delay the steering committee from conducting other business. It also allowed for a more in-depth, direct discussion of the issues and afforded a better opportunity for compromises to be reached. Issues team meetings were open to everyone, but the chairs of the issues teams tried to focus the discussions among those appointed to the team.

Over the course of five years, the EARIP had numerous issues teams. In every instance save two, a supermajority vote was not needed to resolve the dispute. The first exception occurred in the fall of 2009 and involved a dispute regarding whether to fund a study extending earlier work supported by the Guadalupe-Blanco River Authority on the relationship of freshwater inflows to the energetics of whooping cranes at the Aransas National Wildlife Refuge. The proposal for extending the study was sponsored by the Guadalupe-Blanco River Authority. When the steering committee was not able to reach consensus on the funding decision, the issue was referred to an issues team that also was unable to reach consensus.[33] At the November EARIP meeting, a supermajority vote was taken, and the proposal to fund the study was defeated.[34]

The second exception came at a crucial meeting of the EARIP on November 7, 2011. At that meeting, the steering committee was to decide whether to recommend the habitat conservation plan and the supporting documents for final approval by the Edwards Aquifer Authority Board of Directors. The recommendation passed with one objection and one abstention.[35] The sole objector waived the issues team process.

Nonetheless, the consensus process had unintended consequences. Because there were twenty-six members on the steering committee, it would take twenty votes to affirmatively move forward, but only seven votes were needed to block a decision. Therefore, what emerged very quickly were voting blocs. The San Antonio Water System met routinely before steering committee meetings with representatives of Bexar County, the Bexar Metropolitan Water District, East Medina County Special Utility District, Alamo Cement, San Antonio River Authority, City Public Service, and Regional Clean Air & Water.[36] This group almost always voted as a bloc. The San Antonio Water System clearly provided strong leadership for this bloc.[37]

A second, more loosely knit bloc emerged, and it consisted of the Guadalupe-Blanco River Authority, Texas Parks and Wildlife Department, Texas Living Waters, San Marcos River Foundation, Guadalupe Basin Coalition, Dow Chemical, Texas Bass Federation, and New Braunfels Utilities. They often voted as a bloc. No single steering committee member provided the leadership for this group. Initially, the Guadalupe-Blanco River Authority seemed to provide the leadership of this bloc. Over time its leadership role appeared to recede as other members assumed that role.

With both groups being capable of blocking any action, the bloc votes were essentially vetoes that had the potential for creating an unsolvable impasse. Any impasse, particularly early in the process, could have the potential to be fatal to the entire effort because it could prevent progress on any issue, create gridlock, reopen old wounds, and provoke retaliation on subsequent issues. Thus, the potential for bloc vetoes ultimately made the primary objective in decision making to be avoiding impasse rather than achieving consensus. As will be illustrated later, the power of bloc vetoes made the timing of votes and the need for one-on-one discussions very important.

The Expert Science Subcommittee

Senate Bill 3 required the steering committee to appoint an expert science subcommittee composed of an odd number of members, between seven and fifteen.[38] The members had to have technical expertise regarding the aquifer system, the threatened and endangered species that inhabit the system, springflows, or the development of withdrawal limitations. The Senate Bill 3 deadline for getting this subcommittee in place was December 31, 2007.

When I started work in mid-December 2007 as program manager, the process of selecting the members of the science subcommittee was well under way. It quickly became apparent, even at this late stage in the selection process, that this issue had the potential to be a real problem. The views of the scientists in the region regarding the aquifer were well known. Rightly or wrongly, few were considered to be without bias. Because of the importance of the subcommittee, the different interest groups each believed that getting a subcommittee favorable to its views was essential to a successful outcome for the EARIP process.

At the EARIP meeting on September 6, 2007, the attendees began discussing the selection of members for the subcommittee.[39] Stakeholders were asked to submit candidates for membership on the subcommittee. A work group was established to develop guidelines and criteria for selecting the members.

By November, approximately forty nominations had been received.[40] After the work group had categorized them by skill set and experience, the steering committee members were asked to rank the candidates.

In December, armed with the rankings, the work group met to consider a recommendation on the subcommittee membership. It could not reach agreement on fifteen scientists but recommended that the steering committee appoint the five highest ranked biologists and the five highest ranked hydrologists along with Susan Aragon-Long from the US Geological Survey (USGS). To lessen concern about possible bias on the subcommittee, the work group also recommended that the work of the subcommittee be subjected to independent scientific review.

At the EARIP meeting on January 10, 2008, the steering committee considered the recommendations of the work group. After lengthy discussions, the steering committee appointed to the science sub-committee, by consensus, the top six applicants from the steering committee straw poll, without regard to expertise, as well as Susan Aragon-Long.[41] The six scientists included Robert Mace, from the Texas Water Development Board; Tom Brandt, from the US Fish and Wildlife Service; Sam Vaugh, from HDR Engineering, Inc.; Norman Boyd, from the Texas Parks and Wildlife Department; Glenn Longley, from Texas State University; and Mary Musick, retired from the Texas Commission on Environmental Quality. With respect to the remaining membership slots, the steering committee compromised and asked the subcom-mittee it had just appointed to recommend eight additional members for consideration by the steering committee. The steering committee also agreed that the work of the subcommittee would be subjected to independent peer review, if money were available.

On February 5, 2008, the science subcommittee made the following recommendations for the eight remaining slots on the subcommittee:

HYDROLOGISTS
- Alan Dutton (University of Texas at San Antonio)[42]
- Rene Barker (Texas State University)
- Ron Green (Southwest Research Institute)
- John Waugh (San Antonio Water System)

BIOLOGISTS
- Robert Edwards (University of Texas–Pan American)[43]
- Jackie Poole (Texas Parks and Wildlife Department)
- Ed Oborny (Bio-West, Inc.)
- Bryan Brooks (Baylor University)[44]

At the EARIP meeting on February 14, 2008, despite the agreement of the San Antonio Water System and Guadalupe-Blanco River Au-thority, the steering committee was unable to reach consensus on the science subcommittee recommendation.[45] After a strategic break to allow for discussion of the issue, the steering committee accepted the recommendations by consensus but only after agreeing to add Charles Kreitler to the subcommittee as a nonvoting member.[46] The subcommittee was then ready to go to work on the specific charges given to it by the legislature in Senate Bill 3.

The Texas Legislature charged the science subcommittee with preparing, by December 31, 2008, initial recommendations regarding

- designation of a separate San Marcos pool, evaluating how such a designation would affect existing pools, and determining the need for an additional well to measure the San Marcos pool, if designated;
- the necessity of maintaining minimum springflows, as well as conducting a specific review of the necessity to maintain a flow to protect federally listed species; and
- whether adjustments should be made in the trigger levels for the San Marcos Springs flow for the San Antonio pool.[47]

These recommendations were completed and submitted to the EARIP on November 13, 2008.[48] The science subcommittee did not recommend designating a separate San Marcos pool, at least until the relationships among rainfall, recharge, downgradient water levels, and springflow became more predictable. It also found that minimum springflows are required within the context of a system flow regime for the federally listed species at Comal and San Marcos Springs. Finally, the science subcommittee found that the critical period management triggers for the San Marcos Springs should not be adjusted at that time.

This report was peer reviewed by an independent panel of scientists assembled by the Sustainable Ecosystems Institute.[49]

The Texas Legislature also required the science subcommittee to analyze the species requirements with respect to springflows. This charge included establishing, if appropriate, separate critical period management withdrawal reduction levels and stages for different pools of the aquifer as needed to maintain target springflows and aquifer levels. The subcommittee submitted its report to the EARIP in December 2009.[50]

Based on the analyses it conducted, the science subcommittee determined that the following flow regime would "sustain an overall trend of maintaining or increasing the population of the aquatic communities of the Comal and San Marcos springs":

COMAL SPRINGS FLOW REGIME
- Long-term average flow: 225 cubic feet per second
- Minimum six-month average flow: 75 cubic feet per second
- Minimum one-month average flow: 30 cubic feet per second with no flow below 5 cubic feet per second

SAN MARCOS SPRINGS FLOW REGIME
- Long-term average flow: 140 cubic feet per second
- Minimum six-month average flow: 75 cubic feet per second
- Minimum one-month average flow: 60 cubic feet per second with no flow below 52 cubic feet per second

The science subcommittee used an existing groundwater flow model to develop withdrawal reductions and stages for critical period management that would meet or exceed all of the three flow criteria for each of the two springs. The model showed that withdrawals needed to be reduced 85 percent in a single stage to achieve all of the requirements of the flow regime. The report of the science subcommittee was peer reviewed by an independent panel of scientists assembled by Annear Associates, LLC.[51]

The flow regimes developed by the science subcommittee were intended to maintain or increase a species population—a *recovery* objective for the listed species—not to ensure that the flows would not jeopardize the species, as was required for the approval of the habitat conservation plan. Further, the determination of the science subcommittee did not take into account the effects of the minimization and mitigation measures that would be put in place in the habitat conservation plan. Thus, the recommendations it made were not directly relevant to the flow targets that the EARIP had to establish, but they nonetheless had a sobering effect on the EARIP deliberations. Those recommendations brought home the reality that, at some point, the magnitude of the required cuts would be too great to be satisfied by diversification of water supplies by the San Antonio Water System and too expensive for smaller municipalities to afford. New aquifer management strategies had to be developed if the EARIP were to succeed.

The work of the science subcommittee was quite remarkable. According to the peer review, "The Subcommittee was given a difficult and complex assignment and did a thorough job of data assimilation, analysis, evaluation, and recommendation development using widely accepted scientific methods."[52] Their discussions all took place during open meetings, and the presentations they received and the fruits of their efforts were posted on the EARIP website. Moreover, EARIP participants and the public were allowed to provide written and oral comments throughout the process.

It required a tremendous amount of focus and energy to produce the reports, particularly in the time frames set out for them. The members of the subcommittee completed their work on time and without compensation. Were the biases that some feared manifested in the process? In a few cases, the answer would be yes; it would be naïve to expect people who have worked so long on aquifer science issues to be able to park their previous work and conclusions at the door. But, for the most part, they functioned as a team and encouraged contrary views to be expressed in their reports. They did not always agree, but they made the extra effort to work through areas of disagreement and to reach consensus. They truly were dedicated individuals.

Some of the success of the subcommittee can be attributed to the leadership. Dr. Robert Mace, a highly respected hydrologist from the Texas Water Development Board, chaired the preparation of both reports. He commanded the respect of both the biologists and hydrologists on the subcommittee, and that respect enabled him to help them find a consensus position. Susan Aragon-Long, from the US Geological Survey, managed the activities of the subcommittee and participated in the discussions. She was a master at keeping the members focused, on time, and on schedule—most of the time with only gentle nudging.

8 : TACKLING THE MINIMUM FLOW ISSUE

The Edwards region is out of time. If the problems aren't worked out, the water battles of recent years will seem like a taffy pull compared to the nightmare that is headed our way.
— Bruce Davidson (*San Antonio Express-News*, December 10, 2006)

With the Texas Legislature having put the cap and statutory critical period management withdrawal reductions in place, two key contentious issues confronted the EARIP: (1) the minimum springflows necessary to protect the listed species and (2) how to ensure that springflows would not fall below the requisite minimum flows. The Edwards Aquifer Area Expert Science Subcommittee defined the term "minimum flows" to mean "flow events that occur infrequently, have a magnitude sufficient to maintain critical ecological functions . . . , and do not last long enough to stress the system beyond a point where it can recover naturally."[1]

The issue of whether something less than continuous flows (that is, something that could cause the springs to cease flowing) would be acceptable in a scheme to protect the listed species was not really an issue in the EARIP process. The science subcommittee had already found that some minimal level of continuous flow was necessary to protect the species.[2] That was also the conclusion reached by Judge Bunton and the US Fish and Wildlife Service on many occasions. Accordingly, the EARIP now had to determine what the minimum flows had to be to avoid jeopardy.

Determining the Minimum Flows Necessary to Protect the Listed Species

Early in 2008 the Fish and Wildlife Service began encouraging the EARIP to use a formal "structured decision-making" process to develop biological models from which new "take" and "jeopardy" flow levels could be derived.[3] The FWS had used this process in other contexts to arrive at biologically based decisions and wanted to extend it to jeopardy determinations. The US Geological Survey (USGS), another agency within the Department of the Interior, had developed expertise in working with and teaching the strategic decision-making process within the federal government.[4] The FWS was determined to have the EARIP retain its sister agency to employ the process for the EARIP.

"Structured decision making" is a systematic way to approach complex problems, with emphasis on identifying and evaluating management or policy options. It begins with the use of a carefully organized, facilitated, transparent process for making decisions based on explicit questions, analysis, and decision criteria. The objective is to "get around the track as fast as you can the first time" and then build iteratively on that first effort.[5]

At the request of the Fish and Wildlife Service, several presentations were given on the structured decision-making process and its use in developing biological models.[6] In April 2008 the steering committee formed the Biological Modeling Work Group to make recommendations on developing a biological model regarding "take" and "jeopardy flow levels."[7]

In May 2008, the Biological Modeling Work Group recommended that the EARIP authorize the development of the biological model for informing the "take" and "jeopardy" analysis in conjunction with the US Fish and Wildlife Service.[8] It further recommended that the steering committee ask the US Geological Survey to submit a scope of work and cost estimate proposing specific steps that could be completed by March 31, 2009, to develop that analysis. In developing the scope of work, the USGS was told to assume that a structured decision-making process would be used to document the process. Finally, the work group recommended that, regardless of whether or not the survey was the contractor, the process used to develop a biological model for the "take" and "jeopardy" analysis would be open and transparent, that is, consistent with a structured decision-making process.

By consensus, the steering committee accepted the recommendations of the Biological Modeling Work Group.[9]

A PUSH FOR STRUCTURED DECISION MAKING

On May 14, 2008, George Ozuna, supervisory hydrologist in the San Antonio office of the US Geological Survey, notified me that the agency would not submit the requested proposal.[10] He explained that other commitments of the USGS would not allow it to dedicate the amount of time that would be required to complete any significant work by the deadline of the EARIP.

On May 16, I spoke with Adam Zerrenner, Joy Nicholopoulos, and George Ozuna regarding the decision of the US Geological Survey not to submit a proposal.[11] Ozuna explained that key personnel would not be available to begin that work until later in the year, possibly December. Nicholopoulos made it clear that the Fish and Wildlife Service required that the USGS prepare the biological model and that it would not allow a project to be started by someone else and then handed over to the USGS at a later date. After some discussion, she agreed to consider allowing the EARIP to use someone like Dr. Thom Hardy, in collaboration with other scientists, to develop the biological models so long as the USGS had project oversight, participated in the process, and subsequently assumed the primary role.[12]

On May 27 Joy Nicholopoulos, Adam Zerrenner, and George Ozuna called Robert Potts, EARIP chair and general manager of the Edwards Aquifer Authority, for a second opinion. Nicholopoulos told him the FWS believed that, to enable it to have confidence in the results, the US Geological Survey would, from the outset, have to take full responsibility for developing the biological model. In addition, she said she was willing to go to Senator Glenn Hegar to explain why the FWS believed it was necessary to extend the Senate Bill 3 deadlines to allow this process to occur. Lastly, she said that the FWS did not have the funds to pay for the work of the survey USGS but would support EARIP efforts to get federal grants to defray some of the costs.

The next day, Ozuna attended the meeting of the Biological Modeling Work Group.[13] He told the work group that it would be late spring 2009 before the process of considering the biology actually started. The winter and early spring would be spent establishing the basis for the structured decision-making process—defining goals and objectives. After the biological work was started, it would probably take two to three years to complete. He estimated that it would be about two years before the EARIP would even have enough information for the science subcommittee to address the criteria related to withdrawal reduction levels and critical period management and for the EARIP to use in developing actions for the habitat conservation plan. When pressed, Ozuna conceded that the work of the USGS would probably cost close to $1 million.

The work group reported to the steering committee about concerns that waiting for the development of the biological model would cause the Senate Bill 3 deadlines to be missed.[14] It reminded the steering committee that an effort to extend the deadlines would be contentious and could threaten the success of the EARIP process. Accordingly, the work group recommended that the EARIP consider attempting to get the Fish and Wildlife Service to agree to a process that would use Hardy and other scientists to develop biological models that would allow the EARIP to proceed with its obligations under Senate Bill 3 and that would provide useful input to the FWS in making the "jeopardy" and "take" determinations.

At the June 12 EARIP meeting, Nicholopoulos gave a presentation to the EARIP indicating that the "U.S. Fish and Wildlife Service prefers the Structured Decision-Making process to determine take and jeopardy levels through the EARIP." She argued, without elaboration, that the US Geological Survey was *"uniquely qualified"* to "provide for an open and inclusive process—collaborative modeling that involves all stakeholders—transparency."[15]

Nicholopoulos warned that, if the EARIP needed to develop flow numbers to meet the deadlines in Senate Bill 3, then it should do so. However, she could not provide assurances that any flow numbers developed outside of the structured decision-making process would be comparable to the results of "take" and "jeopardy" developed through that process or that the information developed outside the process would be usable by the FWS in the structured decision-making process. But, she said, if the EARIP conducted an analysis of flow regimes outside the structured decision-making/biological modeling process, the Fish and Wildlife Service wanted the USGS to oversee those efforts.

After Nicholopoulos's presentation, the steering committee agreed by consensus that Hardy would analyze the flow needs of the species that would be used by the science subcommittee to address the charges in Senate Bill 3. They also agreed that the USGS could oversee Hardy's work so that the information would be more likely to be used by the Fish and Wildlife Service in making the "jeopardy" and "take" determinations.

Soon after the decision, Nicholopoulos wrote to Senator Hegar. Although her letter did not specifically ask him to intervene, the message was conveyed subtly:

As you may know the U.S. Fish and Wildlife Service attended a structured decision-making workshop in February 2008 at the National Conservation Training Center to establish a structured process that would allow the Service to work with the RIP to determine take and jeopardy levels for the listed species. The structured decision-making process by nature is an open and inclusive process that involves stakeholders in the decision making process. The Service believes that it would be advantageous for the RIP to utilize this process to maintain the RIP's long-term success through buy-in of all stakeholders as it moves forward in developing the Habitat Conservation Plan for the Edwards Aquifer.[16]

The decision by the steering committee not to fully acquiesce to the development of the biological model was significant and may have changed the dynamics of the interaction between the Fish and Wildlife Service and the EARIP in a positive manner. The FWS ultimately determines if a habitat conservation plan satisfies the issuance criteria; the "take" and "jeopardy" determinations are critical parts of that determination. An applicant for an incidental take permit routinely provides information in the habitat conservation plan that is used in the "take" and "jeopardy" determination of the FWS without using the structured decision-making process. Nonetheless, the opportunity to actually participate in the decision-making process, in even a non-decisional role, theoretically would allow more direct input to the FWS on this decision.

In this case, however, participation came at a high price. First, allowing the US Geological Survey to do the work would most certainly force the EARIP to miss the deadlines, not just by a little but probably by years. Moreover, the steering committee was well aware that the USGS was notoriously late in providing project deliverables and was almost always over budget. The committee members also were quite aware that other recovery implementation programs, dominated by federal interests, had taken many, many years to complete.

Many of those involved in the EARIP placed a great deal of importance on achieving the deadlines. This concern was not just because meeting them was required by Senate Bill 3, as Nicholopoulos seemed to assume, but because the nonpumpers had already conceded increasing the pumping caps—the withdrawal caps had already been enacted into law—and they were unwilling to allow resolution of the continuous minimum flow issue, which had gone unresolved for fifteen years, to be delayed further.

Another concern of the EARIP was that it would have to fund the work. Ozuna had conceded that the cost of the process would probably be close to $1 million. While the Fish and Wildlife Service might try to assist the EARIP in getting a grant for some of the bio-modeling, the EARIP was skeptical regarding whether federal funding was likely to materialize in the near term, if at all. Moreover, the EARIP would still have to find funding for the remainder of the work, as well as for the development and evaluation of the measures that would be needed to put together the habitat conservation plan, that is, to prepare not only the plan itself but also other documentation necessary to apply for the incidental take permit. It was also paradoxical that the FWS claimed to not have the money to fund the structured decision-making process but intended to use that process in making the "take" and "jeopardy" determinations if the EARIP did use that process.

Finally, no one had any illusions that the final decision on "take" and "jeopardy" would not be made exclusively by the Fish and Wildlife Service. However, some could not understand why the FWS would not have confidence in the results if the biology were developed by the EARIP with the participation of the US Geological Survey.

After the Fish and Wildlife Service decided to use Hardy, the role of the FWS in the EARIP process appeared to change. FWS representatives still attended all of the meetings and gave many useful presentations on habitat conservation plans and related topics, but it no longer tried to direct the process. The EARIP was starting to take ownership of the process. Regardless of whether the decision was wise, in the overall scheme of things, for the EARIP to begin assuming ownership of the process was an enormous step forward toward reaching consensus.

PAYING FOR THE HARDY STUDY

Having decided how to proceed, the EARIP then had to find a way to pay for the study. On July 17, 2008, the EARIP applied for a grant from the Texas Water Development Board to cover 50 percent of the costs of the research necessary to determine the biological needs of the federally listed species.[17] Through an understanding reached with the Texas Water Development Board, the EARIP acknowledged that the grant, if approved, would constitute "TWDB's full contribution" to the EARIP, absent a specific appropriation from the legislature.[18]

On August 25, 2008, the Texas Water Development Board approved a grant of $127,470 for the Edwards Aquifer Recovery Implementation Program. The grant would be used to pay 50 percent of the estimated cost of Hardy's study.[19] The remainder of the costs of the Hardy study and the US Geological Survey participation in that study would be paid by the San Antonio River Authority, San Antonio Water System, Edwards Aquifer Authority, and the Guadalupe-Blanco River Authority.

No decision was made to retain the consultants recommended by the Fish and Wildlife Service to facilitate a structured decision-making process because no funds were available at that time to do so.[20]

INITIAL SPRINGFLOW TARGETS

On December 16 and 17, 2008, Hardy met with Dr. Jean Cochrane of the US Geological Survey Patuxent Wildlife Research Center to discuss how the biological models for the listed species populations would be designed and conducted to help support the US Fish and Wildlife Service decision making and the EARIP flow analysis. The full team, including Cochrane, met in San Marcos, Texas, in mid-January 2009, to develop the first prototypes of these conceptual models, to consider various technical issues such as modeling scale and spatial components, and to plan the next steps in model development and data collection. In all, an eclectic mix of forty-seven scientists and stakeholders attended the meeting.

One of the initial steps in the development of the biological model was the creation of "influence diagrams" that depicted the various impacts on the listed species—an approach used in the structured decision-making process.[21] Consistent with the approach of a structured decision-making process, each iteration of the diagram would add complexity. Similar influence diagrams were developed for each listed species in the aquifer area.

After extensive data collection, analysis, modeling, and joint discussion, in July 2010 Hardy told the EARIP that his current thinking was to recommend using as flow targets forty to fifty cubic feet per second at Comal Springs and fifty-five to sixty cubic feet per second at San Marcos Springs.[22] He cautioned, however, that these numbers were not final.[23] Subsequently, Hardy agreed to do another model run to examine the biological effects of maintaining minimum flows at thirty cubic feet per second at Comal Springs and forty-five cubic feet per second at San Marcos Springs over the period of the drought of record to better define a range of acceptable flows.[24]

Hardy presented the preliminary results of his team's study to the EARIP on September 9, 2010.[25] Ed Oborny from Bio-West participated in that presentation. Hardy and Oborny agreed that the extensive mitigation and minimization measures being developed in the EARIP were essential to protect the listed species during periods of low flow and had to be part of any flow target. They also agreed that flows of thirty cubic feet per second at Comal Springs and forty-five cubic feet per second at San Marcos Springs would be the lowest minimum flows that would be adequate to ensure that the listed species could survive a repeat of the drought of record and retain the potential for recovery.[26] This view was conditioned on the assumption that increased flows of eighty cubic feet per second for two to three months would be used to ensure that the minimum flows did not continue for longer than six months.

The ensuing discussion of minimum flows did not generate any agreement on the issue. Thus, rather than asking for objections and having to face the reality of impasse, the EARIP took a straw vote to gauge the general sentiment regarding use of the flow minimums described by Hardy and Oborny. Fifteen steering committee members voted that they would support a minimum flow of thirty cubic feet per second at Comal Springs and forty-five cubic feet per second at San Marcos Springs with the recommended pulses. Seven steering committee members voted that they would oppose these minimum flows. Four members did not vote. The issue clearly was not close to resolution.

The discussions on the appropriate minimum flow levels for the Comal and San Marcos Springs were scheduled to continue on September 23 and 24. I feared that there would be no resolution of this issue; the momentum toward impasse was growing. Thus, before the meeting, I encouraged the steering committee and stakeholders to remember that, at the end of the day, the goal was to ensure that the species and their habitats were protected; flows were a means to that end, not the end itself.[27] Specific flow numbers are simply surrogates for biological conditions that are apt to occur over a range of flow conditions. Accordingly, I urged them to avoid impasse by not engaging in an untimely and unnecessary battle over what was the *most* appropriate flow number but, rather, to use the best data available to define a range of flow targets and, thereafter, to improve those data to define the specific minimum flows through the adaptive management process during the permit term.

Specifically, I recommended that the EARIP consider the following phased approach for developing and implementing the habitat conservation plan: (1) make an initial decision now on a reasonably narrow but acceptable range of minimum flows, (2) stack up "non-engineered" options that get the simulated flows as close as possible to those flow ranges and commit to closing the remaining gap with an engineered solution, (3) implement "non-engineered" options and mitigation and minimization measures as soon as possible after issuance of the permit, (4) make decisions to establish more precise minimum flows during the permit term through the adaptive management process, (5) make changes or adjustments to the actions during the permit term based on the decisions on the minimum flows and other information developed in the adaptive management process, and (6) agree to implement the engineered solution if determined to be necessary by the adaptive management process.

After extensive discussion of this "phased approach" on September 23, the steering committee took a straw vote to get an indication of support. Nineteen members voted that they would support this approach. The Guadalupe-Blanco River Authority did not support the approach. Six members did not indicate a position but appeared during discussions not to oppose a phased approach.[28]

Further discussion of the phased approach was held in abeyance, and the discussions were refocused on trying to reach consensus on springflow targets. This attempt, not surprisingly, did not prove to be fruitful. Those who had objected to the minimum flows presented by Hardy and Oborny generally believed that these flows would not be adequately protective without an additional "buffer" or safety factor for managing uncertainty. Some did not understand how Hardy had moved from his initial views in July (springflow targets of forty to fifty cubic feet per second at Comal Springs and fifty-five to sixty cubic feet per second at San Marcos Springs) to flow targets of thirty cubic feet per second at Comal Springs and forty at San Marcos Springs. However, the principal concern was that the minimum springflows were expressed as monthly averages—that is, that significantly lower flows could be experienced during any given month. They argued that Oborny and Hardy had made it clear that springflows lower than those they had proposed should be avoided.[29]

After repeated attempts to find a compromise, the meeting broke up after 5:00 p.m. If we weren't at impasse, we were definitely very close to it. The next morning, various groups met early to see if some traction could be gained for a new approach. However, all sides were willing to go to impasse on this issue when the entire group convened.[30] After further discussion among the entire group, there was no apparent movement—at least not in a positive direction. Frankly, I couldn't see where future discussions could constructively lead.

At that point, Myron Hess, an attorney from the National Wildlife Federation, asked to get representatives of the two big factions together to make one last attempt to break the impasse. He urged, in a theme that would often be repeated, *"We have come too far to fail."* Within thirty to forty minutes, Hess made a proposal on behalf of the conferees to allow the consultants to use in evaluating actions the following minimum flows:

COMAL SPRINGS
- thirty cubic feet per second (monthly average)
- thirty cubic feet per second (daily average)
- fifty cubic feet per second (daily average)

SAN MARCOS SPRINGS
- forty-five cubic feet per second (monthly average)
- forty-five cubic feet per second (daily average)
- sixty-five cubic feet per second (daily average)

Calvin Finch confirmed that the San Antonio Water System agreed with the compromise. After further discussion, the compromise proposal was approved by consensus.[31]

Recently, Finch indicated that when the small groups met, both sides were surprised at how close they were on the issue. As he put it, "we were there," but both sides had to vent their frustrations with the other before agreement could be reached.[32]

The following day, Weir Labatt sent an e-mail to Carter Smith, a colleague and the executive director of the Texas Parks and Wildlife Department. Labatt wrote, "It is almost a miracle that occurred late

Friday morning after a seemingly widening impasse the previous day and one half. I truly believe that the relationships built over the past 3 years made this compromise possible."[33]

Later, the EARIP would revisit and adopt the use of the phased approach. But at this point, they turned to developing actions to achieve the minimum springflow targets to which they had agreed. And, momentum for the time being would be on their side; after all, they had agreed that the EARIP had "come too far to fail."

The Evolution of the Bottom-Up Strategy

In December 2009, the EARIP started discussing possible measures that could be implemented to protect springflow. Initially, most of the discussions involved the feasibility of using engineered solutions, such as storing water in quarries or constructing structures to enhance recharge during drought. One option that received significant attention was a "recharge and recirculation" program that would place water into recharge structures, recover the recharge from the previous year, and recirculate it to the recharge structures to allow the water to remain in the aquifer until specified drought triggers occurred. It was a program that had been extensively studied by the Edwards Aquifer Authority since 2004.[34]

In November 2009 the EARIP authorized a study by HDR Engineering, Inc., to compile information regarding potential projects for springflow enhancement, including Type II recharge structures, run-of-river diversions, run-of-river diversions with storage, storage of water in quarries or other facilities for timed recharge during drought, and "recharge and recirculation."[35] The San Antonio Water System agreed to fund 50 percent of the cost of the study.[36]

Carol and Kirk Patterson were true believers in the potential of "recharge and recirculation" to solve the water supply problem in the region. They were zealous in their advocacy, and they probably dominated the process too much at the early stages, as they worked every angle to advance the cause of their proposed solution. But EARIP allowed the time to be spent to ensure that the potential of the approach was thoroughly vetted.

At the EARIP meeting in February 2010, Kirk Patterson gave a presentation on the conceptual framework for the recharge and recovery program.[37] A meeting was held on April 21, 2010, to formulate the technical assumptions for the recharge and recirculation option. Prior to the meeting, Kirk Patterson had submitted a document entitled "Recharge and Recirculation Basic Option Package" for consideration at the meeting. A "general consensus" was reached at the meeting on the assumptions to be used in the evaluation of the recharge and recirculation program. The assumptions included four optimization modeling runs.[38]

At a workshop on June 14, HDR Engineering and a subcontractor, Todd Engineers, presented their evaluation of the recharge and recirculation option and a conceptual engineering and preliminary cost analysis of the other options evaluated. The recharge and recirculation option, including the four optimization runs, was not able to maintain continuous springflow at Comal Springs during modeling simulations of a repeat of the drought of record.[39] Moreover, it was a very expensive option—projected to cost more than $1 billion (including annual operating costs) over the life of a twenty-five-year permit.[40] The conceptual engineering evaluation of the other options revealed that the engineered solutions were all very expensive and tended to have problems in implementation.

After the presentations, the steering committee asked HDR Engineering to evaluate two engineered options, three trade-off options, and one "combination" option that did not focus exclusively on engineered solutions.[41] The two engineered options included: (1) the injection of water stored in an aquifer storage and recovery (ASR) facility in the Carrizo Aquifer in Wilson County into the Edwards Aquifer between Cibolo Creek and Comal Springs using three assumptions regarding the critical period management withdrawal floor for stage IV (340,000, 320,000, and 286,000 acre-feet) and (2) one additional optimization run for the recharge and recirculation option.

The trade-off options involved: (1) developing a well field and pumping 66,700 acre-feet of water obtained through irrigation permits and storing it in the Twin Oaks aquifer storage and recovery facility of the San Antonio Water System in exchange for additional pumping reductions in Bexar County; or (2) constructing an aquifer storage and recovery facility, storing water from selected Type II recharge structures, and providing the stored water to San Marcos or New Braunfels in exchange for additional pumping reductions.

The combination option included the following elements: (1) using selected Type II recharge structures to enhance recharge, (2) creating a "dry year option," (3) storing water (forty thousand acre-feet) in the aquifer storage and recovery facility owned by the San Antonio Water System to offset deeper pumping reductions, and (4) funding a brush management program with the water conserved being "stored" in Canyon Lake for recharge during severe drought.[42]

HDR Engineering presented the results of the requested evaluation on September 9, 2010.[43] The following is a brief summary of the results:

- The recharge and recirculation option still was unable to provide continuous springflow during a repeat of the drought of record conditions.
- Among the trade-off options, none was able to achieve continuous springflows under the assumptions used.
- With respect to the ASR options, all of the variations were able to ensure continuous springflows. However, the ASR approach was able to ensure a minimum of only 30 cubic feet per second of springflow if the stage IV critical period management floor was 286,000 acre-feet.
- The combination package evaluated was not able to ensure continuous minimum springflow; in this scenario, the Comal Springs ceased to flow for seventeen months during a repeat of the drought of record.

All of the engineered solutions were prohibitively expensive, especially considering the small amount of time that they might be needed. The combination package also was expensive, but the costs were substantially reduced if the Type II recharge structures were omitted.[44]

After considering the HDR presentation, the steering committee reached general agreement to use a "bottom-up" approach that combined a number of "non-engineered" options (e.g., the dry-year option and regional conservation) to attain the minimum flow targets. If the non-engineered options were not adequate to attain the minimum flow targets, a small engineered option would be added to close the gap. The EARIP, however, was not able to reach agreement on a specific package of non-engineered options primarily because of differing views as to whether a reduction in the critical period management floor from 340,000 to 320,000 acre-feet should be included among the non-engineered options to protect springflow.

The San Antonio Water System strongly opposed the 320,000 floor in the EARIP even though it had accepted the use of a 320,000-acre-foot floor for critical period management reductions during the 2005 legislative session. The Guadalupe-Blanco River Authority was equally strong in its insistence that the 320,000-acre-foot floor would not allow the package to be adequately protective and instead pushed for evaluating a floor at 286,000 acre-feet (a 50 percent reduction from the 572,000 acre-foot cap) as one of the non-engineered elements.[45]

A work group was established to discuss whether the use of the San Antonio Water System aquifer storage and recovery facility could be optimized to improve the benefit to springflow.[46] At the first meeting of that work group, an important suggestion was made by Karl Dreher, the new general manager of the Edwards Aquifer Authority.[47] He suggested that the 320,000-acre-foot floor not be considered as a replacement for the current stage IV critical period management reductions but instead be used as a new stage V reduction that would be triggered only after the other critical period management reductions and any other aquifer management measures, such as the dry-year option, had been in put in place but had failed to maintain springflow. In short, it would be an emergency measure triggered only after all else had failed.

At the EARIP meeting on September 23, it was agreed to have HDR analyze the effects of the following "bottom-up" package: dry-year option (now being referred to as the voluntary irrigation suspension program option or VISPO); San Antonio Water System aquifer storage and recovery with the trade-off strategy; brush management, purveyor, and agricultural water conservation programs; and stage V emergency critical period management withdrawal reductions to at least 320,000 acre-feet.[48] Subsequently, the agricultural conservation and brush management elements were deferred for consideration as part of the adaptive management process during the implementation of the habitat conservation plan.[49]

HDR Engineering presented the results of its evaluation at the EARIP meeting on October 21, 2010. The results showed that implementation of the four elements of the bottom-up package (regional conservation, VISPO, the San Antonio Water System aquifer storage and recovery program, and stage V emergency reductions) resulted in continuous flows at both springs. Moreover, the simulations showed that the monthly average springflows approximated the monthly average minimum flow targets for both springs.[50]

At this point, it was apparent that a package of flow protection measures had been developed that probably would be acceptable to the EARIP steering committee and stakeholders; however, no formal vote was taken to adopt the bottom-up package. Instead, the steering committee agreed to further refine the four options and asked me to prepare another memorandum for the November meeting regarding the phased approach.[51]

At the EARIP meeting on January 28, 2011, after the flow protection measures had been refined, HDR Engineering presented its final analysis of the bottom-up package. With implementation of the flow protection measures during a repeat of the drought of record, the minimum springflow projected for Comal Springs for phase I was 27 cubic feet per second (monthly average), and springflow fell below the 30 cubic feet per second monthly average target only for two months. At San Marcos Springs, the simulated minimum monthly average springflow for phase I was 50.5 cubic feet per second—well above the 45 cubic feet per second monthly average flow target.

Dr. Thom Hardy and Ed Oborny then discussed the effect of the minimum flow regimes during a repeat of the drought of record.[52] Hardy concluded, and Oborny concurred, that the springflows presented by HDR would not appreciably reduce the likelihood of survival and recovery of the listed species over the first seven years of the habitat conservation plan, even if a repeat of drought of record were to occur during that time, so long as all recommended measures were implemented to restore and protect the habitat of the listed species.[53]

After these presentations, a motion was made and seconded to approve the use of the phase I bottom-up package in preparing the habitat conservation plan and developing costs of implementing the plan. The package consisted of: (1) a regional water conservation program, (2) a VISPO program, (3) the San Antonio Water System aquifer storage and recovery program, (4) stage V restrictions, (5) minimization measures, (6) a robust monitoring and adaptive management program, and (7) supplementary support for the Fish and Wildlife Service National Fish Hatchery and Training Center in San Marcos to develop refugia to provide a safety net if the other measures did not provide the expected protection for the listed species. The Guadalupe-Blanco River Authority and Regional Clean Air & Water objected to the motion, so an issues team was appointed.[54]

At the issues team meeting, consensus was reached with respect to a restated decision that approved the bottom-up package for purposes of preparing the habitat conservation plan and developing estimates of the costs of implementing the plan by expressly identifying the items that needed to be completed prior to consideration of the package for final adoption. The steering committee approved the recommendation of the bottom-up issues team, with the two objectors abstaining.[55]

MINIMIZATION MEASURES

The EARIP also addressed the issue of what non-flow related measures it would implement to satisfy the requirement that the applicant for an incidental take permit must "minimize and mitigate" the impacts of any "take" to the "maximum extent practicable."[56]

Work groups developed specific measures for the steering committee to consider. These work groups consisted for the most part of scientists from the Fish and Wildlife Service, Texas Parks and Wildlife Department, Texas State University, and the River System Institute, as well as consulting firms such as Bio-West, working with the representatives of the cities of New Braunfels and San Marcos, where the measures would be implemented.

The measures the EARIP adopted included habitat restoration, replacement of exotic vegetation with native vegetation favored by the listed species, maintenance of dissolved oxygen through removal of decaying aquatic vegetation during low flows, sediment removal, predator control, and fountain darter gill parasite control. To protect Texas wild-rice from recreational impacts, the Texas Parks and Wildlife Department created state scientific areas—zones in which recreation and other activities are restricted during flow conditions below 120 cubic feet per second.[57] Water quality measures included an incentive program for low impact development, best management practice implementation, support for coal tar sealant bans, and expanded water quality monitoring.[58]

In addition to satisfying the issuance criteria for an incidental take permit, these minimization measures are important because they have the ability to ameliorate the effects of drought on the listed species and were thus an element of the recommended flow protection measures.

BIOLOGICAL GOALS AND OBJECTIVES

The US Fish and Wildlife Service requires habitat conservation plans to contain measurable biological goals and objectives.[59] The biological goals define the expected outcome of the implementation of the habitat conservation plan. For example, the plan for the Edwards region must indicate the quantity and quality of habitat of each spring ecosystem. The biological objectives are the management objectives for attaining the biological goals. One objective would be, for example, providing the flows necessary to achieve and maintain the quantity and quality of the habitat prescribed by a biological goal.

In the case of the phased approach employed by the EARIP, Hardy had determined that the phase I flow protection package, if the full suite of minimization measures were implemented, would be protective of the species during the first seven years of the permit. However, the Fish and Wildlife Service, in deciding whether to approve a habitat conservation plan, must also evaluate the long-term effects of the entire action, not just the effects of the first phase of the action.

On February 28, 2011, Bio-West presented a conceptual approach for developing the long-term biological goals and objectives for each species. The goals generally were expressed in terms of habitat quantity or population numbers. For example, with respect to the fountain darter, the biological goal would be expressed both as areal coverage of vegetation (i.e., habitat) and as population goals. The biological objectives to achieve those goals would be expressed in terms of management objectives (e.g., the amount of habitat restoration) and minimum springflow objectives. After extensive discussion, the EARIP steering committee approved the general approach with two abstentions.[60] The approval, however, was qualified by the condition that the next iteration of the concept should consider the comments of Jackie Poole, from the Texas Parks and Wildlife Department, regarding the goal for Texas wild-rice.

After discussions between Ed Oborny of Bio-West and Jackie Poole, a final set of biological goals and objectives was presented to the steering committee on May 17, 2011, along with comments from the Texas Parks and Wildlife Department.[61] The steering committee approved the biological goals and objectives as amended to address the specific goal for Texas wild-rice proposed by the Texas Parks and Wildlife Department.

The minimum springflow objective for fountain darters and certain other listed species is 45 cubic feet per second (monthly average) at Comal Springs and 52 cubic feet per second (monthly average) at San Marcos Springs.[62] These objectives are simply the monthly average flow targets for each spring system in phase I but corrected to reflect an equivalent daily average flow. In addition, the minimum flow objectives are not to exceed six months in duration, followed by 80 cubic feet per second (daily average flows) for three months. Further, the flow objective includes, for Comal Springs, a long-term average spring-flow of 225 cubic feet per second and, for San Marcos Springs, a long-term average springflow of 140 cubic feet per second.

Because the minimum springflow objective may require ensuring more flow than during phase I, the EARIP also had to come up with presumptive phase II measures that it would implement, if needed, to ensure that the habitat conservation plan achieved the long-term biological goals. The decision regarding whether any additional measures were needed would be based on the best available science *at that time*, would rely heavily on information developed in a robust adaptive management process, and would be supported by the independent analyses of the National Academy of Sciences.

On June 9, 2011, the steering committee agreed to a presumptive measure proposed by the San Antonio Water System.[63] The measure involved continuation of the phase I measures and expanded use of the San Antonio Water System aquifer storage and recovery facility by taking advantage of a west-side pipeline extension that was under construction in 2014. If expanding the availability of the aquifer storage and recovery facility did not fully meet the minimum flow objectives, the balance would be obtained through alterations to the conservation measures, including an increase in stage V withdrawal reductions.

HDR Engineering evaluated the bottom-up package with the presumptive phase II measure.[64] It reported that, with the measure, the bottom-up package would provide enough flow to meet the minimum springflow objectives. If the presumptive phase II measure were implemented using the west-side pipeline extension alone, the minimum monthly average would drop below forty-five cubic feet per second (monthly average) for only three months during a simulated repeat of the drought of record, with forty-two cubic feet per second as the lowest flow predicted by the modeling. The springflow at San Marcos Springs would fall below fifty-two cubic feet per second, but only for one month, with that springflow being fifty-one cubic feet per second.

Through the adaptive management process, the west-side pipeline extension alone may prove adequate to meet the minimum springflow objective. If not, the modeling shows that, with a 47 percent critical period management stage V reduction and the presumptive measure, springflow at Comal Springs would be forty-seven cubic feet per second. The minimum monthly average springflow at San Marcos Springs was projected to be fifty-two cubic feet per second.

How the EARIP will achieve the eighty cubic feet per second pulses and the long-term flow objectives will be resolved through the adaptive management process.

9 : FUNDING AND ALLOCATING COSTS

Show me the money!
— *Jerry McGuire* (TriStar Pictures, 1996)

The EARIP stakeholders anticipated that it would get federal money, at least to pay for the implementation of the habitat conservation plan. After the EARIP process had started, Dr. Joy Nicholopoulos clarified that the US Fish and Wildlife Service did not traditionally provide funding for recovery implementation programs.[1] She explained that, in other recovery implementation programs, most of the funding was funneled through the Bureau of Reclamation, a participant in many of those programs. She cautioned that, if federal funding was to come to the EARIP, the group needed to consider how and through which agency it would obtain the money.

Following up on Nicholopoulos's advice, the EARIP in early 2008 began exploring the possibilities of federal funding for the implementation of the habitat conservation plan. Weir Labatt, Jerry James, Todd Votteler, and I met with staff working for members of the congressional delegation in the region, including staff for US senators John Cornyn and Kay Bailey Hutchison, and US representatives Charles Gonzalez, Ciro Rodriguez, and Lloyd Doggett. Although they were very receptive to the meetings, as well as knowledgeable about the Edwards Issue, their message was uniform and not encouraging. It was not possible to get an appropriation until there was a specific project, and their offices typically were unwilling to sponsor legislation to fund studies for projects. However, as we got deeper into 2008, the message took a far more problematic turn because the appropriation being sought would be considered an "earmark," and there would be no more earmarks in the foreseeable future. They suggested that our best hope was to try to find an agency to include us within its budget. With budgets being cut, however, this option did not seem to offer very much hope.

The EARIP would revisit the possibility for federal funding later in the process. However, as reality sank in, the EARIP turned its initial efforts toward obtaining the money needed to manage the EARIP process, to conduct scientific studies to support the decision-making process, and to retain the consultants to prepare the habitat conservation plan and associated documentation.

Project Management Costs

Senate Bill 3 had not provided any money for the operation of the EARIP. Instead, it directed the Edwards Aquifer Authority and other stakeholders, including the state agencies, to provide "money as necessary to finance the activities" of the EARIP.[2] The steering committee agreed that the Edwards Aquifer Authority and the four state agencies would contribute twenty-five thousand dollars annually toward the cost of the EARIP process. In addition, the San Antonio River Authority, Guadalupe-Blanco River Authority, and San Antonio Water System agreed to contribute the same amount. Other stakeholders volunteered to make smaller contributions.[3] The program management costs for the EARIP included salaries and benefits, office space and expenses, and travel for the program manager and support personnel.

Over the life of the EARIP, the participants paid $1,030,291.35 in project management costs. Those costs did not include the costs of scientific studies to support the decision-making process and the cost of consultants to prepare the habitat conservation plan and associated documentation. Texas A&M University was designated by Senate Bill 3 to provide administrative support for the EARIP, although the EARIP was responsible for the cost of that support. Initially, the EARIP agreed to pay Texas A&M University 25 percent of the funds received for the EARIP, whether from the stakeholders or any other source, as indirect costs for administering the program.[4] Subsequently, Robert Potts and state senator Glenn Hegar worked successfully with Texas A&M University to get the indirect costs it incurred reduced from 25 percent to 5 percent.[5]

Scientific Support for EARIP Decision Making

With the project management costs covered, the EARIP turned its attention to obtaining money for scientific research and preparing the habitat conservation plan. At the urging of Adam Zerrenner, supervisor of the Austin field office of the Fish and Wildlife Service, in September 2008 the EARIP applied for a habitat conservation planning assistance grant under section 6 of the Endangered Species Act. The EARIP application sought $1,417,500 to pay for both consulting help in preparing the habitat conservation plan and the documentation required by the National Environmental Policy Act, as well as the costs related to hiring facilitators to assist with the EARIP decision-making process. The grant, if awarded, would require a cost-share from the EARIP of 25 percent of the total costs awarded by the Fish and Wildlife Service.

Senator John Cornyn and Representatives Charles Gonzalez, Lloyd Doggett, Ciro Rodriguez, and Lamar Smith sent letters of support for the section 6 grant application.[6] On April 21, 2009, the Fish and Wildlife Service awarded the EARIP a grant for $1,417,500. The FWS share of the grant was $1,063,125. The EARIP share was $354,375.

Because of the uncertainty of obtaining the section 6 grant, the significant cost-sharing required even if the grant was funded, and the need for additional scientific studies, the EARIP, while the grant application was pending, set up a work group consisting of Jerry James, Con Mims, Weir Labatt, and me to try to obtain funding from the legislature, which was in session in 2009. The work group was given a short leash in its discussions with the legislature. All positions it took had to be cleared with the steering committee in advance and a report of all contacts provided to the steering committee within five business days.[7]

The work group's goal was to obtain up to $1,692,000 in funding to cover the costs of developing the habitat conservation plan, including the cost of scientific research to assist in the decision-making process.[8] We believed this amount was the minimum needed to put together the habitat conservation plan if no section 6 grant funds were available. Senator Hegar agreed to sponsor the funding and rider appropriation in the Senate budget process. State senators Hegar, Judith Zaffirini, Leticia Van de Putte, Jeff Wentworth, and Carlos Uresti sent a letter to Senator Steve Ogden, chair of the Senate Committee on Finance, on February 3, 2009, supporting our request. Our further efforts to gain support for the legislation were coordinated through Senator Hegar's office.[9]

Due to a miscommunication with the House sponsor, the funding request did not get into the House budget bill. Accordingly, on April 15, 2009, Jerry James contacted Justin Unruh, chief of staff and legislative director for Representative Geanie Morrison (Victoria), to discuss whether Representative Morrison would introduce a floor amendment adding the language appropriating the nearly $1.7 million for use by the EARIP into the House budget bill. Representative Morrison agreed to do so.

When we were notified that the Fish and Wildlife Service had approved the section 6 grant, Jerry James immediately notified Lisa Craven, Senator Hegar's chief of staff. On April 22, 2009, she told James that Senator Hegar did not want to amend the appropriation for the EARIP in the Senate budget. Hegar said that he wanted to be sure that EARIP had the money it needed to complete its work. He said that, after the budget conference had been completed, an accountability system would be put in place so that any money not used by the EARIP would be returned to the Texas Water Development Board, which would be distributing the appropriation through its grant program.[10]

On April 23, 2009, Jerry James and I met with Lisa Craven and Justin Unruh to discuss Senator Hegar's proposed approach. Afterwards, we met with Shelly Botkin and David Kinsey, senior budget advisor for House Speaker Joe Straus, to discuss the approach and to stress the importance of the additional funding for the EARIP process.[11]

While James, Labatt, and I were at the Capitol on April 30, 2009, we serendipitously ran into Kirby Brown from the Texas Wildlife Association, a stakeholder in the EARIP. He suggested that we meet with staff for Representatives John Otto and Jim Pitts, who both were conferees on the budget bill.[12] We were able to get brief meetings with their staff during which we asked for their representatives' support in the conference committee for the EARIP budget item in the Senate committee substitute for budget bill. We were told that the conferees would be discussing the part of the bill containing that item at 8:00 a.m. the next day and were asked to provide a one-page briefing paper regarding the funding request no later than close of business on April 30. We made it just under the wire, which prompted the thought that it was better to be lucky than good.

The budget containing the EARIP item was passed by the legislature and signed by the governor. That item directed the Texas Water Development Board to allocate out of Water Assistance Fund No. 480 up to $1,692,500 for grants and studies for the Edwards Aquifer Recovery Implementation Program.[13] This allocation was to include money for the nonfederal share of the section 6 habitat conservation planning assistance grant; the project management contributions of the Texas Parks and Wildlife Department, Texas Department of Agriculture, and

Texas Commission on Environmental Quality ($25,000 for each agency for the biennium); the cost of peer review of scientific work; as well any other nonproject management costs necessary for the timely completion of the habitat conservation plan.

Funding Implementation of the Habitat Conservation Plan

After agreement had been reached on the elements of the habitat conservation plan in 2011, we stepped "once more unto the breach" and again explored the possibility of seeking federal funds. On February 15, 2011, Rick Illgner, Calvin Finch, Todd Votteler, Weir Labatt, and I met in Albuquerque with Dr. Benjamin Tuggle, the regional administrator for Region 2 of the Fish and Wildlife Service, and some of his staff to seek their help in obtaining funding.[14] We reminded him that many of the participants had entered into the EARIP because of the potential for receiving federal support. We also explained that the habitat conservation plan would direct a significant amount of money toward the National Fish Hatchery and Training Center in San Marcos and that the Fish and Wildlife Service and Department of Defense were significant users of the aquifer and yet did not, like other users, pay aquifer management fees. Tuggle was enthusiastic in his praise for the progress the EARIP had achieved. He said that he believed there was what he called a federal role in this habitat conservation plan and that he would do what he could to help us obtain some assistance.

Tuggle was helpful in setting up a meeting on July 21, 2011, with Rowan Gould, deputy regional administrator; Gary Frazier, assistant director of Endangered Species Program; and others on his staff, as well as representatives of the Department of the Interior in Washington, D.C. The EARIP representatives were again greeted with praise and enthusiasm for what we had accomplished.[15] Once again, the representatives of federal agencies could offer no real encouragement about funding due to cuts in their budgets. They were equally pessimistic about the prospects for obtaining funding from other agencies.

Having again been given no encouragement regarding the prospects for federal funding, the EARIP team's emphasis shifted to coming up with other ways to pay for the implementation of the habitat conservation plan. It was obvious that the annual cost of implementing it would be substantial. Although, with refinement, the cost would decrease considerably, in late 2010 the annual price tag was estimated to average approximately $30 million over the first seven years of the habitat conservation plan implementation.[16] Thus, it was not surprising that the decision regarding how to fund the implementation of the habitat conservation plan would be the most contentious obstacle the EARIP faced.

In October 2010, the steering committee appointed a funding work group.[17] It consisted of representatives from the Guadalupe Basin Coalition (Tom Taggart), Guadalupe-Blanco River Authority (Todd Votteler), and City of Victoria (Jerry James) on behalf of the nonpumping interests, as well as representatives of the San Antonio Water System (Calvin Finch), Bexar County (Kerim Jacaman), and the City of Garden Ridge (Jim Bower) for the pumper interests. The Nueces River Authority (Con Mims), Texas Water Development Board (Weir Labatt), and the representative of the Edwards Aquifer region ratepayers/general public (Kirk Patterson) also were appointed to the work group. Subsequently, Adam Yablonski was added to the work group to represent the agricultural interests. The meetings, however, were open to anyone who wished to attend.

The first meeting of the work group was held on November 8, 2010. The lines were already clearly drawn at the outset.

The representatives of the pumpers believed that the downstream interests were significant beneficiaries of the flow protection measures in the habitat conservation plan. They argued that the fifty/fifty split in Senate Bill 1477 with respect to the costs of reducing the withdrawal cap from 450,000 to 400,000 acre-feet was the appropriate split for the costs of the habitat conservation plan as well because it reflected the legislature's view of the relative benefits obtained from the aquifer. The pumpers also argued that the recreational activities that were important to the economies of San Marcos and New Braunfels derived significant benefits from the additional springflow provided by the flow protection measures. The San Antonio Water System viewed those activities as contributing significantly to the threats to the listed species and thus argued that those impacts should be reflected in the cost sharing.

Not surprisingly, the downstream interests saw the allocation issue differently, pointing fingers at the City of San Antonio for failure to diversify its water supplies, which allowed it to enjoy some of the lowest water rates in the state while other municipalities, such as San Marcos and New Braunfels, had diversified and incurred higher water rates as a result.[18] They argued that most if not all of the costs of the habitat conservation plan should be paid by the pumpers through the aquifer management fees that the Edwards Aquifer charged permit holders to finance administrative expenses and programs.[19]

Irrigated agriculture was an interested but cautious spectator in the debate because aquifer management fees for those users were capped at two dollars per acre-foot by statute. The irrigators were there to make clear that they had no intention of compromising with respect to that cap.

The arguments over the costs grew heated, and neither the success in putting together the bottom-up package, nor the "come too far to fail" theme, nor the win/win attitude that got the EARIP through so many issues softened the rhetoric. As 2011 began, the work group had narrowed the funding options to two:

- a regional authority established by the state legislature to receive and distribute a sales tax set by the state;
- a funding allocation between the Edwards Aquifer pumpers and the nonpumpers whereby pumpers would pay additional aquifer management fees and nonpumpers would pay a fixed amount per year.[20]

The sales tax option was favored because it spread the costs more equitably over the entire area that benefited from the aquifer. After discussion, the steering committee unanimously endorsed having the Funding Work Group continue to pursue both options.

THE SALES TAX OPTION

On January 28, 2011, the steering committee received recommendations from the Funding Work Group regarding the concept of a regional sales tax.[21] Under that concept, the Texas Water Development Board would receive and disburse the sales tax. The tax receipts would be used to pay for the implementation of the habitat conservation plan and other water-related projects, such as those connected to the Guadalupe Basin environmental flows process. The latter was included to provide additional justification for broadening the geographic scope of the sales tax. Most importantly, from the political perspective, the sales tax would not go into effect unless it was approved by the voters of the affected region.

The other basic elements of the sales tax proposal were as follows:

- The sales tax would be collected in the counties in the current boundaries of the Edwards Aquifer Authority jurisdiction and all counties contiguous to the lower Guadalupe and San Antonio Rivers.
- The sales tax would be authorized for up to one-quarter of 1 percent and allow the collection of one-eighth of 1 percent to fund the habitat conservation plan, conditioned on the approval of a majority of the voters in the jurisdiction of the district.
- The remaining one-eighth of 1 percent for the water-related projects would be available if the projects were authorized by the legislature and approved by a majority of all voting citizens in the counties.
- This sales tax was to be in addition to the 2 percent sales tax that localities and municipalities were already authorized to collect.[22]

The representative of the Edwards Aquifer region municipal ratepayers/general public objected to the use of a sales tax, and the issue was sent to an issues team. At a meeting of that body on February 4, 2011, consensus was reached with one abstention regarding a restated decision ensuring that alternative funding mechanisms would be considered while the EARIP pursued the regional sales tax option.[23]

On February 10, 2011, the Funding Work Group Issue Team presented a recommendation to the EARIP. After extensive discussion, the steering committee adopted by consensus, with two abstentions, the following modified restatement of the decision: "The EARIP should ask the Legislature to allow the people of the region to vote on a ¼ of a cent regional sales tax as a funding mechanism for EARIP . . . and other water-related issues with respect to species of concern in the region; provided, however, with respect to the EARIP, it is agreed that proposals for alternative mechanisms to the regional sales tax, not involving a sales tax, will proceed to be developed while EARIP is seeking authority for a regional sales tax from the Legislature, the Governor, and the voters." The steering committee also agreed by consensus, with two abstentions, that the first priority for the money collected through the sales tax would be implementation of the habitat conservation plan, provided that not less than $1.5 million per year would be used to fund the other water-related issues.[24]

To say the least, in the Texas Legislature in 2011 the notion of anything that might be called a tax was likely to be a nonstarter. However, the EARIP was not asking to have the legislature impose the sales tax but simply to allow the voters in the region to decide whether they wanted to pay for the habitat conservation plan through a sales tax or through the fees charged to the aquifer users and downstream beneficiaries. We were able to persuade Senator Wentworth to introduce a bill (Senate Bill 1595) that would have allowed voters in the Edwards region to decide whether to pay for the habitat conservation plan through revenues from a sales tax. Representative John Garza sponsored the same bill in the House (House Bill 2760).

We met with key legislators from the region. While they seemed to understand the importance of the sales tax to the habitat conservation plan and the fact that all we were asking for was to allow the region to vote, few were willing to stick their necks out to support it—at least not without significant political cover. To see if that cover were available, we met with former senator Ken Armbrister, who was then Governor Rick Perry's director of legislative affairs. If the Governor's Office considered it to be a new tax, we knew that we would not get anywhere with the sales tax. When our calls were not returned after the meeting, it was apparent that the Governor's Office was not in favor of the sales tax.

House Bill 2760 had a hearing before House Natural Resources Committee on April 5, 2011. On the advice of Representative Garza and Senator Wentworth, a committee substitute was introduced that limited use of the revenues from the sales tax to just the implementation of the habitat conservation plan. The EARIP sales tax bill did not get a hearing in the Senate, and the committee substitute did not emerge from the House Committee on Natural Resources. At that point, serious discussions resumed regarding the use of aquifer management fees and contributions from the downstream interests to pay for the habitat conservation plan.

A STRATEGIC MISCALCULATION AND A COMPROMISE

Because of the great uncertainty associated with the sales tax, the Funding Work Group continued to explore the use of aquifer management fees with annual contributions from downstream interests to pay for the implementation of the habitat conservation plan. The gulf between the various interests was wide—very wide. No one on either side had any real willingness to alter a firmly held position.

An underlying issue of fairness plagued the ability of the work group to move toward an acceptable solution. Even though irrigated agriculture used or leased about 30 percent of the water from the aquifer each year, aquifer management fees for irrigators were capped at two dollars per acre-foot of water pumped. All of the fees paid to the Edwards Aquifer Authority by the irrigators were consumed in financing the administrative expenses and other programs of the authority. Accordingly, irrigated agriculture would not be paying anything toward the cost of implementing the habitat conservation plan. Further, owners of domestic and livestock wells were exempt from having to obtain permits and, therefore, from paying aquifer management fees. In short, any pumpers' share would be borne entirely by the municipal and industrial permit holders. Moreover, the San Antonio Water System was particularly sensitive to these perceived inequities because the share of any fee increase it paid for the habitat conservation plan would be close to 80 percent.

To move things along, the Funding Work Group asked HDR Engineering to evaluate the impact of springflow protection measures in the habitat conservation plan on groundwater availability and the surface water supplies downstream in the Guadalupe-San Antonio River Basin. HDR gave its report to the Funding Work Group on January 17, 2011.[25] It showed, based on the modeling, that, as a result of the flow measures in the habitat conservation plan, during the worst year of a repeat of the drought of record the groundwater supplies from the aquifer would increase by 75,000 acre-feet while surface water supplies downstream would increase by 21,532 acre-feet.

However, because of junior/senior appropriation rights, the number of surface water users that would benefit from the additional springflow during a severe drought was relatively small. Those who would benefit to any significant extent included the Guadalupe-Blanco River Authority, Seguin Municipal Utilities, DuPont Chemical, and the City of San Antonio (through City Public Service).

Based on the presumed increase in groundwater supplies relative to surface water supplies during the worst year of the drought of record, the San Antonio Water System took the position that 78 percent of the habitat conservation plan costs should be allocated to the pumpers and a 22 percent share allocated to the downstream surface water users.[26] The San Antonio Water System warned that this allocation was not supported by all pumpers because some pumpers still believed the split should be fifty/fifty.

Although acknowledging that the San Antonio Water System proposal constituted progress in the negotiation, the nonpumpers argued that allocating the benefit based strictly on the amount of increased water availability downstream during drought ignored the fact that it would be the pumpers who would be receiving the benefit of the incidental take permit, that is, that the nonpumpers would not be exposed to a lawsuit if the EARIP failed. Under these circumstances, they maintained, it would be a tough sell to get their respective boards and city councils to agree to contribute any significant share, such as 22 percent. They also pointed out that only five surface rights holders in the EARIP receiving such a benefit (in rank order, Guadalupe-Blanco River Authority, City Public Service of San Antonio, Dow Chemical, Invista, and the City of Victoria) were part of the EARIP.[27] It would also be difficult, they argued, to get those who had not participated to contribute voluntarily to the implementation of the habitat conservation plan.

Very quickly the San Antonio Water System began to realize that, if its bargaining position were adopted, City Public Service would have to pay a significant surface water share in addition to increased aquifer management fees. The unintended—and probably unexpected—consequence of the position of the San Antonio Water System created a huge negotiating and political problem for it. City Public Service was a sister agency of the San Antonio Water System. It had a modest groundwater permit for withdrawals from the Edwards Aquifer. City Public Service believed, incorrectly as it turned out, that the surface water use permit it had was strictly a "bed and banks" permit that determined the amount of water it could remove from the San Antonio River based solely on how much water was placed into the river from the wastewater treatment plant operated by the San Antonio Water System. Thus, it believed that the surface water it diverted was not affected by additional springflow.

With the share of the City Public Service surface water benefit being almost as large as the Guadalupe-Blanco River Authority share, it was difficult for the San Antonio Water System to make any change in stance. The timing of the revelation, so late in the negotiations, made it even more difficult for the San Antonio Water System.[28] The discussions of the work group continued, but, perhaps as a result of the miscalculation, no real progress was made.

At the March 15, 2011 meeting of the Funding Work Group, the San Antonio Water System announced that if the regional sales tax option was not enacted by the Texas Legislature during the session of 2011, it was going to propose that all activities toward the completion of the habitat conservation plan be postponed until another attempt to pass the sales tax legislation could be made in 2013.[29]

When the EARIP learned in early April that a hearing was not going to be scheduled on the sales tax in the Senate Natural Resources Committee, it abandoned all efforts on the sales tax. The San Antonio Water System then carried out its threat.

THE PROCESS NEARLY FALLS APART

Attempts to come up with a way to allocate costs between the pumpers and nonpumpers had not been successful. It is probably fair to say that the EARIP was at an impasse.

On April 29, 2011, the EARIP met in Austin. On the agenda, at the request of the San Antonio Water System, was a discussion and possible decision on delaying submission of the habitat conservation plan until after another attempt could be made in the legislature in 2013 to obtain a vote on a regional sales tax. I had prepared a memorandum setting out the considerations of delaying the EARIP.[30] What I did not state there was that I believed that the delay would have serious repercussions. Even making the extraordinarily optimistic assumption that a sales tax would have been popular in the 2013 legislative session, the very earliest that the habitat conservation plan could be submitted to the Fish and Wildlife Service would be 2014. Moreover, that date depended on the voters actually approving the collection of a sales tax. In my view, by that time, all momentum would be lost, and the EARIP simply could not survive the delay.

At the EARIP meeting in April, the San Antonio Water System representative said that it was committed to the process but wanted more time to devise a solution to the funding issue. There was no stated reason as to why it believed the sales tax proposal would fare better in 2013, or, if that did not happen, why attempts to allocate the costs would be any easier in late 2013.[31] The San Antonio Water System dismissed the delay by saying that Senator Hegar did not really intend the deadlines to be firm deadlines.

All of the steering committee members were asked about their position on the San Antonio Water System proposal. The Bexar Metropolitan Water System, Alamo Cement, the representative of the industrial pumping interests, and the representative of a western-sector water utility (East Medina County Special Utility District)—all traditionally strong backers of the San Antonio Water System positions—supported the proposal.[32] Otherwise, the proposal was greeted with concern or outright rejection. No formal vote was taken, but it appeared that the steering committee would continue to work on the funding question and to stay on schedule to submit the habitat conservation plan to the Fish and Wildlife Service in the fall of 2011. I suggested getting the Funding Work Group back together to consider the perspectives discussed at the April meeting and see if it could recommend any new strategies.[33]

The issue of delaying the submission came up again at the next EARIP meeting, in May.[34] Con Mims, who had chaired the EARIP with a steady, calming hand since 2009, asked to have an opportunity to deliver a report on the efforts of the Funding Work Group that included his personal views. He solemnly delivered that report reviewing the status of the work group's deliberations. He said that the "only idea being discussed that could result in a funding solution in time to meet our 2012 deadline is the option of pumpers paying, with contributions being made by non-pumpers." He then concluded with force and presence:

> We in this room have been working for nearly four years to deliver a Habitat Conservation Plan to FWS for its approval.
>
> We constitute the most widely diverse and representative group of people to ever attempt to resolve the endangered species protection issue at Comal and San Marcos Springs.
>
> We have devoted considerable time in establishing complex and comprehensive rules and agreements to guide our work so that it is fair and transparent. These guidance documents, and the desire of everyone involved to succeed, have been the glue holding us together.
>
> We have had firm support of our efforts on the local, regional, state and federal levels. There has been widespread optimism that we will succeed, and our accomplishments to date have supported that optimism.

With the leadership of one of the finest managers I have ever worked with, coupled with the exceptional talent of those participating in this process, we have surmounted difficult decisions, over and over again, and have developed an HCP that seems [*sic*] will accomplish the species recovery and protection this region has sought for over 20 years.

It is expected that we will have spent over $4 million of local, state and federal money by the time our HCP is delivered to FWS.

It is not likely that the working relationships we have forged and the momentum we have achieved will ever happen again.

. . .

We have four options:

a. We can solve this problem, ourselves, by the statutory deadline established, using the inclusive and balanced process we have created,
b. We can turn the matter over to the Edwards Aquifer Authority, with its elected Board, to resolve,
c. We can let the Texas Legislature dictate, or
d. We can let a federal judge control our water resources.

It is clear to me which option is best for the region. We must keep working, because, once more, we, likely, will never be at this point again, as a region.[35]

At my invitation, Senator Glenn Hegar also addressed the stakeholders. He began by expressing his great appreciation for the time, energy, and resources everyone had given over the last several years. But he said that the work of the EARIP was not complete. He stressed, presumably for the benefit of the San Antonio Water System, that the 2012 statutory deadline was real and could not be changed. He urged the EARIP to keep working. In closing, he said that four years ago everyone had asked him how the region could stay together to resolve this issue and that he had replied that he had simple faith that the region could do this. He said that he "still feels that the region can complete its task."[36]

I reported on discussions regarding the ways to reduce project costs, which at that time were estimated to average close to $27 million annually. The prime targets for savings were the San Antonio Water System aquifer storage and recovery option and the VISPO program. If the San Antonio Water System absorbed the cost of depreciation for the use of its aquifer storage and recovery facility, the cost of the ASR element of the bottom-up package would be reduced by $3.22 million. Moreover, the VISPO Work Group reported that VISPO program costs could be reduced by almost $4.5 million by reducing the trigger at the J-17 index well to 635 feet mean sea level and moving the trigger date from September 1 to October 1. If these two changes were made, the total average annual cost of the habitat conservation plan would be less than $20 million. HDR had confirmed that the changes would not affect the effectiveness of the program.

After extensive discussion, Karl Dreher voiced his concerns.[37] As was often the case, the general manager of the Edwards Aquifer Authority strategically waited to speak until the discussions were complete. He predicted that his board would be unlikely to approve a threefold increase in aquifer management fees, which might be required if the full VISPO element were implemented.[38] Therefore, he suggested that the EARIP consider removing the VISPO element from the bottom-up package until it could be paid for and then replacing it with deeper pumping cuts in stages IV and V to maintain the overall protectiveness of the package. He said that, while the VISPO element remained an option for the future, the pumping cuts would remain in place throughout the permit period until the permittees could afford it.

Dreher's eleventh-hour position would have forced a fundamental change in direction for the EARIP. It would have changed the entire bottom-up package rather than just modified one of the elements to reduce costs. The VISPO program was one of the first elements agreed to by the steering committee. It had broad support, including from irrigated agriculture. Pumping cuts on the other hand were extremely unpopular with almost all of the EARIP participants. Indeed, avoiding pumping cuts was the very reason the EARIP began looking at alternative water management strategies.

Sam Vaugh from HDR had told both Dreher and me earlier that, if the VISPO program were replaced by increased stage IV and V pumping cuts, the stage IV cuts would have to be increased from 35 to 45 percent for the Uvalde pool and from 40 to 43 percent for the San Antonio pool. Stage V cuts would be 47 percent for both pools.[39] Dreher did not share Vaugh's analysis with the EARIP. While the San Antonio Water System might have been able to diversify to meet the reductions if the need arose, the same probably was not true of the smaller communities to the west.

We were still at an impasse. The next meeting was scheduled at the San Antonio Water System for June 9, 2011. I had the strong sense that, after that meeting, we would know whether or not Senator Hegar's feeling that the region could complete the task at hand was correct.

Beginning in early 2009, I had started preparing memoranda regarding the difficult issues the stakeholders were discussing and setting out a "straw man" to focus the discussions at the upcoming meeting. I had tried to remain neutral in writing those memoranda.

Soon after the May 17, 2011, EARIP meeting, Calvin Finch, the representative of the San Antonio Water System on the EARIP Steering Committee, approached me. He said that the San Antonio Water System had a proposal to resolve the funding issue and asked me if I would prepare a straw-man memorandum about the proposal. I said that I had always tried to stay neutral in those memoranda and that I did not think it would be a good idea to change now. I offered, however, that if he could get substantial consensus on the proposal, I would prepare another memorandum.

Soon after the call, I heard rumblings that Finch was vetting his proposal and doing a good job in getting support both inside and outside of the San Antonio region. In early June, Finch called me again. He said that he had talked to almost all of the steering committee members, except the Guadalupe-Blanco River Authority. He asked me to mediate a meeting with the Guadalupe-Blanco River Authority. Not to be overly dramatic, but I could not help but feel that, after fifty years, the two key players in the dispute were going to sit down one-on-one and, if all went well, start to put the Edwards Issue to bed once and for all.

The meeting was scheduled for 1:00 p.m. on June 8. The San Antonio Water System was represented by Robert Puente, the president and chief executive officer, and the Guadalupe-Blanco River Authority, by Bill West, the general manager. Also attending for the San Antonio Water System were Chuck Ahrens, vice president for water resources; Calvin Finch; and Robert Macias, a person with knowledge of the operation of the San Antonio Water System aquifer storage facility. Todd Votteler also attended for the Guadalupe-Blanco River Authority. The discussions were friendly but to the point. Finch and Ahrens placed the San Antonio Water System proposal on the table. After one and one-half hours of discussion, the following agreement was reached:

1. The bottom-up package would be used as the basis for the habitat conservation plan at least until a phase II decision was made.
2. The VISPO program would remain in the bottom-up package but would be modified as proposed by the VISPO Work Group to reduce the cost of the program from $8.63 million to $4.17 million.
3. SAWS would absorb the cost of depreciation for the use of the San Antonio Water System aquifer storage and recovery facility, estimated to be $3.22 million. This would reduce the cost of the ASR element of the bottom-up package from $12.55 million to $9.33 million.
4. The municipal and industrial pumpers would pay for the bottom-up package through increases in the aquifer management fees. Municipal and industrial pumpers, along with irrigators, would be able to lease their permitted water rights for use in the San Antonio Water System aquifer storage and recovery facility.
5. The nonpumpers would contribute approximately $1 million annually toward the cost of the bottom-up package.[40] Of the targeted amount, the Guadalupe-Blanco River Authority would contribute $400,000. In exchange, it would expect some yet-to-be-defined level of participation in the management structure under discussion for implementing the habitat conservation plan.
6. The presumptive action for phase II that would be included in the habitat conservation plan will be a strategy involving the San Antonio Water System western extension pipeline that will be designed to ensure springflows of thirty cubic feet per second daily (forty-five cubic feet per second based on a monthly average). To the extent that such a project could not achieve the goals within the constraints of the San Antonio Water System, greater springflow protection would be obtained through additional critical period management pumping cuts in stage V.
7. The EARIP would actively support continued efforts through the 2017 legislative session to obtain a vote on the sales tax to cover the remaining costs of the phase I work and any phase II project that may be needed.[41]

The agreement did not differ significantly from what the San Antonio Water System had proposed earlier in the meeting. The issue that received the most attention at the meeting was the contribution of the Guadalupe-Blanco River Authority and participation of the authority toward implementing the habitat conservation plan. In light of the large increase in aquifer management fees that the San Antonio Water Authority would have to pay, Puente was concerned about his ability to sell the compromise to his board without a significant contribution from the Guadalupe-Blanco River Authority. Bill West responded that the Guadalupe-Blanco River Authority did not have the revenue base to enable it to match the San Antonio Water System contribution. However, he proposed that it would make an annual contribution in an amount that would increase customer rates to about as much as the San Antonio Water System would have to pass on to its ratepayers (approximately $400,000). After further discussion, Puente and West were in agreement. They shook hands and left it to me to finalize the straw-man memorandum for consideration the next day by the steering committee.

The compromise was submitted to the steering committee on June 9, 2011. After I presented the proposal, the San Antonio Water System and the Guadalupe-Blanco River Authority representatives expressed their support for the compromise.[42] The proposal was for the most part favorably received by the steering committee and stakeholders. The City of San Marcos and New Braunfels Utilities, both customers of the Guadalupe-Blanco River Authority, supported the compromise but expressed concern because the river authority would not actually be making the contribution since the cost would be passed on to the customers.

The only significant area of concern was a rebate program of the Edwards Aquifer Authority. As discussed more fully later, beginning in 2006 the Edwards Aquifer Authority had been rebating aquifer management fees paid by municipal and industrial pumpers for water on which they had paid fees but had not actually pumped during the year.[43] The San Antonio Water System, which actually used most of the water it was permitted to pump, did not favor the rebate, but the City of San Marcos and New Braunfels Utilities, both of which had diversified their water supplies years before and typically did not use all of their permitted Edwards water, expressed strong support for keeping the rebate program as part of the Edwards Aquifer Authority decision to raise the aquifer management fees to pay for the habitat conservation plan. Smaller municipalities in the western part of the aquifer region also voiced strong support for the rebate program. However, it was ultimately agreed that the issue of the rebate was not germane to the funding issue and would be left to the Edwards Aquifer Authority Board of Directors when it set the aquifer management fees to cover the implementation of the habitat conservation plan.

After lengthy debate, the steering committee approved, by consensus, the seven funding concepts set out in the "straw-man" memorandum in the habitat conservation plan, provided that the costs shown in the attachment to the memorandum were amended to include the full costs as adjusted by the compromise. Karl Dreher abstained because he again did not know his board members' position on raising aquifer management fees.[44]

The fight with Dreher over the VISPO program was not over. Dreher told me that he wanted to remove the VISPO program because he believed that irrigated agriculture was getting "too good a deal" and would not be paying for any of the habitat conservation plan costs. He carried his fight to the San Antonio Water System and to his board at a retreat scheduled for late June in Bandera, Texas.

Previously, in May, at a meeting of the Funding Work Group, Dreher had announced that he had been having private meetings with the highest officials of the San Antonio Water System but that he was not free to disclose the content of their discussions. He said that he believed we should start looking at the costs as if the VISPO program were not included as one of the elements of the habitat conservation plan. It must have come as a surprise to him to see that the San Antonio Water System was at that time vetting a proposal that expressly included VISPO as an element of the habitat conservation plan.

After the compromise had been approved by the steering committee, Dreher again met with the San Antonio Water System to try to persuade it to back off the compromise and do away with VISPO.[45] Afterwards, Dreher told me that the San Antonio Water System might withdraw support for the compromise because the VISPO program was part of it. This prediction turned out to be false. Calvin Finch, who attended the meeting, told me that it was his impression that Dreher had a tendency to consider the mere failure to reject a proposal, or even the polite recognition of the proposal, to signal agreement with it.[46]

The San Antonio Water System firmly believed that it was time to move or the deal would be lost.[47] Accordingly, in an e-mail entitled "SAWS supports EARIP Bottom Up package," Calvin Finch of the San Antonio Water System made sure that key steering committee members did not think that, because of Dreher's efforts, the system was backing away from the consensus agreement that the EARIP had reached: "In case you have heard otherwise, dismiss it. SAWS made the motion to proceed with the package, and we continue to support it. We are determined to make it work. Join us in encouraging everyone to stay on course. Thanks Calvin."[48]

About two weeks after the approval of the compromise on June 9, the Edwards Aquifer Authority board held its annual two-day workshop in Bandera. The issue of the EARIP habitat conservation plan and, more specifically, the VISPO program were on the agenda. Dreher prepared and distributed a white paper to his board laying out his position that the VISPO program should be removed from the habitat conservation plan.[49] He had been encouraged to present his views by Luana Buckner, the board chair. I was invited to give a presentation on the second day of the workshop regarding the recently approved funding decision. I had invited Weir Labatt and the EARIP chair, Con Mims, to attend the workshop. At my suggestion, Jerry James had invited Senator Hegar to attend and briefed him on the recent decision of the EARIP and on Dreher's objections to that decision.

On June 24, the workshop featured a discussion of the EARIP habitat conservation plan and the VISPO program. Dreher suggested that the EARIP members did not really understand what they were voting on. He said his approach was simply to try "to preserve options for this board" rather than force the board to consider only the single option that the EARIP provided. He said that the habitat conservation plan presented to the board needed only to "*largely*" reflect the "regional consensus" but that it needed to be an option "potentially acceptable to this board." Board chair Buckner made it clear that she was not going to be "bullied into just rubber stamping the habitat conservation plan." She asserted, "Karl's option was not discussed. I was told that everyone would support looking at it."[50]

That evening, Senator Hegar spoke to the board at an informal gathering before dinner. He had made the trip all the way from his home in Katy and would return home that evening. Senator Hegar got his message across: as an elected board, the Edwards Aquifer Authority had an obligation to reach its independent decision regarding the habitat conservation plan, but he hoped that, in doing so, the board would keep in mind that the plan reflected years of work and the consensus of the regional stakeholders, a consensus that had eluded them for many years.

The next morning, I was on the agenda to discuss the habitat conservation plan adopted by the steering committee two weeks earlier. I did so and addressed Dreher's arguments about costs. But I began my presentation by trying to extend the theme struck by Senator Hegar. I told the board members that the EARIP had a duty to make a recommendation to the Edwards Aquifer Authority board that reflected the consensus thinking of the region. That obligation was independent of the Edwards Aquifer Authority board members' duty to decide whether to accept or reject that recommendation. If, after the board received the habitat conservation plan, it wanted changes, then the EARIP would sit down with the authority and see if a compromise could be reached that would satisfy the board and maintain consensus in the region.

Saturday afternoon, Con Mims and Weir Labatt spoke briefly to the board. Mims said that he hoped the board members would ask themselves three questions before considering any changes to the plan presented by the EARIP: "Is this change essential? Is it something you are unable to live without? And can the adaptive management process deal with it?" Labatt said that the "RIP came to consensus because they didn't want pumping cuts. They would rather pay more money."[51]

In the discussion that followed, two directors made points that I believe swayed the outcome of the debate. First, Jerry James said that, although the EARIP would be presenting a complete habitat conservation plan with a recommendation reflecting the consensus of the region, during the development of the plan the "opportunity has always been there to discuss other options."[52]

The second, and most persuasive point, was made by Adam Yablonski, who in my estimation was viewed both by the EARIP and the board as being very thoughtful and fair-minded. He said quite forcefully, "I disagree that [the steering committee] didn't know what they were doing" or "that they didn't know what Karl's option was." He also said, "I feel like they made an informed decision at the meeting." Yablonski pointed out that almost all of the major pumpers were represented on the steering committee. According to Yablonski, the message from the pumpers was "we'd rather pay more than to take [pumping] cuts up front." For him, it would be "hard to tell pumpers 'I know you think you know what you're doing, but it is really more fair for you not to pay so much.'"[53]

After the discussion, the chair informally polled the board members regarding whether or not they believed that they would support the regional consensus or have Dreher try to get the EARIP to amend the plan by removing VISPO in favor of deeper pumping cuts. A quorum of members was not present; however, more than a majority of the members supported the EARIP plan, and only three members, including the chair, favored Dreher's alternative approach.

After the board workshop, Dreher requested an opinion from the general counsel for the Edwards Aquifer Authority as to whether two of the directors who spoke in favor of the EARIP's consensus decision had a conflict of interest with respect to the VISPO issue. Each was an Edwards permitted agricultural water rights holder—one in Medina County and the other in Uvalde County—who could have taken advantage of the VISPO program. It was the general counsel's view that both had a conflict of interest and would need to recuse themselves when the vote on the VISPO program was before the board. Both directors were made aware of the general counsel's view. One of the directors retained a prominent water law attorney, Edmond R. McCarthy Jr. of Jackson, Sjoberg, McCarthy & Wilson, LLP, from Austin. McCarthy's opinion directly conflicted with that of the general counsel. The Edwards Aquifer Authority did not pursue the conflict issue when the habitat conservation plan was brought before the board in December 2011. Subsequently, the board of directors for the authority agreed to reimburse the member who had paid McCarthy's legal fees.

At the September 28 EARIP meeting, triggered by remarks from Dreher about VISPO, the EARIP directed its displeasure at Dreher for his post hoc attacks on the consensus package. Most of the stakeholders' concerns were related to his continued attempts to remove the VISPO program. Dreher admitted raising the conflict of interest issue but said that both of the directors would be allowed to vote. The discussion ended with a very stern warning from Gene Richardson of the Texas Farm Bureau of the potential repercussions if his efforts to remove VISPO were successful.

Closing the Deal

It had been agreed that the applicants for the incidental take permit would be the City of San Marcos, the City of New Braunfels, the Edwards Aquifer Authority, Texas State University, and the San Antonio Water System. A funding and management agreement was drafted to set out the understandings among the applicants as to how the habitat conservation plan would be funded, managed, and implemented.

After the final deal was done, a significant problem arose—whether the funding and management agreement precluded the Edwards Aquifer Authority from issuing a rebate on the aquifer management fees for the habitat conservation plan. Municipal and industrial permit holders paid aquifer management fees at the beginning of a calendar year based on the total amount of groundwater authorized under their permit. Since 2006 the Edwards Aquifer Authority had given municipal and industrial pumpers a rebate on that portion of groundwater authorized but not actually pumped in that year.

By 2011 the rebate had become controversial and was creating budget problems for the Edwards Aquifer Authority. At the workshop in June, Dreher had discussed limiting the rebate to half of the fees paid by the municipal and industrial aquifer users. On September 13, 2011, the Edwards Aquifer Authority Board of Directors voted to keep the rebate program in place for purposes of developing the proposed operating budget for 2012.[54] This decision, however, did not apply to the fee increase for the habitat conservation plan that the board was scheduled to consider in December.

In the EARIP, the rebate had been controversial. But the EARIP stakeholders did not take a position on the rebate, believing it to be too political and not directly related to the issue of protecting federally listed species. It was left up to the Edwards Aquifer Authority to decide one way or another and approve a funding mechanism.

After the city councils of New Braunfels and San Marcos and the Texas State University administration had approved the habitat conservation plan and the supporting documents, on November 16 Karl Dreher invited the applicants to a meeting at the Edwards Aquifer Authority, where he announced that he had a legal opinion from Darcy Frownfelter, the general counsel for the authority, indicating that the funding and management agreement precluded the payment of the rebate on aquifer management fees for the habitat conservation plan.[55] He distributed a copy of that opinion at that meeting. Dreher admitted that he had received this opinion orally from Frownfelter several days before the two city councils met—meetings that he had actually attended and where he could have alerted the councils to the problem. Moreover, Frownfelter, one of the primary drafters of that agreement, had not flagged that issue in the discussions with the other drafters or with the EARIP. Factually correct but perhaps not politically astute, Dreher pointed out that the attorneys of the major players were involved in the drafting of the funding and management agreement and should have figured it out.

The cities of New Braunfels and San Marcos and New Braunfels Utilities were enraged by Dreher's action, not so much because the rebate would not apply to the increased fees charged to pay for the habitat conservation plan but because their city councils had voted to approve the plan, believing as they did that the Edwards Aquifer Authority Board of Directors had the discretion to approve the fee increase with or without the rebate program.

Subsequently, Mary Q. Kelly, one of the authors of the funding and management agreement and a highly respected attorney, challenged the validity of the conclusions in Frownfelter's legal opinion.[56] The cities, meanwhile, began talking with Buckner, chair of the Edwards Aquifer Authority board, and other board members.

On December 13, 2011, the Edwards Aquifer Authority Board of Directors was presented with the program documents, including the funding and management agreement. If the board wanted to allow the rebate to be applied to some or all of the habitat conservation plan fee increase, it would, under the general counsel's legal opinion, have required a vote to amend the funding and management agreement. If such an amendment were approved, the agreement would have had to be submitted again to the other applicants for approval—a result that, at best, would only have delayed the submission of the habitat conservation plan.

The board of directors of the authority voted to approve the habitat conservation plan and implementing agreement. It rejected, however, the funding and management agreement by an 8-to-7 vote.[57] That decision on the funding and management agreement resulted from a split in the board regarding whether a rebate program should be applied to the aquifer management fees for the habitat conservation plan costs. After going into closed session, the board directed Karl Dreher to meet with other applicants and to bring back a workable solution for the rebate issue at a special meeting of the Edwards Aquifer Authority board that they were scheduling for December 28, 2011.

Several meetings with the stakeholders were held prior to the special December 28 board meeting. Board chair Buckner and other directors were instrumental in setting up the meetings. On December 21, an agreement was reached at a meeting in New Braunfels attended by representatives of the cities of San Marcos and New Braunfels, New Braunfels Utilities, the San Antonio Water System, and the Edwards Aquifer Authority. It was agreed that the authority would not apply the rebate to the aquifer management fee increase for the habitat conservation plan. Under the agreement, however, the authority would provide grants out of the Endangered Species Mitigation Fund it maintained for projects that benefited the listed species but were not included in the habitat conservation plan. Specific projects were discussed for which the New Braunfels Utilities and City of San Marcos would be provided grants.[58]

On December 28, 2011, the Edwards Aquifer Authority Board of Directors approved the funding and management agreement by a vote of 15 to 0. The habitat conservation plan and supporting documents were submitted to the US Fish and Wildlife Service along with the incidental take permit application on January 5, 2012.[59] The FWS provided a few comments on the plan in May 2012. It approved the incidental take permit application and habitat conservation plan, essentially without change, on March 18, 2013.

The EARIP had done the job given to it by the legislature—on time and by consensus. I was finally able to exhale.

10 : REFLECTIONS

We few, we happy few, we band of brothers.
— William Shakespeare, *Henry V*

T he Edwards Aquifer habitat conservation plan was a historic achievement for the region. It provided the solution to the last, and probably most difficult, problem in resolving the Edwards Issue, and it brought an end to decades of acrimony and litigation over the use of the Edwards Aquifer. The plan fulfilled the task assigned to the Edwards Aquifer Authority by providing protection required by the federal Endangered Species Act for eight listed species in the Comal and San Marcos ecosystems. It did so while recognizing the ever-growing need for water in the region. It ended the threat of a federal takeover of the aquifer—the "blunt axe" that had hung over local authorities responsible for the water supply of the region.

Water issues are inherently difficult to solve. The Edwards Issue was particularly complex because of the semiarid, drought-prone climate, the number of widely divergent interests involved, and the length of the controversy. Any process that can work through all of these difficulties, reach a solution by consensus, and get political buy-in by the region deserves at least some attention as a historic achievement. Add to that, the problem was solved in Texas, where private property interests are inviolate and where rancor between the parties is rivaled only by that of a Texas-Oklahoma football game and is almost as much fun. If the Edwards Aquifer habitat conservation plan is not a historic achievement, it surely comes close.

Why the EARIP Succeeded Where Other Attempts Failed

After the EARIP process had been completed, many people asked me how it was able to solve the Edwards Issue when all earlier efforts had failed. The opportunity to study the history of the Edwards Issue and to reflect upon the EARIP process has given me insight into the answer to this question. The procedural tools the EARIP created to help those involved reach consensus have been discussed here. They provide part of the answer. However, at a more fundamental level, the EARIP succeeded because: (1) it benefited from the "infrastructure" that had been created in response to those earlier failed efforts, (2) it was able to effectively use the tools that were available to it, and (3) it earned the commitment of the stakeholders to solve the Edwards Issue.

THE INFRASTRUCTURE

Past efforts to resolve the Edwards Issue set the stage for the success of the EARIP. Unlike earlier efforts, the EARIP did not have to struggle without an agency that had authority to regulate the aquifer. The lack of such an agency was a major obstacle facing the Regional Water Resource Plan, the Texas Water Commission, and even Judge Lucius Bunton himself. Moreover, the Edwards Aquifer region had become accustomed to operating without the rule of capture. After a decade of regulation by the Edwards Aquifer Authority, the fears of the agricultural interests regarding the substitution of a regulatory regime for the old rule of capture had not materialized. As discussed earlier, the irrigators were no longer fighting the notion of regulation but were involved in the process of refining that regulation to make it more suitable to their needs. Indeed, in a relatively short time, Luana Buckner, general manager of the Medina County Underground Water Conservation District and one of the leaders of the "western insurrection" from 1989 through 1992, had become chair of the Edwards Aquifer Authority Board of Directors.

The specific tasks facing the EARIP were better and more narrowly defined than those facing the earlier groups attempting to resolve the Edwards Issue. More than a decade earlier Michael Spear and Judge Bunton had encouraged the region to prepare a habitat conservation plan. Senate Bill 3, however, *directed* the EARIP to prepare such a plan. The requirements for a habitat conservation plan are quite clear and specific. Moreover, Senate Bill 3 narrowed the issues by resolving the withdrawal cap and the critical period management issues and by establishing unambiguously the objective for the EARIP—a plan that provided protection for the listed species even during a repeat of the drought of record.

Further, Senate Bill 3 set specific deadlines for the EARIP to meet in developing that plan. While other efforts, such as those of John Hall, set deadlines for completing negotiations, the 2012 deadlines for completing the habitat conservation plan and for solving the continuous minimum flow issue were an essential part of the compromise that resulted in Senate Bill 3. Therefore, as a part of the compromise, failure to meet those deadlines had potential consequences, such as a federal lawsuit or legislative intervention during the 2013 session. The internal deadlines were also valuable because they provided milestones by which the stakeholders could gauge their progress and keep the EARIP focused on the task at hand.

THE TOOLS

The legislature gave the EARIP the essential tools to allow the program decision-making process to be based on the best available science. Senate Bill 3 required the EARIP to create and use an expert science subcommittee and set out specific questions that were pertinent to the decision-making process. Requiring that the program answer these questions went a long way toward avoiding the "my science versus your science" debate.

Further, when the EARIP was created, there was concern about the lack of science to support the process. However, at the critical time, the legislature provided the money needed to actually develop the science. That money funded the work of Dr. Thomas Hardy of the River Systems Institute at Texas State University, Ed Oborny of Bio-West, HDR Engineering, and Todd Engineers, which went a long way toward addressing the concern about the lack of science. Moreover, with the money from the legislature, the EARIP was able to commission additional scientific studies.[1]

Although acquiring additional data was important to the decision-making process, it was equally important that the process allowed the EARIP participants to discuss and better understand the existing science. The results and conclusions of much of the work commissioned by the EARIP were presented and discussed by the participants. Allowing an opportunity for a deeper understanding of the existing science was particularly important because many of the stakeholders did not have the background to fully understand some of the highly technical aspects of the work and thus benefited from an opportunity to hear a discussion of the work and to ask their own questions. In many instances the EARIP participants were also afforded the opportunity to provide comments on the work. Moreover, meetings of the science subcommittee were open to all. Subcommittee meetings often featured scientific presentations on issues related to the tasks at hand, and they were well attended by the EARIP participants.

Most importantly, the reports of the science subcommittee were peer reviewed by independent scientific review panels. In addition, Hardy's critically important work was also peer reviewed by the science subcommittee. The independent peer review was instrumental in getting the buy-in of EARIP participants on the scientific work and, I believe, was important to the Fish and Wildlife Service evaluation of the habitat conservation plan. It focused the debate on the policy implications of the science—not on the validity of the work itself—and kept the arguments about who would perform the scientific work to a minimum. Peer review took time and it was rather expensive, but it was worthwhile. If we had not taken the time, the EARIP might have gotten bogged down in arguments about the value of the available science.

Senator Glenn Hegar's support was also essential to the success of the EARIP. He and Representative Robert Puente secured passage of the legislation creating the program. Senator Hegar effectively used the carrot-and-stick approach to keep the EARIP team focused. During the process, he met on numerous occasions with the EARIP—sometimes to encourage, sometimes to gently scold. With the help of others, such as Representative Doug Miller, Senator Hegar helped get the EARIP the money needed to fund the science work that was essential to the decision-making process. To their credit, he and Representative Miller did not throw us out of their offices when we announced our interest in legislation for a sales tax—although I am sure the thought crossed their minds, probably more than once.

THE PEOPLE

The ultimate answer as to why the journey of the EARIP was successful is not to be found only in the infrastructure issues or the external tools. *The stakeholders were committed to finding a solution.* At the outset, in creating the memorandum of agreement, they wrestled with what "consensus" meant and, in adopting it, committed themselves to abiding by the process *they had created.*

They also committed the time to make the process work. The EARIP met for the better part of a day in regular meetings each month from February 2007 through November 2011. Not infrequently, the EARIP met twice a month. With work groups, subcommittees, issues teams, and workshops, it was possible for the participants in the EARIP to have found themselves in a meeting at least once a week. The effort was significant for the individuals involved but also for the organizations that had to commit those resources.

Beginning with the memorandum of agreement and building with each decision they made and each crisis they avoided, the stakeholders restored the trust that had been lost over the previous decades. Con Mims, who I hold in the highest regard and for whom the word "gentleman" is an understatement, nailed it when he said, "It is not likely that the working relationships we have forged and the momentum we have achieved will ever happen again."

I believe Myron Hess's "We have come too far to fail" declaration exemplifies the restoration of trust in the region. Recall that the environmental community was skeptical of the EARIP from the start. They believed that they had largely been excluded from the Senate Bill 3 process. I believe it was entirely possible that if the steering committee had not been enlarged, the environmental community might have walked. If a lawsuit were to have come, it would have probably been brought by an environmental plaintiff, as it was in 1991. In this context, Hess's statement takes on real significance.

Even more importantly, though, when Hess made that statement and the stakeholders responded to it, the stakeholders assumed *ownership of the process*. Further, the decision on springflow targets he facilitated gave the process momentum at a critical juncture. That momentum was enough to carry the EARIP through many tough issues until it ran into the funding issue.

The notion of compromise permeated almost all of the relations among stakeholders in the process. The San Antonio Water System had the potential to be the "800-pound gorilla" in this process.[2] For the most part, however, that potential was not realized. Dr. Calvin Finch was the San Antonio Water System representative on the steering committee. He was a tough negotiator, but he had a true sense of compromise coupled with an uncanny sense of when to compromise to close the deal.

The EARIP also was fortunate to have persons who, at very key moments, exhibited leadership in the search for consensus. Although that could be said of almost any of the stakeholders in the EARIP, it was Jerry James, Weir Labatt, and Jim Bower who really stood out. James was a strong advocate for the City of Victoria, but he understood the importance of compromise and the consequences of failure. He was widely trusted and respected for his ability to find the middle ground.

Weir Labatt, the representative of the Texas Water Development Board, had been dealing with water issues involving the Edwards Aquifer since 1987. But he spoke from his heart as well as his long experience. He provided a sobering voice in the search for consensus and kept urging the team not to allow the EARIP to be added to the long list of missed opportunities to provide solid water management for the region.

Jim Bower represented the City of Garden Ridge, which had no interest in a specific outcome—except that the EARIP be successful. Bower firmly believed in ensuring that the process was fair and that procedures were followed. His outspoken devotion to the integrity of the process was important in reaching a successful outcome.

Still, some of the stakeholders did not appreciate the value of compromise or the principles of openness and transparency that were the hallmarks of the EARIP. For example, Karl Dreher joined the Edwards Aquifer Authority only in March 2010, just six months prior to becoming the authority representative to the EARIP. He had thus not gone through the earlier stages of the EARIP process or been influenced by its consensus-based, open, and transparent philosophies. He was extraordinarily adept technically and had a keen understanding of groundwater issues. With an engineer's precision, he would decide what was the best answer, and that decision, in his mind, had to be what the EARIP adopted. Dreher seemed to prefer working behind the scenes, particularly with the San Antonio Water System, to try to achieve his view. The problem was that the San Antonio Water System in general and Calvin Finch in particular understood the value of consensus. Consensus does not always result in the absolutely best solution, but it does typically yield a solution that is apt to have longevity.

Other Factors Affecting the EARIP Decision-Making Process

In addition to the value placed on consensus, five aspects of the EARIP effort had a significant effect on the overall success of the process.

THE PHASED APPROACH

The decision to adopt the phased approach was perhaps one of the more important factors in allowing the EARIP to reach consensus.

The EARIP had excellent modeling simulations to predict the likely effects of low flows on the species and their habitats, but very little observational data existed to support the modeled results. This lack of data created uncertainty. For example, the tolerance of aquatic vegetation to reduced flow conditions is an unknown. We do not know when and where fountain darters move when the vegetation decays. We do not know the relationship of the fountain darter's food source to low-flow conditions. Even if the native vegetation can tolerate a particular flow, the fountain darter's food source may be lost before that flow level is reached.

In the face of such uncertainties, it was difficult for many participants in the EARIP to agree to a particular flow target. In the absence of observational data, many insisted on conservative flow targets. Others found the conservatism unwarranted, particularly in light of the low frequency of low-flow events and the high cost of ensuring that flow targets would be met.

By adopting the phased approach, supported by a robust adaptive management process, the EARIP stakeholders did not have to resolve all of the complex technical issues that were rife with uncertainties.[3] The phased approach allowed decisions to be made on the best information available during the EARIP process with the knowledge that further development of the science would occur and that any adjustments necessary would be based on the best information available at that later time.

FACILITATION

As they discussed use of the structured decision-making process, the EARIP steering committee explored using a facilitator to assist in developing the biological model and in making other decisions. In March 2009 the steering committee created a work group to identify and make recommendations regarding the facilitator.[4] The work group uniformly agreed that a facilitator would be better suited than a mediator for EARIP decision making, particularly if a structured decision-making process were to be used.

The work group went through an arduous but thoughtful process of preparing a request for proposals for the facilitation and evaluating those proposals. The process was not easy because the views of the group's members as to what was needed in a facilitator were quite divergent and tightly held. One of the issues that provoked significant discussion was whether the facilitator needed to have experience in the structured decision-making process. All of the discussions were cordial, frank, and productive. As an often exhausted observer of the process, I could see the debate itself strengthening the bonds of trust among the stakeholders, just as it had done during the preparation of the memorandum of agreement.

The request for proposals expressly sought facilitators with experience in the structured decision-making process. The EARIP received ten highly qualified responses to the request for proposals. Much to everyone's surprise, no one who responded to the request for proposals had specific experience with the structured decision-making process. The persons who the Fish and Wildlife Service had recommended to facilitate such a process and who had given a presentation to the EARIP declined to submit a proposal. In telephone interviews, the candidates said that their facilitation informally used some elements of structured decision making but that they had never used the formal structure of that process.

The process of winnowing down the list of candidates was rigorous. Finally, after a series of telephone interviews, the work group invited three candidates for face-to-face interviews. After these interviews, in September 2009, the steering committee selected Joe McMahon of Collaborative Processes out of Denver to facilitate the discussions. McMahon teamed with Patrick Field from the Massachusetts Institute of Technology. They were both very skilled facilitators, got along well with the participants, and contributed positively to the process by helping to organize and stimulate discussions and to catalog the information being discussed.

Ultimately, however, the EARIP stakeholders realized that what they had actually needed were mediators, not facilitators, as well as an approach that was more fluid and less structured. In addition, both McMahon and Field had obligations to other projects, and they were not conveniently located to allow frequent, short visits to the region. Their lack of availability became a problem as the pace of the process accelerated. Thus, with time, Collaborative Processes' involvement with the EARIP diminished. I believe few, if any, in the EARIP regret the decision to select Collaborative Processes, although many may regret the decision to limit the search only to facilitators.

As program manager, I had conducted most of the EARIP meetings before Collaborative Processes was hired. Beginning in June 2010, at the request of the EARIP chair, I became "more engaged in the facilitation process."[5] As Collaborative Processes' role diminished, I assumed more of the mediator/facilitator role.

I believe that the memoranda I prepared throughout the process assisted EARIP decision making by framing the issues for the group and, thus, focusing the stakeholders on the issue at hand. I am not sure how the memoranda got started. I think, quite honestly, I started writing them initially for myself, to figure out what was going on. I am sure that, to the extent they were useful, it was because I was viewed as neutral, and the memoranda were perceived as neutral. Regardless, anyone who worked with this "herd of cats" learned very quickly that they were not going to be led anywhere they did not want to go.

Another contribution I made was keeping the EARIP moving. I was always concerned that, if we slowed down too much, we would lose momentum and start heading down rabbit trails. The deadlines were valuable tools in imparting a sense of urgency, although the stakeholders seemed to recognize on their own that a fast pace was important.

Finally, just as a blind hog finds an acorn now and then, I was also able to anticipate the potential for impasse and divert the group in another direction until they felt ready to tackle the issue again. From the outset, I met with the various stakeholders individually or in small groups. I initiated the meetings when I could foresee a potential problem, but much of the time the meetings were requested by the stakeholders themselves. Wherever it might be helpful, I set up meetings of small groups of stakeholders to try to avoid areas with the potential for impasse.

THE US FISH AND WILDLIFE SERVICE

Jerry James told me, and I believe he is correct, that "the important thing about the recovery implementation program was that it gave the stakeholders the tools they had been lacking in 2005 to get the job done."[6] It provided an effective forum for addressing the continuous minimum flow issue and a decision maker to evaluate the results of those efforts. It also brought many stakeholders into a decision-making role in the process rather than an advisory role, such as that performed by the Biology Advisory and Citizens' Advisory teams used by the Edwards Aquifer Authority in its earlier attempt to create a habitat conservation plan. Finally, as a regional program, it helped to bring the springs communities and Texas State University into the pro-

cess, thus facilitating the inclusion of measures such as habitat restoration, removal of sediment, and exotic species in the habitat conservation plan.

In addition, establishing a recovery implementation program ensured the meaningful involvement of the US Fish and Wildlife Service
in creating the habitat conservation plan. The service guided the process in the earliest stage, educated the EARIP team in the intricacies of
the Endangered Species Act, and encouraged the stakeholders in their
efforts. Indeed, Dr. Benjamin Tuggle, the administrator for Region 2
of the service, attended an EARIP meeting in August 2009 to offer encouragement and committed Region 2 staff to assist the process. Adam
Zerrenner, supervisor of the Austin field office, attended most if not all
of the EARIP meetings for the first two years and as frequently as his
schedule allowed thereafter. Moreover, service staff from the Region 2
office and from the Austin field office regularly attended the EARIP
meetings. It is not uncommon for field office staff to attend meetings
regarding the development of a habitat conservation plan. Indeed,
that occurred in the earlier attempt of the Edwards Aquifer Authority
to develop such a plan. It is difficult to overstate, however, the value of
having decision makers in actual attendance as the stakeholders express their widely divergent perspectives and struggle with the difficult
issues that had to be addressed to solve the Edwards Issue.

While the EARIP did not take full advantage of all of the tools the
Fish and Wildlife Service offered, such as collaborative learning and
structured decision making, the FWS exercised flexibility and wisdom
in allowing the EARIP to take ownership of the process rather than in-
sisting that the EARIP operate in a particular way. Indeed, the EARIP
was not typical of earlier recovery implementation programs that involved a large contingent of federal agencies and states.

I believe the Fish and Wildlife Service accepted our decisions in
large part because the EARIP process stayed true to the principles of
consensus, inclusiveness, openness, and transparency. The success of
the EARIP should dispel any notion that the FWS or the much-vilified
Endangered Species Act lacks the ability to facilitate the resolution of
complex, regional problems involving endangered species.

THE LACK OF FEDERAL FUNDING

As indicated earlier, there is little question that the EARIP stakeholders anticipated receiving federal money, at least to pay for the im-

plementation of the habitat conservation plan. Dr. Joy Nicholopoulos in her early outreach presentations probably contributed to those expectations by overselling the prospects for that funding. Her presentations contained a slide that showed a very simple, straightforward process, making it appear that there was almost certainly a pot of gold at the end of a successful recovery implementation program.[7] If that slide alone did not create an expectation of federal funding, it was followed by a series of slides listing examples of other recovery implementation programs obtaining funding that ranged from $30 million to $323 million.

Nicholopoulos gave her presentation to the San Antonio Water System Board of Trustees on November 7, 2006.[8] According to Calvin Finch, the part of her presentation that stood out was the discussion of the ability of other recovery implementation programs to obtain federal funding and her suggestion that similar funding opportunities might be available if the EARIP were established.[9] Senator Hegar was clear with respect to his expectations: the "federal government will put in federal dollars."[10] The senator stated that, "when you look at this process, there is a tremendous amount of federal dollars that can become available. It will cost a lot to address these issues, but that amount is there as long as the federal government wants to do this. . . . As a state, we don't have this resource."[11]

The failure to obtain federal funding for the implementation of the habitat conservation plan caused problems for the EARIP. "Where's the federal government?" was a constant refrain during the funding discussions. Federal funding was important not only because it would have helped reduce the significant costs the aquifer users would have to pay but also because of a firmly held belief that a federal contribution was dictated by the equities of the circumstances. Both the US Fish and Wildlife Service, through fish hatcheries, and the Department of Defense, through military installations in San Antonio, were users of the aquifer. Neither, however, was required to get a permit and thus did not have to pay aquifer management fees. Further, because the Department of Defense has to comply with the requirements of the Endangered Species Act, it would benefit significantly from the protection the EARIP habitat conservation plan would provide the species. Moreover, the EARIP would be paying $1.68 million to the National Fish Hatchery and Training Center in San Marcos to substantially subsidize the operation of a refugia there. For these reasons, the lack of federal funding for the program made many parties view the federal government as the quintessential free rider.

I believe Nicholopoulos was sincere in her encouragement regarding the prospects for federal funding, but she may have lost track of the fact that other recovery implementation programs had one or more large federal agencies that had direct access to the budget appropriation process. In the end, it probably was the failing economy, shrinking budgets, and sequestration that prevented the EARIP from obtaining federal funding. But try explaining that to a high-level executive or official who had made the decision to participate in the EARIP on the expectation of finding a pot of gold at the end of a successful process.

THE DROUGHT OF 2011

A belief (perhaps *superstition* is a better word) in the water community is that no big decisions or initiatives occur during times of abundant rainfall. Representative Puente certainly thought that to be the case in 2005, when he explained why the House did not act on Senate Bill 3: "It was one of those things where I think you have to have a drought and a budget surplus to pass a bill like that. . . . It had lots of support, but there wasn't the urgency to do it."[12] The ability of John Birdwell, of the Texas Water Commission, to get agreement on a regional emergency drought plan and his inability to obtain a long-term regional plan were influenced by the "significant rainfall" in the region in the late summer of 1990.[13]

It is widely believed that 2011 was one of the driest, hottest single years of drought.[14] Concern about the drought, I believe, weighed on the stakeholders' minds as they struggled to resolve the funding issues, particularly when they decided not to delay the submission of the incidental take permit. The issue of how to respond to the drought was discussed by the EARIP throughout 2011. In addition, I am sure that it did not escape the stakeholders' awareness that the threat of third-party litigation is far more likely to be realized during severe drought.

In November 2007, when I accepted the job of program manager of the EARIP, I was leaving a job with the Department of Justice, where I was a successful environmental attorney, to manage a group in which no one had any expectations of success or any burning desire to be civil to the persons sitting next to them unless they were allies. I honestly did not have a clue of how to bring people together. I wasn't exactly well known as someone who had much patience or who knew how to get along well with others. Moreover, I really did not have any notion about what I was going to do. I took the job because I knew that this group had a chance to solve a very important problem and that I was being given the chance to be part of that solution.

After the EARIP adopted the habitat conservation plan, I told the group, "I am proud to be part of the solution."[15] I meant that then, and I mean it today. I will always remember that there was a time when we stood together, disparate yet unified, transcending individual, deeply held perspectives for the greater good of the threatened and endangered species and the future generations of the region.[16]

APPENDIX 1
PARTICIPANTS IN THE EDWARDS AQUIFER
RECOVERY IMPLEMENTATION PROGRAM

The thirty-nine stakeholders listed below executed the 2007 memorandum of agreement with the US Fish and Wildlife Service regarding participation in the Edwards Aquifer Recovery Implementation Program.

Statutory Steering Committee Members
1. Edwards Aquifer Authority
    Robert Potts
    Velma Danielson
    Karl Dreher
    Rick Illgner
2. Texas Commission on Environmental Quality
    Cary Betz
    Herman Settemeyer
3. Texas Parks and Wildlife Department
    Cindy Loeffler
    Colette Barron
4. Texas Department of Agriculture
    Cary Dupuy
    Kelley Faulk
    Mike McMurry
5. Texas Water Development Board
    Weir Labatt
    Matt Nelson
6. San Antonio Water System
    Dr. Calvin Finch
    Chuck Ahrens
7. Guadalupe-Blanco River Authority
    Dr. Todd Votteler
    Bill West

8. San Antonio River Authority
     Steve Raabe
     Mike Gonzales
9. South Central Texas Water Advisory Committee
     Gary Middleton
     Bob Keith
10. Bexar County
     Joe Aceves
     Kerim Jacaman
11. CPS Energy
     Scott Smith
     Sam Hemle
     Kimberly Stoker
12. Bexar Metropolitan Water District (or its successor)
     Humberto Ramos
     Al Rocha
13. A representative of a holder of an initial regular permit issued to a
     retail public utility located west of Bexar County (appointed by
     the Edwards Aquifer Authority)
          East Medina County Special Utility District
               Bruce Alexander
               Bob Lee
14. A representative of a holder of an initial regular permit issued
     by the Edwards Aquifer Authority for industrial purposes
     (appointed by the authority)
          Alamo Cement
          Buck Benson
15. A representative of a holder of an industrial surface water right in
     the Guadalupe River Basin (appointed by the Texas Commission
     on Environmental Quality)
          Dow Chemical
               Kristen Soto
               Gena Leathers
16. A representative of a holder of a municipal surface water right in
     the Guadalupe River Basin (appointed by the Texas Commission
     on Environmental Quality)
          City of Victoria
               Jerry James

17. A representative of a retail public utility in whose service area the Comal Springs or San Marcos Springs is located
> New Braunfels Utilities
>> Roger Biggers
>> Melani Howard
18. A representative of a holder of an initial regular permit issued by the authority for irrigation (appointed by the commissioner of agriculture)
> Gilleland Farms
>> Rader Gilleland
>> Adam Yablonski
19. A representative of an agricultural producer from the Edwards Aquifer region (appointed by the commissioner of agriculture)
> Guadalupe County Farm Bureau
>> Ray Joy Pfannstiel
>> Herman Harris
20. A representative of environmental interests from the Texas Living Waters Project (appointed by the governing body of that project)
> Myron Hess
> Tyson Broad
21. A representative of recreational interests in the Guadalupe River Basin (appointed by the Texas Parks and Wildlife Department)
> Texas Bass Federation
>> Tim Cook
>> Carl Adkins

Steering Committee Members Added by the EARIP
1. A representative of a holder of an Edwards Aquifer Authority initial regular permit issued to a small municipality (population under fifty thousand) located east of San Antonio
> City of Garden Ridge
>> Jim Bower
>> Tony Zugay
2. A representative of Edwards Aquifer region municipal ratepayers/general public
> Regional Clean Air & Water
>> Kirk Patterson
>> Carol Patterson

3. A representative of Guadalupe River Basin municipal ratepayers/
general public
    Guadalupe Basin Coalition
      Tom Taggart
      Gary Spence
4. A representative of a conservation organization
      San Marcos River Foundation
        Dianne Wassenich
5. A representative of the Nueces River Authority
      Con Mims
      Kirby Brown

Stakeholders

1. Aquifer Guardians in Urban Areas
2. City of New Braunfels
3. City of San Marcos
4. Comal County
5. Dan Laroe
6. Greater Edwards Aquifer Alliance
7. Greater San Antonio Chamber of Commerce
8. Dr. John M. Donahue
9. Larry Hoffman
10. Mary Q. Kelly
11. Preserve Lake Dunlap Association
12. South Texas Farm and Ranch Club
13. Texas Wildlife Association

Steering Committee Officers

2008
Chair: Robert Potts, Edwards Aquifer Authority
Vice Chair: Cindy Loeffler, Texas Parks and Wildlife Department
Secretary: Steve Raabe, San Antonio River Authority

2009–2011
Chair: Con Mims, Nueces River Authority
Vice Chair: Myron Hess, National Wildlife Federation
Secretary: Steve Raabe, San Antonio River Authority

APPENDIX 2

THE ENDANGERED SPECIES ACT

The Endangered Species Act (ESA) gives the federal government authority to protect threatened and endangered species from both federal and nonfederal actions.[1] The US secretary of the interior, through the US Fish and Wildlife Service, or the secretary of commerce, through the National Marine Fisheries Service (NMFS), administers and enforces the Endangered Species Act.[2] For the purposes of this book, the most pertinent provisions of the Endangered Species Act are in sections 9 and 10(a) of the act, described below. Section 7(a)(2) is also relevant to the EARIP, so a discussion of it is appended as well.

Section 9
Section 9 of the ESA prohibits the "take" of listed endangered fish and wildlife.[3] "Take" is defined as "to harass, harm, pursue, hunt, shoot, wound, kill, trap, capture, or collect or to attempt to engage in any such conduct."[4] "Harm" includes significant habitat modification that actually kills or injures a listed species through impairing essential behavior such as breeding, feeding, or sheltering.[5] To establish a violation of section 9, the plaintiff must prove that the defendant was the proximate cause of the "take."[6]

Listed plants are not subject to the "take" prohibition in section 9. However, under section 9, plants listed as endangered may not be imported into or exported from the United States, removed from or damaged on federal property, used in commercial activities, or damaged or removed from any area in knowing violation of any state law or regulation.[7]

Enforcement of fish and wildlife violations under section 9 may come in the form of civil penalties.[8] Knowing violations may trigger criminal fines and imprisonment of less than one year, as well as injunctions.[9] Citizen suits are also allowed to enjoin any violation of the act or to compel action of the interior secretary.[10]

Courts have found that the actions or failures to act on the part of a regulatory agency may violate the Endangered Species Act.[11] For example, the US Court of Appeals for the First Circuit found that the fishing regulations of the State of Massachusetts caused a "take" of the endangered northern right whale.[12] The state had authorized gillnet and lobster pot fishing in the whales' critical habitat, but the NMFS had issued a final interim rule proposing to modify those fishing practices, as entanglement with fishing gear was a leading cause of depletion of the whales.[13] The court found that the Endangered Species Act not only prohibits the acts of a person causing a take but also bans the acts of a third party that bring about the taking, a situation known as vicarious liability. The court concluded that "a governmental third party pursuant to whose authority an actor directly exacts a taking of an endangered species may be deemed to have violated the provisions of the Endangered Species Act."[14]

Section 10(a)

Section 10(a) of the Endangered Species Act provides, under certain circumstances, relief from federal or citizen suits alleging violations of section 9. For example, permits may be issued that allow a taking if such taking is incidental to, and not the purpose of, the carrying out of an otherwise lawful activity.[15] These permits are referred to as incidental take permits.

An incidental take permit must have an approved conservation plan, commonly known as a habitat conservation plan.[16] The habitat conservation plan must specify the likely impact of the taking, the steps the applicant will take to minimize and mitigate such impacts and the funding available for the steps, the alternative actions considered and the reason why such alternatives are not being used, and other measures the interior secretary may require as necessary or appropriate.[17] An incidental take permit will be issued if the interior secretary finds that the taking will be incidental; the applicant, to the maximum extent practicable, will minimize and mitigate the impacts of the taking; the applicant ensures funding for the habitat conservation plan; the taking will not appreciably reduce the likelihood of the survival and recovery of the species in the wild; and the applicant ensures that the habitat conservation plan will be implemented.[18]

While the Endangered Species Act does not prohibit the taking of listed plants on nonfederal land, a habitat conservation plan may need to include conservation measures to protect listed plant species, as the Endangered Species Act requires that the Fish and Wildlife Service consider, in the section 7 biological opinion regarding issuance of the permit, impacts to any listed species, including plants.[19] Once an incidental take permit has been issued, so long as the permittee complies with the terms of the permit, the service may not require the commitment of additional funding or resources from the permit holder for changed or unforeseen circumstances.[20] This is often referred to as the "no surprises" rule.

The issuance of an incidental take permit is a federal action subject to section 7 of the Endangered Species Act.

Section 7(a)(2)

Section 7(a)(2) requires all federal agencies, in consultation with the Fish and Wildlife Service, to ensure that any action "authorized, funded, or carried out" by an agency is "not likely to jeopardize the continued existence of any endangered or threatened species or result in the destruction or adverse modification" of designated critical habitat.

While the Endangered Species Act does not define "jeopardy," federal regulations define it as "to engage in an action that reasonably would be expected, directly or indirectly, to reduce appreciably the likelihood of both the survival and recovery of a listed species in the wild by reducing the reproduction, numbers or distribution of that species."[21] To determine whether the effects of the incidental take will appreciably reduce the likelihood of the survival and recovery of the listed species, the direct and indirect effects of the action and the cumulative effects are aggregated and compared to the environmental baseline.

It is important to note that, unlike the prohibition in section 9 of the Endangered Species Act that applies to individual members of a listed species, the section 7(a)(2) analysis looks at the effects of the action on the species as a whole.

The ESA describes critical habitat as those areas that contain the "physical or biological features (1) essential to the conservation of the species and (2) which may require special management considerations or protection."[22] The Fish and Wildlife Service regulations identify the "constituent elements" of critical habitat to include "those that are essential to the conservation of the species," such as "roost sites, nesting grounds, spawning sites, feeding sites, seasonal wetland or dryland, water quality or quantity, host species or plant pollinator, geological formation, vegetation type, tide, and specific soil types."[23]

The results of the section 7 consultation are documented in biological opinions developed by the Fish and Wildlife Service. A biological opinion is the document that sets out the opinion of the service regarding whether or not the action complies with the jeopardy and critical habitat standards.

APPENDIX 3

TEXAS WATER LAW

A root cause of the dispute over the use of the Edwards Aquifer is an outgrowth of the difference in the way Texas managed groundwater and surface water resources. A fundamental tenet of hydrology is that groundwater and surface water are interconnected resources. This tenet is embodied in the concept of the hydrological cycle. Many, if not most, western states recognize and manage these interconnected resources together—a regulatory process known as conjunctive management.[1]

But not Texas. In Texas, prior to 1993, groundwater use was governed almost exclusively by the "rule of capture." Under this doctrine, established by Texas courts, a landowner would be free to capture and use as much water as could be beneficially used without waste.[2] Moreover, this common law privilege generally could be exercised without regard for any negative impacts to adjacent landowners or springflows.[3] The rule of capture was known as the rule of the biggest pump, that is, the one with the biggest pump could take all the water. Befitting of Texas, that rule exemplified the wild, wild West of water law.

Until 2012, it was not clear who owned the groundwater, but it was clear that the state had the authority to regulate the resource, at least when it was brought to the surface.[4] In 1949, the Texas Legislature created underground water conservation districts, which generally had the authority to promulgate rules for conserving, protecting, recharging, and preventing waste of groundwater.[5] Few such districts were created, though, and those that were largely tended to issues such as subsidence.

Surface water is broadly defined to include the ordinary flow, underflow, and the tides of every flowing natural watercourse in the state. Storm water and floodwater found within natural lakes, rivers, and streams are also state waters.[6] As is common in most western states, including Texas, surface waters are governed by the "prior appropriation doctrine."[7] Under this doctrine, the State of Texas owns all surface water in trust for the benefit of citizens, subject to a state-granted right to use.[8] Through an administrative process, the state grants permission, based on seniority, to beneficially use the water.[9] The lower segment of the Guadalupe River surface water is regulated now by the Texas Commission on Environmental Quality. In the early 1990s, the authority to regulate surface water resided in a predecessor agency, the Texas Water Commission.

APPENDIX 4
ELEMENTS OF THE BOTTOM-UP APPROACH

The EARIP took a "bottom-up" approach to developing the measures to ensure flow protection, starting with simpler and less costly elements and layering on additional elements until the springflow targets were met. The bottom-up package consists of four elements: a regional conservation program, an irrigation suspension program (referred to as VISPO), the SAWS ASR program, and stage V emergency withdrawal reductions.

Regional Water Conservation Program
The San Antonio Water System has one of the best water conservation programs in the nation. Likewise, cities such as San Marcos have made great advances with their programs. However, water conservation programs have not been implemented meaningfully across the entire Edwards Aquifer region or been developed to target exempt domestic and livestock wells. The Regional Water Conservation Program in the habitat conservation plan was designed to address these gaps.

The goal of the Regional Water Conservation Program is to provide incentives to conserve twenty thousand acre-feet per year of permitted or exempt Edwards Aquifer withdrawals, primarily in areas where conservation efforts have not been put in place. In exchange for technical assistance and incentives for implementing the various measures, one-half of the conserved water must remain in the aquifer, unpumped, for fifteen years to benefit springflow levels and contribute to species protection.

Patterned on the San Antonio Water System conservation program, the Regional Water Conservation Program focuses on implementation of incentive programs encouraging: (1) reduction of "lost water" through leak detection, (2) installation of high-efficiency plumbing fixtures and high-efficiency toilets, (3) a large-scale commercial/industrial retrofit rebate, and (4) efficient landscape irrigation using reclamation collection projects.

The program has modest impacts on springflows during a repeat of the drought of record. However, encouraging conservation is an important element in protecting the Edwards Aquifer and was, for that reason, included in the phase I package.

Voluntary Irrigation Suspension Program Option (VISPO)

The use of a dry-year option was not a new strategy to protect springflow. A dry-year option was one of the points of the five-point plan that had been presented to the Texas Water Commission by the region and included by the Texas Water Commission in the preferred strategies proposed in the concept paper the commission issued in 1992.

Early in 1997, the Edwards Aquifer Authority actually implemented a pilot irrigation suspension program for the Edwards Aquifer region.[1] The program used a reverse auction to select the participants for inclusion in the program.[2] The program enrolled 9,669 acres, mainly in Medina and Uvalde Counties, at a cost to the authority of about $234 per acre included in the program.[3] The program was funded by contributions from throughout the region.[4] The effectiveness of the program was difficult to evaluate because the region experienced a wet spring in 1997, and even irrigators not enrolled in the program applied little or no irrigation water.

VISPO is a voluntary dry-year option program that minimizes the impacts of incidental take from low springflows by paying irrigators (who voluntarily participate in the program) to suspend their pumping of aquifer water for irrigation purposes during drought.

The goal for VISPO is to achieve and maintain a total program enrollment of forty thousand acre-feet per year over the fifteen-year term of the permit. Irrigation permit holders are allowed to enroll less than their full permitted volume; however, their withdrawals will be monitored by real-time automated meters installed by the Edwards Aquifer Authority.

Irrigators were offered the option of committing to the program for either five- or ten-year terms. The payment structure was designed to encourage the longer commitment.

FIVE-YEAR PROGRAM
- A standby fee of $50 per acre-foot that increases 1.5 percent per year will be paid to the enrollee every year of the term, regardless of aquifer conditions.

- A fee of $150 per acre-foot that increases 1.5 percent per year will be paid for each year when temporary pumping suspensions are required.

TEN-YEAR PROGRAM
- A standby fee of $57.50 per acre-foot for years one through five and $70.20 per acre-foot for years six through ten will be paid to the enrollee every year of the term, regardless of aquifer conditions.
- A fee of $172.50 per acre-foot for years one through five and $210.60 per acre-foot for years six through ten will be paid for each year when temporary pumping suspensions are required.

The EARIP relied heavily on input from the agricultural community in designing the payment schedules. The intent was not necessarily to make the irrigators whole for not pumping but to provide them reasonable, but attractive, compensation for not pumping.

The suspension of pumping by the participants in the program is triggered if the J-17 index well in Bexar County is at or below 635 feet mean sea level on the annual trigger date of October 1. This date provides irrigators, and businesses affected by the decisions made by irrigators, ample time to make crop-planting and other business decisions.

San Antonio Water System Aquifer Storage and Recovery Program

Aquifer storage and recovery is a technology that, in the case of the San Antonio Water System, involves pumping water from the Edwards Aquifer and storing it in the Carrizo Aquifer at the Twin Oaks Aquifer Storage Recovery facility that the system operates in southern Bexar County.[5]

The specific objectives of the program are to protect springflow during the drought of record by: (1) reducing pumping totals by 50,000 acre-feet by not pumping water leased by the EARIP; (2) storing up to 126,000 acre-feet of the leased water in the San Antonio Water System aquifer and storage facility; (3) reducing total pumping by the San Antonio Water System by up to 46,300 acre-feet per year during drought-like conditions; and (4) returning water from the aquifer and storage facility to the water system to "offset" pumping reductions made by the San Antonio Water System.

The triggers for forbearance are when the ten-year average annual recharge is 500,000 acre-feet and there is a ten-day average aquifer level of 630 feet mean sea level. The first trigger is set where the ten-year rolling average was in 1947, when the drought of record began. Because the amount of the pumping cuts and the offset are also closely patterned after conditions similar to the drought of record, it is very much a program to prevent the springs from going dry, as they did in 1956. Because of the way the trigger is set, it may not afford protection during smaller but still very significant droughts.

Stage V Pumping Cuts

Under the habitat conservation plan of the EARIP, the program included a new emergency stage V pumping reduction of 44 percent, applicable in both the San Antonio and Uvalde pools. The stage V reductions were viewed as emergency measures because they were triggered only after the other critical period management reductions and any other aquifer management measures had been in place. For the San Antonio pool, stage V would be triggered by a combination of monthly average J-17 levels below 625 feet above mean sea level or springflows of either 45 cubic feet per second, based on a ten-day rolling average at Comal Springs, or 40 cubic feet per second, based on a three-day rolling average. The Uvalde pool would trigger stage V reductions when the J-27 index well water level dropped to 840 above feet mean sea level.

NOTES

Copies of most documents cited in the text are in the possession of the author. Some documents, such as the pre-1988 newspaper references from the *San Antonio Express-News* and *San Antonio Light* and the voluminous *Report of the United States Commission–Texas*, the Espey, Huston & Associates report of 1986, and G. P. Kiel's *History of the Canyon Dam*, can be found in the Texana collection of the San Antonio Public Library. The Texas Water Plans can be found on the website of the Texas Water Development Board. The minutes of the San Antonio City Council can be found on the City of San Antonio website on the city clerk's page. Although I have copies of many of the legislative documents, they all can be found on the website of the Texas Legislature. The Edwards Aquifer Authority website also contains some of the documents cited.

Part I. The "Edwards Issue"

1. An acre-foot of water is 325,851 gallons and is approximately the amount a family of four or five would use in a year.

2. See app. 3 for a brief discussion of Texas water law.

3. Edwards Aquifer Authority, *Edwards Aquifer Authority hydrologic data report for 2011, No. 12–04*, October 2012. The lowest recharge for this region was 43,700 acre-feet in 1956. The highest pumping during the drought of record also occurred in 1956, when a total of 321,100 acre-feet of water was withdrawn from the aquifer.

4. Todd Hayden Votteler, "Water from a stone: The limits of the sustainable development of the Texas Edwards Aquifer" (PhD diss., Southwest Texas State University, 2000).

5. The federally listed species include the fountain darter, San Marcos salamander, San Marcos gambusia, Texas blind salamander, Peck's cave amphipod, Comal Springs dryopid beetle, Comal Springs riffle beetle, and Texas wild-rice. See app. 2 for a brief discussion of the Endangered Species Act.

6. See Board of Water Engineers v. City of San Antonio, 283 S.W.2d 722, 723 (Tex. 1955). This decision recognized that the city of San Antonio faced a serious water-supply problem by reason of a large and rapid increase in population and water consumption within and around the corporate limits.

7. See Edwards Aquifer Authority, *Edwards Aquifer Authority hydrologic data report for 2011*, 27–28.

8. Espey, Huston & Associates, Inc., "Executive summary of the water availability study for Guadalupe and San Antonio River Basins," February 1986, available at the San Antonio Public Library.

9. Ibid.

Chapter 1. "What's Past Is Prologue"

The chapter title is a line from Shakespeare, *The tempest,* act 2, scene 1.

1. William Feathergill Wilson, *History of water in the San Antonio River Valley,* Alamo Area Council of Governments, September 1970, 19–20.

2. Charles R. Porter Jr., *Spanish water, Anglo water: Early development in San Antonio* (College Station: Texas A&M University Press, 2009).

3. *The report of the United States Study Commission–Texas: A report to the president and Congress,* part III, 1962, 190–91; Texas Board of Water Engineers, *A plan for meeting the 1980 water requirements of Texas,* May 1961, 145–52.

4. See San Antonio City Council and Edwards Underground Water District Board of Directors, "Regional water resource plan for the Edwards Aquifer," September 1988 (hereafter cited as "Regional water resource plan"), 44, available at edwardsaquifer.org.

5. G. P. Kiel, *A history of the Canyon Dam* (Seguin, Tex.: Guadalupe County Historical Commission, 1992).

6. Ibid., 42.

7. Gregg Eckhardt, "Canyon Lake and the Guadalupe River," Edwards Aquifer website, http://www.edwardsaquifer.net/canyon.html.

8. Kiel, *History of the Canyon Dam,* 42.

9. City of San Antonio v. Texas Water Commission, 407 S.W.2d 752 (1966).

10. San Antonio River Authority, "A brief in support of the SARA-GBRA water exchange plan," September 14, 1963.

11. "GBRA gives OK to water talks," *Victoria Advocate,* February 15, 1963.

12. Lila Cockrell, interview by author, San Antonio, Tex., December 27, 2013.

13. "CWB reservoir proposal blockbuster," *San Antonio Express-News,* July 17, 1963.

14. Roy Grimes, "San Antonio to file bid for dams on 3 rivers, GBRA, LCRA due to fight," *Victoria Advocate,* July 18, 1963.

15. San Antonio River Authority, "Brief in support of the SARA-GBRA water exchange plan."

16. Texas Water Development Board, *Texas water plan,* November 1968, 14–15.

17. Robert Van Dyke, general manager, San Antonio City Water Board, to Mr. Fred Pfeiffer, San Antonio River Authority, February 10, 1970; Commissioner Ellis L. Armstrong, Bureau of Reclamation, to Secretary of the Department of Interior, March 15, 1972; Minutes of the regular meeting of the San Antonio City Council, September 2, 1972.

18. Minutes of the regular meeting of the San Antonio City Council, April 18, 1974.

19. David Tomlin, "CWB keeps options open on Cibolo," *San Antonio Express-News,* April 16, 1974 (quoting Cockrell).

20. David Tomlin, "CWB steps towards suspending project," *San Antonio*

Express-News, May 15, 1974; Minutes of the regular meeting of the San Antonio City Council, August 8, 1974.

21. Public Law 93–493, October 27, 1974.

22. Kiel, *History of the Canyon Dam,* 63.

23. Ibid. See also Minutes of the regular meeting of the San Antonio City Council, May 27, 1976.

24. Jan Jarboe, "3 salons oppose San Antonio water pact," *San Antonio Light,* May 8, 1976.

25. Minutes of the regular meeting of the San Antonio City Council, May 27, 1976.

26. Ibid.

27. Roddy Stinson, "To all of the Cisneros bashers: Henry was not the culprit," *San Antonio Express-News,* May 14, 1992; Minutes of the regular meeting of the San Antonio City Council, May 27, 1976.

28. John MacCormack, "GBRA Guadalupe agency, city in water face-off; Different priorities pit river authority San Antonio in long-running struggle," *San Antonio Express-News,* May 17, 1992 (quoting Cockrell).

29. Water Resources Task Force, *Report to the Planning Commission: A program for long-range water resource development,* 1979.

30. Resolution No. 79–35–74, adopting a water policy and requiring the Water Board of Trustees to proceed with steps necessary to secure construction of the Applewhite Reservoir, July 19, 1979.

31. Minutes of the regular meeting of the San Antonio City Council, September 2, 1971.

32. Minutes of the special meeting of the San Antonio City Council, June 30, 1981.

33. Minutes of the regular meeting of the San Antonio City Council, May 14, 1981.

34. "Regional water resource plan," 47.

35. Acts 1959, R.S. ch. 99, 1959, Tex. Gen. Laws 173.

36. Robert Hasslocher, interview by author, San Antonio, Tex., January 16, 2014.

37. "Memorandum of understanding, Edwards Underground Water District and City of San Antonio, November 1983," executed by Henry Cisneros, mayor, City of San Antonio, and Robert C. Hasslocher, board chair, Edwards Underground Water District, January 12, 1984.

38. Carl F. Raba, chair of the Technical Advisory Committee, to Robert Hasslocher, chair of the Edwards Underground Water District, and Mayor Henry Cisneros, March 21, 1986.

39. City of San Antonio and Edwards Underground Water District, *San Antonio regional water resources study,* April 1986, 3.

40. "Joint resolution," attachment E to "Regional water resource plan."

41. "Regional water resource plan," 54–55.

42. "Joint resolution," 4–5.

43. See Minutes of the regular meeting of the San Antonio City Council, March 5, 1987.

44. Resolution No. 87–12–14, Minutes of the regular meeting of the San Antonio City Council, March 5, 1987.

45. Act of 1959, R.S. ch. 99, 1959, Tex. Gen. Laws 173 *as amended*, § 17A. On August 23, 1988, the Edwards Underground Water District Board of Directors approved the "Edwards Underground Water District Drought Management Plan." It called for specific water use reductions when aquifer levels, springflows, and rainfall dropped below specified historical averages. The plan also mandated that subsequent reductions would be triggered only by lower aquifer levels and springflows, not reduced rainfall, which would prompt water use restrictions.

46. Regarding the parking lot agreement: Hasslocher interview; Rodney Reagan, telephone interview by author, January 21, 2014.

47. Hasslocher interview.

48. Rebecca Q. Cedillo, interview by author, San Antonio, Tex., May 29, 2014.

49. "Regional water resource plan," 12–16.

50. "Joint resolution," 4.

51. "Regional water resource plan," 16.

52. Ibid., 30.

53. The Applewhite project was recommended in part because it was the only project that could have been completed by the year 2000. "Regional water resource plan," 31.

54. "Regional water resource plan," 195.

55. Ibid., 34.

56. "Uvalde farmers vow to sink regulation of aquifer water," *Houston Chronicle*, May 21, 1988.

57. Hasslocher interview.

58. Quoted in "Uvalde farmers vow to sink regulation of aquifer water," *Houston Chronicle*, May 21, 1988.

59. Con Mims, executive director, Nueces River Authority, to the Honorable B. J. Wynne, III, chair, Texas Water Commission, September 20, 1988; Hasslocher interview.

60. Tom Bower, "Task force OKs water plan as opposition keeps brewing," *San Antonio Express-News*, July 8, 1988.

61. Henry G. Cisneros, mayor of the City of San Antonio, and Robert C. Hasslocher, chair of the Edwards Underground Water District, transmittal letter "To the citizens of the Edwards region," July 1988.

62. City of San Antonio Ordinance 67605, July 28, 1988; Tom Bower, "City approves Edwards plan," *San Antonio Express-News*, July 29, 1988.

63. Edwards Underground Water District, Resolution and Order No. 09–88–096, September 13, 1988; Tom Bower, "Board OKs $1.6 billion water plan," *San Antonio Express-News*, September 14, 1988.

64. Quotations from Tom Bower, "Board OKs $1.6 billion water plan," *San Antonio Express-News,* September 14, 1988.

65. Reagan interview.

66. Jim Woods and Susie Phillips Gonzalez, "Water district drawing up curbs in aquifer case," *San Antonio Express-News,* November 14, 1991 (quoting Wolff).

67. Hasslocher interview.

68. Rodney Reagan, telephone interview by author, January 21, 2014; Greg Rothe, telephone interview by author, January 14, 2014; Weir Labatt, interview by author, San Antonio, Tex., January 16, 2014.

69. Reagan interview.

70. "Edwards Aquifer district board OKs withholding of water plan," *Austin American-Statesman,* January 19, 1989.

71. Henry Krausse, "Medina, Uvalde counties vote to leave Edwards water district," *Austin American-Statesman,* January 22, 1989.

72. See, e.g., Sierra Club v. Babbitt, Testimony of John Hall, "Transcript of Proceedings," November 18, 1992, 231–32.

73. Henry Krausse, "Water proposal supporters want pumpage limits enforced," *Austin American-Statesman,* January 31, 1989.

74. Henry Krausse, "Water use bill set for Edwards Aquifer," *Austin American-Statesman,* February 21, 1989.

75. Henry Krausse, "Cisneros, foes wage water war for lawmakers," *Austin American-Statesman,* April 6, 1989.

76. John H. Specht, general manager, Guadalupe-Blanco River Authority, to Mr. [*sic*] Manuel Lujan Jr., secretary, US Department of the Interior, June 15, 1989. On February 27, 1990, the authority issued a second notice of intent to sue regarding violations of the Endangered Species Act. John H. Specht, general manager, Guadalupe-Blanco River Authority, to the Honorable Manuel Lujan Jr., secretary, US Department of the Interior, February 27, 1990.

77. Two landowners who were recipients of the notice filed suit against the secretary of the interior seeking a declaratory judgment that section 9 of the Endangered Species Act was unconstitutional as applied to the listed species living at or immediately downstream of the San Marcos and Comal Springs. Shields v. Babbitt, 229 F.Supp. 638 (W.D. Tex. 2000). The main issue was whether Congress had the power to regulate these species, found exclusively in Texas, under the commerce clause of the US Constitution. Judge Lucius D. Bunton found that Congress had that power. The US Court of Appeals for the Fifth Circuit, however, vacated the lower court decision and remanded the case to Judge Bunton with instruction to dismiss because the case was not justiciable. Shields v. Babbitt, 289 F.3d 832 (5th Cir. 2002).

78. In re: The adjudication of rights of water in the Edwards Aquifer, No. 89–0381 (22nd Dist. Ct., Hays County, Tex., June 15, 1989). In 1988, the Guadalupe-Blanco River Authority released a monograph setting out the legal and technical support for contentions that the Edwards Aquifer was an underground river.

Guadalupe-Blanco River Authority, *The Edwards Aquifer: Underground river of Texas* (Seguin, Tex.: Guadalupe-Blanco River Authority, 1988).

79. The case was removed to the US District Court for the Western District of Texas. The district court subsequently remanded the case back to state court under a legal doctrine known as Burford abstention. Guadalupe-Blanco River Authority v. City of Lyle, 937 F.2d 184 (5th Cir. 1991). The US Court of Appeals for the Fifth Circuit, however, vacated the judgment of the district court and remanded the case back to the state district court.

80. Tom Bower, "Catfish farm planning to expand production," *San Antonio Express-News*, August 15, 1991.

81. Dwight Silverman, "Water gusher spilled over into aquifer fight," *Houston Chronicle*, November 15, 1992. In October 1991 the Edwards Underground Water District, the San Antonio River Authority, and Bexar County filed suit in state district court claiming the catfish farm was polluting the Medina River with fecal coliform bacteria. At the request of the Texas Water Commission, Pucek shut down the well until a wastewater discharge permit could be obtained. Pucek filed a claim to some 48,000 acre-feet of water as part of the Edwards Aquifer Authority permitting process. The Edwards Aquifer Authority granted Pucek a permit for 22,500 acre-feet. In December 2000 the San Antonio Water System acquired 10,000 acre-feet of Pucek's permitted water for approximately $9 million, plus a lease on all additional rights for $25 an acre-foot for five years and a right of first refusal to purchase those rights. Jerry Needham, "SAWS buys catfish farm; Utility adds to aquifer rights," *San Antonio Express-News*, December 6, 2000. Subsequently, the San Antonio Water System paid $1,750 an acre-foot for 3,125 acre-feet of additional rights. Jerry Needham, "Fish farmer hooks even more money; SAWS buys more rights from Pucek and his partner," *San Antonio Express-News*, May 21, 2003.

82. Recitals in "Agreement relating to meeting on October 2, 1989."

83. Mary Q. Kelly, memorandum to Edwards Underground Water District Board of Directors, "Closed meeting held August 23, 1989, 9:00 a.m. at the Edwards Underground Water District," August 28, 1989.

84. Buck Wynne, chair of the Texas Water Commission, participated in the October 2 meeting. Mary Q. Kelly, memorandum to file, "Report of meeting held October 2, 1989, at 2 p.m., EUWD conference room," October 6, 1989.

85. Suzanne McAuliffe, "Closed meetings flow on water," *San Antonio Light*, August 26, 1989.

86. Rick Casey, "Lawyers to upstage Krier's water group," *San Antonio Light*, September 22, 1989.

87. Weir Labatt, city council member, District 9, and chair, City Council Water Task Force, to Lila Cockrell, mayor, City of San Antonio, "Report on discussions with Guadalupe-Blanco River Authority, Friday," October 6, 1989.

88. Lila Cockrell, mayor, to participants, "Discussions with GBRA, Friday, October 6, 1989," October 6, 1989.

89. Mary Q. Kelly, memorandum to file, "Report of meeting held 2:00 p.m., Monday, October 9, 1989, in the Edwards Underground Water District conference room," October 13, 1989.

90. Mary Q. Kelly, memorandum to the Litigation Committee, "Report of meeting held 2:00 p.m., Friday, October 20, 1989, in the Edwards Underground Water District conference room," October 23, 1989.

91. Technical Advisory Panel, "Technical factors in Edwards Aquifer use and management," February 15, 1990, 6, 8 (quote).

92. John A. Folk-Williams, Western Network, "Final report: The Edwards Aquifer dispute resolution project," undated. See also John A. Folk-Williams to Michael Spear, regional director, US Fish and Wildlife Service, Region 2, June 28, 1992.

93. Tom Bower, "Aquifer dispute returns to solons; Mediator: Parties unwilling to move," *San Antonio Express-News*, March 10, 1991 (including quotes).

94. Diana R. Fuentes, "Aquifer report fails to win recommendation," *San Antonio Express-News*, January 8, 1991.

95. Commissioner John Birdwell to Kenneth Ikels, chair of the Edwards Underground Water District Board, attachment to letter, November 1989.

96. Minutes of the meeting on February 26, 1990, Special Committee on the Edwards Aquifer, 4.

97. David Matustik, "Aquifer plan calls for mandatory water restrictions," *Austin American-Statesman*, July 3, 1990.

98. Texas Water Commission, "Draft emergency action plan," attached to Edwards Underground Water District, Resolution and Order No. 07–90–12, "Emergency action plan," July 11, 1990. The plan explained that the Edwards Underground Water District Drought Management Plan, authorized by House Bill 1942, "does not have the flexibility and areal coverage to effectively address the current drought situation."

99. David Matustik, "Aquifer plan calls for mandatory water restrictions," *Austin American-Statesman*, July 3, 1990.

100. "Areas OK emergency drought proposal for Edwards Aquifer," *Houston Chronicle*, July 10, 1990; "Groups approve plan for Edwards Aquifer," *Victoria Advocate*, July 10, 1990.

101. Minutes of the regular meeting of the San Antonio City Council, July 5, 1990; Greater San Antonio Area Citizens Committee on Water, "Report to the mayor and city council," March 1992.

102. Edwards Underground Water District, Resolution and Order No. 07–90–12, "Emergency Action Plan," July 11, 1990; "Aquifer board OKs emergency use restrictions," *Austin American-Statesman*, July 12, 1990.

103. Michael Spear, regional director, US Fish and Wildlife Service Region 2, to Commissioner John Birdwell, Texas Water Commission, July 5, 1990.

104. John E. Birdwell, commissioner, Texas Water Commission, to Mr. Michael J. Spear, regional director, US Fish and Wildlife Service Region 2, August 3, 1990.

105. Texas Water Commission, Permit to Appropriate State Water, No. 3914, October 20, 1982.

106. "Regional water resource plan," 187.

107. Minutes of the regular meeting of the San Antonio City Council, July 21, 1988; "San Antonio reservoir OK'd," *Houston Chronicle,* July 23, 1988.

108. Tom Bower, "Applewhite foes win EUWD seats; Patterson scores big victory," *San Antonio Express-News,* January 20, 1991.

109. Jim Wood, "Applewhite foes meet requirements for vote," *San Antonio Express-News,* February 22, 1991.

110. Minutes of the regular meeting of the San Antonio City Council, February 28, 1991 (Ordinance 73214); City of San Antonio, "Ordinance 73583 declaring the results of the canvass of the special municipal election held on May 4, 1991, on a proposed initiative ordinance to abandon the Applewhite Reservoir project," May 6, 1991; Tom Bower, "Water board plan blasted by Wolff; Others on council less critical of reservoir-only proposal," *San Antonio Express-News,* May 31, 1991.

Chapter 2. John Hall and the Edwards Underground River

1. Ric Jensen, "Year of the woman," *Texas Water Resources* 18, no. 4 (winter 1992). According to this source, "In recent Texas history, few policymakers [have] exerted a greater influence on crafting the State's water and environmental policies than Governor Ann Richards." Ibid., 2.

2. See Stefanie Scott, "Water boss Hall willing to make political waves; Shy family man with a mission stands his ground in aquifer fight," *San Antonio Express-News,* June 7, 1992.

3. Dave McNeely, "Hall's induction a shining symbol of politics gone right," *Austin American-Statesman,* May 30, 1991; Bill Dawson, "Water panel shift hailed as protecting aquatic life," *Houston Chronicle,* June 13, 1991.

4. Stefanie Scott, "Water boss Hall willing to make political waves; Shy family man with a mission stands his ground on aquifer fight," *San Antonio Express-News,* June 7, 1992.

5. Tom Bower, "Low price of water in San Antonio likely to be an issue," *San Antonio Express-News,* January 3, 1992.

6. John Hall, chair, Texas Water Commission, to the Honorable Daniel Morales, Texas attorney general, "Request for expedited opinion; § 28.011 Texas Water Code," September 13, 1991; Op. Tex. Att'y Gen. No. 0–3205, 1941.

7. Attorney General Opinion, Op. Tex. Att'y Gen. No. DM-54, letter to the Honorable John Hall, November 4, 1991.

8. Section 28.011 authorizes the Texas Water Commission to "make and enforce rules and regulations for conserving, protecting, and distributing underground, subterranean, and percolating water."

9. Subsequently, in March 1992 Attorney General Morales, in response to a request from state senator John Montford, qualified his opinion to make clear that

the *opinion* would be insufficient legal authority for the Texas Water Commission to attempt to regulate the use of groundwater on the basis of section 28.011. In a letter to Secretary of the Interior Manuel Lujan, Attorney General Morales explained: "As explained in the letter to Senator Montford, DM-54 opined on the technical issue whether § 28.011 of the Texas Water Code was a constitutional delegation of authority to the Texas Water Commission. As I stated in the last sentence of the first paragraph of DM-54, I did not and have not opined as to the actual scope of authority delegated by § 28.011, nor have I opined on the issue of how to harmonize Chapter 52 of the Texas Code (which specifically provides for underground water regulation by local underground water districts) with § 28.011." Dan Morales, attorney general, to the Honorable Manuel Lujan, secretary, Department of the Interior, March 14, 1992.

10. Tim Lott, "Mayor to mediate talks on Edwards Aquifer," *Austin American-Statesman,* November 7, 1991; Tom Bower, "Aquifer factions seek agreement," *San Antonio Express-News,* November 27, 1991.

11. Labatt quoted in Tom Bower, "SA has plan to halt water war; Proposal calls for users to pay farmers not to irrigate during drought," *San Antonio Express-News,* January 4, 1992; Kathy Glasgow, "S.A. offers to limit aquifer pumping; Policymakers seeking water," *San Antonio Express-News,* January 24, 1992.

12. Tom Bower, "SA has plan to halt water war; Proposal calls for users to pay farmers not to irrigate during drought," *San Antonio Express-News,* January 4, 1992 (including Lytle quote).

13. Tom Lott, "Aquifer negotiations hit snag," *Austin American-Statesman,* February 1, 1992 (including Labatt quote).

14. Tom Lott, "Water agency takes over aquifer management efforts," *Austin American-Statesman,* February 6, 1992.

15. Texas Water Commission, "Avoiding disaster: An interim plan to manage the Edwards Aquifer," February 18, 1992.

16. Ibid.

17. Ibid.

18. Hall quoted in Tom Bower, "Hall waits for water settlement," *San Antonio Express-News,* February 26, 1992.

19. Chair John Hall and Commissioners Pam Reed and Peggy Garner to all parties interested in the management of the Edwards Aquifer, April 2, 1992; Tom Bower, "State unveils 'peace plan' for aquifer; Water chief gives warring sides until April 14 to agree to pact," *San Antonio Express-News,* April 3, 1992.

20. Texas Water Commission, "Agreement regarding implementation and enforcement of an interim management plan for the Edwards Aquifer and a long-term water management plan for the south-central Texas region," April 2, 1992.

21. Ibid., 7–10.

22. "Aquifer battle comes to point," *San Antonio Express-News,* April 11, 1992; "San Antonio ready to fight state, U.S. control of aquifer," *Austin American-Statesman,* April 11, 1992.

23. M. J. Spear, regional director, US Fish and Wildlife Service Region 2, to John Hall, chair, Texas Water Commission, March 26, 1992, 2–3. See app. 2 for a discussion of what constitutes "jeopardy."

24. M. J. Spear, regional director, US Fish and Wildlife Service Region 2, to John Hall, chair, Texas Water Commission, March 26, 1992, 2–3.

25. Ibid., attachment, 1–3.

26. Texas Water Commission, "A resolution urging the U.S. Fish and Wildlife Service to consider the public health, safety, and welfare, and economic well-being of the region in establishing springflow goals at Comal Springs," April 15, 1992.

27. 17 Tex. Reg. 2,949 (April 24, 1992).

28. Jim Wood and Don Driver, "San Antonio officials boiling over state's action," *San Antonio Express-News,* April 16, 1992.

29. Wolff quoted in "Water panel takes temporary control of Edwards Aquifer," *Dallas Morning News,* April 16, 1992.

30. Stefanie Scott, "Water war swirling around springs," *San Antonio Express-News,* May 17, 1992. ("Sierra Club, unsatisfied with the Texas Water Commission's takeover plan for the Edwards Aquifer, says it will accept no less than guaranteed springflows to protect endangered species thriving on aquifer-fed springs." Ibid.); Tom Bower, "Farmers steamed at aquifer plan," *San Antonio Express-News,* June 21, 1992; Ralph Winingham, "Medina, Uvalde owners in fighting mood over water rights," *San Antonio Express-News,* August 30, 1992.

31. City of San Antonio v. the Texas Water Commission, No. 92–07029 (261st Dist. Ct., Travis County, Tex. May 15, 1992).

32. In an attempt to prevent the commission from taking control of the aquifer, former mayor Cisneros urged the city to take the lead in negotiating with other interests in the region. He warned that he knew of "one corporation that has invested $100 million in manufacturing here whose management is now wondering if they did the right thing, based on the potential for a water crisis." Quoted in Scott Huddleston, "Cisneros urging new water talks; Ex-mayor says state may back off aquifer control if city takes lead," *San Antonio Express-News,* May 14, 1992. See also L. A. Lorek, "USAA warns water jeopardizing plant," *San Antonio Light,* June 17, 1992. (Robert McDermott, board chair of USAA, one of the largest employers in San Antonio, threatened to move out of the state a planned $35 million financial center unless USAA had "certainty of a water supply." Ibid.) Cisneros urged, "I don't think you should wait for a study to be completed; let's build a plan with what we know and not let everything hang. Somebody needs to take the lead and play the role of statesman." Quoted in Scott Huddleston, "Cisneros urging new water talks; Ex-mayor says state may back off aquifer control if city takes lead," *San Antonio Express-News,* May 14, 1992.

33. San Antonio Water System, "Comments on behalf of San Antonio/Bexar County regarding the Texas Water Commission's proposed permanent rules,"

June 18, 1992; Tom Bower, "Water czar, city council lock horns over aquifer; Hall stresses cooperation, stays mum on S.A.'s share of water," *San Antonio Express-News,* April 24, 1992.

34. Cliff Morton, chair of the San Antonio Water System Board of Trustees, memorandum to City Council, "Texas Water Commission's proposed rules regulating the Edwards Aquifer," June 18, 1992.

35. Tom Bower, "In water rule," *San Antonio Express-News,* May 31, 1992.

36. "San Antonio, state officials reach accord in Edwards Aquifer dispute," *Dallas Morning News,* June 19, 1992; Patrick Crimmins, "City flashes thumbs-up to state aquifer plan," *San Antonio Light,* June 19, 1992; "San Antonio, Water Commission officials agree on aquifer control," *Austin American-Statesman,* June 19, 1992.

37. "San Antonio, state officials reach accord in Edwards Aquifer dispute," *Dallas Morning News,* June 19, 1992; Minutes of the regular meeting of the San Antonio City Council, June 18, 1992; Tom Bower, "S.A. council reacts favorably to feud-settling aquifer plan," *San Antonio Express-News,* June 19, 1992.

38. Minutes of the regular meeting of the San Antonio City Council, June 25, 1992 (Morton quote); San Antonio City Council, Resolution No. 92–27–23, June 25, 1992.

39. San Antonio Water System, "Comments on behalf of San Antonio/Bexar County regarding the Texas Water Commission's proposed permanent rules," June 18, 1992.

40. Hall quoted in Tom Bower, "S.A. agrees to back deal capping aquifer pumping," *San Antonio Express-News,* June 26, 1992.

41. Tom Bower, "50% cut in pumping touted to save springflow," *San Antonio Express-News,* June 25, 1992; David Thorkildsen and Paul D. McElhaney, Texas Water Development Board Report 340, "Model refinement and applications for the Edwards (Balcones Fault Zone) Aquifer in the San Antonio region, Texas," July 1992, 22.

42. Texas Water Commission, "Water management plan for the Edwards Underground River," July 6, 1992, 3–5.

43. Tom Bower, "S.A. agrees to back deal capping aquifer pumping," *San Antonio Express-News,* June 26, 1992.

44. Texas Water Commission, "Water management plan for the Edwards Underground River," July 6, 1992, 3–5.

45. The San Antonio Water System estimated that the permitting approach would mean approximately 170,000 acre-feet annually for the San Antonio Water System; 80,000 acre-feet for other municipal and industrial Bexar County users; 180,000 acre-feet for irrigators in Bexar, Medina, and Uvalde Counties; and 20,000 acre-feet for other pumpers, including Comal and Hays Counties. Patrick Crimmins, "City flashes thumbs-up to state aquifer plan," *San Antonio Light,* June 19, 1992; Tom Bower, "Aquifer plan divide water among users," *San Antonio Express-News,* August 27 1992.

46. Texas Water Commission, "Water management plan for the Edwards Underground River," July 6, 1992, 4–5; Hall quoted in Tom Bower, "S.A. agrees to back deal capping aquifer pumping," *San Antonio Express-News,* June 26, 1992.

47. Steve Cullinan, "Notes from meeting with TWC 5/19/92."

48. Tom Bower, "Federal official says plan for aquifer on right track," *San Antonio Express-News,* July 8, 1992.

49. See Texas Water Commission, "Water management plan for the Edwards Underground River," July 6, 1992; Tom Bower, "Federal official says plan for aquifer on right track," *San Antonio Express-News,* July 8, 1992.

50. Tom Bower, "Federal official says plan for aquifer on right track," *San Antonio Express-News,* July 8, 1992.

51. "Uvalde spoofs 'Edwards River' with glowing tubes," *San Antonio Express-News,* April 21, 1992.

52. Texas Water Commission, Public comments on Edwards underground river rules chapter 298, Testimony of M. L. Stolte, June 30, 1992, 115–16; Rothe interview.

53. Texas Water Commission, Public comments on Edwards underground river rules chapter 298.

54. Ralph Winingham, "Medina tries to heal water-war wounds," *San Antonio Express-News,* August 10, 1992.

55. John Hall, interview by author, Austin, Tex., August 19, 2013.

56. Henry quoted in Tom Bower, "Aquifer plan divides water among users," *San Antonio Express-News,* August 27, 1992.

57. GBRA statement quoted in Tom Bower, "Aquifer rules to be unveiled today seen changing S.A. lifestyle," *San Antonio Express-News,* August 26, 1992.

58. M. J. Spear, regional director, US Fish and Wildlife Service Region 2, to John Hall, chair, Texas Water Commission, August 19, 1992.

59. Ibid.; Sierra Club v. Babbitt, Testimony of John Hall, "Transcript of proceedings, November 18, 1992, 3–225; Bruce Hight, "Federal regulator backs plan for aquifer," *Austin American-Statesman,* August 21, 1992; Texas Water Commission, "Water management plan for the Edwards underground river," July 6, 1992, 3–4.

60. Spear quoted in Todd Ackerman, "Federal official backs plan for Edwards Aquifer," *Houston Chronicle,* August 21, 1992.

61. Sierra Club v. Babbitt, "Amended findings of fact and conclusions of law," para. 32; Sierra Club v. Babbitt, Testimony of Paul Thornhill, "Transcript of proceedings," November 16, 1992, 157.

62. David Thorkildsen and Paul D. McElhaney, Texas Water Development Board Report 340, "Model refinement and applications for the Edwards (Balcones Fault Zone) Aquifer in the San Antonio region, Texas," July 1992. See also Edwards Aquifer Authority, "Draft Edwards Aquifer Authority habitat conservation plan," July 2004, as amended on September 21, 2004, app. H, table 4–1.

63. Hall quoted in Tom Bower, "Aquifer plan divides water among users," *San Antonio Express-News,* August 27, 1992.

64. Wolff quoted in Jim Wood, "Wolff toasts water rules," *San Antonio Express-News*, August 27, 1992.

65. Patrick Crimmins, "Legislature hooks aquifer battle as panel OKs rules," *San Antonio Light*, September 10, 1992; Clayton quoted in Mike Ward, "Aquifer limits imposed amid flood of protests," *Austin American-Statesman*, September 10, 1992; 17 Tex. Reg. 6,601 (September 25, 1992).

66. All quotes from the new water rules are from 17 Tex. Reg. 6,601 (September 25, 1992).

67. 17 Tex. Reg. 6,601 (September 25, 1992). According to Hall, "Should the Legislature pass any new law regulating the Edwards Aquifer, the Water Commission would be prepared to repeal any rules we have put into place." Tom Bower, "Aquifer 'river' ruling comes under assault; Lawmaker vows to thwart panel," *San Antonio Express-News*, May 6, 1992.

68. McFadden v. Texas Water Commission, No. 92–052–14 (331st Dist. Ct., Travis County, Tex., September 11, 1992).

69. "State legislator seeks to protect water sources; Panel limits on aquifer were rejected by judge," *Dallas Morning News*, September 14, 1992.

70. Quoted in David Anthony Richelieu, "John Hall tells real fright tale," *San Antonio Express-News*, September 24, 1992.

71. Subsequently, on September 10, 1993, the Texas Water Commission withdrew the rules. 18 Tex. Reg. 6,241 (September 17, 1993). In proposing to withdraw the rules, the commission explained it was taking this action because the legislature subsequently had found that the Edwards Aquifer was not an underground river and it had created the Edwards Aquifer Authority to manage use of the aquifer. 18 Tex. Reg. 5,057 (August 3, 1993). In 1993, in Senate Bill 1477, the Texas Legislature found "that the Edwards Aquifer is a unique and complex hydrological system, with diverse economic and social interests dependent on the aquifer for water supply. In keeping with that finding, the Edwards Aquifer is declared to be a distinctive natural resource in this state, a unique aquifer, and not an underground stream." Senate Bill 1477 § 1.01(a). Subsequently, the Texas Fourth Court of Appeals dismissed the appeal as moot.

72. Perry and Hall quoted in Diana R. Fuentes, "Perry alleges state may have conspired with feds in aquifer takeover," *San Antonio Express-News*, September 16, 1992.

73. "Water, agriculture officials at odds over Edwards Aquifer," *Dallas Morning News*, September 19, 1992.

74. Bruce Hight, "Federal regulator backs plan for aquifer," *Austin American-Statesman*, August 21, 1992.

75. Alisa Shull, telephone interview by author, December 12, 2013.

76. Sierra Club v. Babbitt, Testimony of Michael Spear, "Transcript of Proceedings," November 17, 1992, 51–52.

77. Michael J. Spear, telephone interview by author, December 27, 2013.

78. 17 Tex. Reg. 6,601 (September 25, 1992).

79. San Antonio Water System, "Comments on behalf of San Antonio/Bexar County regarding the Texas Water Commission's proposed permanent rules," June 18, 1992, 7.

80. Sierra Club v. Babbitt, "Transcript of proceedings," November 17, 1992, 106.

81. John Hall, interview by author, Austin, Tex., September 19, 2013.

82. Luana Buckner, interview by author, San Antonio, Tex., January 6, 2014.

Chapter 3. Judge Lucius Bunton and *Sierra Club v. Babbitt*

1. John Specht, former general manager of the Guadalupe-Blanco River Authority, claimed that the motivation of the authority in *Sierra Club v. Babbitt* was to protect the water resources of the Guadalupe River Basin. Todd H. Votteler, "Raiders of the lost aquifer? Or, the beginning of the end to fifty years of conflict over the Texas Edwards Aquifer," *Tulane Environmental Law Journal* 15, no. 70 (2004): 257, 274; "Fish service official tells about 2 letters," *San Antonio Express-News*, November 18, 1992 (reporting that Specht testified that, in joining the lawsuit, "his agency was fighting to maintain springflows for the sake of the river's base flow"). The Fish and Wildlife Service characterized the notice of intent to sue as an "attempt [by the Guadalupe-Blanco River Authority] to invoke the Endangered Species Act to achieve some degree of ground water regulation." John F. Turner, director, US Fish and Wildlife Service, to the Honorable William P. Clements Jr., governor of Texas, December 14, 1989.

2. The Guadalupe-Blanco River Authority, the municipal governments of San Marcos and New Braunfels, New Braunfels Utilities, Green Valley Special Utility District, Atascosa Rural Water Supply Corporation, Bexar Metropolitan Water District, and others intervened on the side of the plaintiffs. The Texas Department of Agriculture, Texas Water Commission, Texas Parks and Wildlife Department, the City of San Antonio, the Greater San Antonio Builders Association, USAA, Living Waters Artesian Springs, Ltd., several farmers, and others intervened on behalf of the defendant.

3. Kim Smith, "Humor, fairness rule in Bunton's courtroom," *Odessa American*, June 10, 1996.

4. Ralph K. M. Haurwitz, "Judge's speedy manner, wit make court a breeze," *Austin American-Statesman*, July 22, 1996. The "walking-on-water" photograph accompanied a feature entitled "The water crisis," which appeared in the *San Antonio Express-News* on July 24, 1994. Roy Bragg wrote the article on Bunton.

5. See Sierra Club v. Babbitt, 995 F.2d 571, 573 (5th Cir. 1993).

6. See, e.g., San Antonio Water System, "The need for Edwards Aquifer management legislation," December 16, 1992.

7. Tom Bower, "Sierra Club's aquifer demands seen fueling loss of jobs in S.A.; Billions of dollars at stake in water trial's outcome, testimony shows," *San Antonio Express-News*, November 20, 1992.

8. See Sierra Club v. Lujan, 1993 WL 151353 (W.D. Tex.) (May 26, 1993), *sub nom,*

Sierra Club v. Babbitt, 995 F.2d 571 (1993). The US Fish and Wildlife Service and the City of San Antonio and other defendant-intervenors filed an appeal in the US Court of Appeals for the Fifth Circuit. See Tom Bower, "Uvalde irrigators, Alamo City, agency will appeal ruling," *San Antonio Express-News,* March 5, 1993. Subsequently, the federal defendants agreed to dismiss their appeal if the plaintiffs agreed to certain semantic changes in the finding and judgment of the district court. See Sierra Club v. Babbitt, "Federal defendants' and plaintiffs' joint motion to clarify the judgment and findings," May 10, 1993; Tom Bower and Susie Phillips Gonzalez, "Deal near in aquifer lawsuit," *San Antonio Express-News,* April 23, 1993; Sierra Club v. Babbitt, 995 F.2d 571, 574 (5th Cir. 1993). On May 26, 1993, Judge Bunton amended his original judgment. On July 2, 1993, the Fifth Circuit dismissed the appeals of San Antonio and the other defendant-intervenors. The Fifth Circuit found that once the FWS service, the actual defendant in the case, dismissed its appeal, the defendant-intervenors lacked standing to prosecute the appeal. Ibid., 575. The court found that Judge Bunton's decision was "of no consequence to them" and would not affect them in any future litigation. Ibid.

9. Sierra Club v. Babbitt, 995 F.2d 571, 574 n.4 (5th Cir. 1993).

10. Sierra Club v. Babbitt, "Amended judgment" (hereafter cited as "Amended judgment"), 6 (emphasis in original).

11. Sierra Club v. Babbitt, "Amended findings of fact and conclusions of law" (hereafter cited as "Amended findings"), May 26, 1993, para. 26, 53, 80, 91, 140, 199, 202, 204.

12. See, e.g., "Amended findings," para. 98.

13. "Amended judgment," 3–4.

14. Ibid., 2–3.

15. Sierra Club v. Babbitt, "Springflow determinations regarding 'take' of endangered and threatened species," April 15, 1993; Sierra Club v. Babbitt, "Springflow determinations regarding survival and recovery and critical habitat of endangered and threatened species," June 15, 1993. The Fifth Circuit granted the request of the federal government for a partial stay of the court order on April 2, 1993, to allow the Fish and Wildlife Service more time to prepare determinations regarding "jeopardy" and "adverse modification."

16. Sierra Club v. Babbitt, "Springflow determinations regarding 'take' of endangered and threatened species," April 15, 1993, 2.

17. Sierra Club v. Babbitt, "Springflow determinations regarding survival and recovery and critical habitat of endangered and threatened species," June 15, 1993.

18. Sierra Club v. Babbitt, "Texas Water Commission's submission of management plan for the Edwards Aquifer," March 1, 1993.

19. Sierra Club v. Babbitt, "Texas Water Commission recommendation: The Edwards Aquifer," 2 (citing "Amended findings," para. 38, 214).

20. Sierra Club v. Babbitt, "Texas Water Commission's submission of manage-

ment plan for the Edwards Aquifer," March 1, 1993 (citing "Amended findings," para. 35, 36, 37, 96, 104, 105, 106, 155, 165, and 214).

21. Sierra Club v. Babbitt, "Texas Water Commission recommendations: The Edwards Aquifer," March 1, 1993.

22. Ibid.

Chapter 4. Senate Bill 1477 and the Creation of the Edwards Aquifer Authority

1. Tom Bower and Ralph Winingham, "Water panel joins Medina in floating an aquifer plan," *San Antonio Express-News*, October 12, 1992; David Anthony Richelieu, "John Hall tells real fright tale," *San Antonio Express-News*, September 24, 1992.

2. Susie Phillips Gonzalez, "Morton says new agency possible," *San Antonio Express-News*, November 20, 1992.

3. Susie Phillips Gonzales, "Lawmakers from Bexar offered briefing on Edwards proposal," *San Antonio Express-News*, December 24, 1992.

4. Stefanie Scott, "Aquifer war heads for legislature; Area water groups hire lobbyists for spring showdown in Austin," *San Antonio Express-New*, January 3, 1993.

5. Stefanie Scott, "Puente files measure to regulate pumping from Edwards aquifer," *San Antonio Express-News*, March 10, 1993.

6. Representative Puente also introduced a bill that would have abolished the Guadalupe-Blanco River Authority. House Bill 2540 was referred to the House Natural Resources Committee, but no further action was taken. The issue, however, reemerged in Senate Bill 1477, as discussed later.

7. Stefanie Scott and Tom Bower, "Aquifer water war compromise reached, but blessing from irrigators absent," *San Antonio Express-News*, April 28, 1993.

8. Debbie Hiott, "Edwards Aquifer compromise preserves springs, officials say," *Austin American-Statesman*, April 29, 1993; Bruce Hight, "Bill limiting aquifer pumping hits Senate," *Austin American-Statesman*, May 6, 1993.

9. Armbrister and Reagan quoted in Stefanie Scott and Tom Bower, "Aquifer water war compromise reached, but blessing from irrigators absent," *San Antonio Express-News*, April 28, 1993.

10. Sims quoted in Stefanie Scott, "Texas Legislature: Senate panel OKs aquifer-limit bill," *San Antonio Express-News*, May 8, 1993.

11. Stefanie Scott, "Texas Legislature: Senate hears water plan testimony," *San Antonio Express-News*, May 7, 1993.

12. Robert Puente, interview by author, San Antonio, Tex., February 11, 2014.

13. Puente quoted in Stefanie Scott, "Aquifer bill to remove name from measure," *San Antonio Express-News*, May 8, 1993.

14. House Research Organization Bill Analysis, "CSSB 1477 by Lewis and SB 1744 by Armbrister," May 24, 1993.

15. Stefanie Scott, "Texas Legislature conferees facing off over aquifer," *San Antonio Express-News*, May 28, 1993.

16. Diana R. Fuentes, "Proposal," *San Antonio Express-News*, June 12, 1993.

17. Act of May 30, 1993, 73rd Leg., R.S., ch. 626, 1993, Tex. Gen. Laws 2350, as amended (hereafter cited as Senate Bill 1477 or the EAA Act).

18. Senate Bill 1477 created the South Central Texas Water Advisory Committee (often referred to by its acronym, SCTWAC), made up of representatives of twenty downstream counties, to interact with the Edwards Aquifer Authority when issues related to downstream water rights are addressed. EAA Act § 1.10 (a). Members are appointed by county commissioners and city councils in the region. Ibid.

19. Senate Bill 1477 § 3.03.

20. Tom Bower, "Leave—job in jeopardy," *San Antonio Express-News*, June 23, 1993; Stefanie Scott, "House votes to save Guadalupe-Blanco board," *San Antonio Express-News*, May 16, 1995.

21. Tom Bower, "Struggles for job," *San Antonio Express-News*, June 19, 1993.

22. Act of May 16, 1995, 74th Leg. R.S., ch. 524, § 1, 1995 Tex. Gen. Laws 3280.

23. EAA Act § 1.16(a).

24. Ibid., § 1.16(e).

25. Ibid., §§ 1.14(b) and (c), § 1.21(a).

26. Ibid., §§ 1.21(b), 1.14(d).

27. Ibid., § 1.16(e).

28. Ibid., §§ 1.29(a)(1), 1.29(a)(2).

29. EAA Act § 1.14(h).

30. "Amended findings," para. 190.

31. Technical Advisory Panel, "Technical factors in Edwards Aquifer use and management," February 15, 1990, 6.

32. EAA Act § 1.26.

33. James P. Turner, acting assistant attorney general, Civil Rights Division, to the Honorable John Hannah Jr., secretary of state, November 19, 1993. See also Jay Jordan, "State disappointed in federal rejection of aquifer proposal," *Austin American-Statesman*, November 21, 1993.

34. On March 9, 1994, the State of Texas filed suit in the US District Court for the District of Columbia seeking to reverse the Department of Justice decision. The state filed a motion for summary judgment, which was denied by the court on October 20, 1994. State of Texas v. United States of America, 866 F. Supp. 20 (D.D.C. 1994). Trial was set for June 5, 1995.

35. Richards quoted in Stefanie Scott, "Richards decries ruling on Aquifer," *San Antonio Express-News*, November 23, 1993.

Chapter 5. Sharpening the "Blunt Axe" of Federal Intervention

1. Tom Bower, "Aquifer dilemma remains," *San Antonio Express-News*, November 20, 1993.

2. Sierra Club v. Babbitt, "Order on motion to appoint a monitor," December 10, 1993.

3. Sierra Club v. Babbitt, "Order appointing Joe G. Moore, Jr. as monitor," February 25, 1994.

4. Bunton quoted in Tom Bower, "S.A. fears losing aquifer control," *San Antonio Express-News,* March 3, 1994.

5. Sierra Club v. Babbitt, "Motion of plaintiffs the Sierra Club and Clark Hubbs for leave to file amended and supplemental complaint," April 15, 1994.

6. Sierra Club v. Babbitt, "Order on motion for leave to file amended and supplemental complaint," May 5, 1994.

7. Sierra Club v. Babbitt, "Motion for additional relief," May 12, 1994.

8. Sierra Club v. Babbitt, "Order on motion for additional relief," June 3, 1994. On August 1, 1994, the court monitor submitted the "Emergency withdrawal reduction plan" for the Edwards Aquifer.

9. Susie Phillips Gonzalez, "Mayor names 26 to study future of water in S.A.," *San Antonio Express-News,* November 23, 1993.

10. Minutes of the special meeting of the City Council of the City of San Antonio, May 9, 1994.

11. Resolution No. 94–26–29 and Ordinance 80,186, both in Minutes of the regular meeting of the City Council of the City of San Antonio, May 19, 1994.

12. Ordinance 80,187, Minutes of the regular meeting of the City Council of the City of San Antonio, May 19, 1994; Jim Wood, "Voters to get 2nd chance at Applewhite," *San Antonio Express-News,* May 20, 1994.

13. Jerry Needham, "GBRA directors back Applewhite reservoir," *San Antonio Express-News,* June 16, 1994; Roy Bragg, "The water crisis," *San Antonio Express-News,* July 26, 1994.

14. Tom Bower, "Aquifer summit called by feds; Seek to create plan to protect species," *San Antonio Express-News,* June 22, 1994; Cindy Tumiel, "Fed aquifer summit drawn into the battle over Applewhite," *San Antonio Express-News,* June 23, 1994.

15. Sierra Club statement quoted in Roy Bragg, "Sierra Club rips reservoir, offers," *San Antonio Express-News,* August 10, 1994.

16. Sierra Club v. Babbitt, "Order on motion for (1) additional information needed for emergency withdrawal reduction planning and (2) water supply planning," August 11, 1994.

17. Cindy Tumiel, "Voters: 'No means no'; City leaders slapped with stunning defeat on Applewhite," *San Antonio Express-News,* August 14, 1994.

18. Lynnell Burkett, "Feasibility of water plan questioned; Final augmentation report to be released next week," *San Antonio Express-News,* July 29, 1994; Sierra Club v. Babbitt, "Amended findings," para. 149–54.

19. Sierra Club v. Babbitt, "Order on the Sierra Club's second motion for additional relief," March 6, 1995.

20. Sierra Club v. Babbitt, "Order directing the monitor to create a panel," September 30, 1994.

21. Joe G. Moore Jr., court monitor, and Todd H. Votteler, assistant to the court monitor, "Draft habitat conservation plan for the Edwards Aquifer," June 23, 1995. The draft habitat conservation plan contained thirteen elements: (1) protection of water quality, including over the recharge zone; (2) water conservation; (3) reuse of treated wastewater; (4) control of the giant rams-horn snail and other harmful species; (5) use of Medina Lake water for municipal, industrial, and military purposes; (6) duplication of the Seco Creek Watershed Water Quality Project in thirteen counties; (7) establishment of recharge structures on flowing streams across the region; (8) importation of groundwater from the Carrizo-Wilcox Aquifer; (9) importation of additional surface water from the Guadalupe River into the Edwards Aquifer region for municipal, industrial, and military use; (10) aquifer storage and recovery in the Carrizo-Wilcox Aquifer; (11) importation of surface or groundwater from the Colorado River Basin; (12) drought management plans; and (13) removal of listed species to refugia. Ibid., 5–7.

22. See Sierra Club v. Babbitt, "Order directing the monitor to create a panel," September 30, 1994, 1.

23. Sierra Club v. Babbitt, "Order on the Sierra Club's second motion for additional relief," March 6, 1995, 4.

24. Ibid., 11. On March 31, 1995, a Revised Emergency Withdrawal Reduction Plan for the Edwards Aquifer was filed with the court. Joe G. Moore, Jr., court monitor, and Todd H. Votteler, assistant to the court monitor, "Revised emergency withdrawal reduction plan," March 31, 1995.

25. Sierra Club v. Babbitt, "Order on the Sierra Club's second motion for additional relief," March 6, 1995.

26. Sierra Club v. Babbitt, "Motion for leave to file amended complaint," April 10, 1995; Sierra Club v. Babbitt, "Order," May 8, 1995.

27. State of Texas and Danny McFadden, Tommy Walker, and Carl Muecke, "Application of petitioners for a writ of mandamus," May 24, 1995.

28. The panel consisted of counsel for the San Antonio Water System, irrigators, the Atascosa Rural Water Supply Corporation and Green Valley Special Utility District, the Edwards Aquifer Authority, and City of New Braunfels. Roy Bragg, "Aquifer panel given 10 days to work deal," *San Antonio Express-News*, May 20, 1995.

29. See, e.g., Stefanie Scott, "Aquifer bill dies in House," *San Antonio Express-News*, May 29, 1995; Stefanie Scott, "Edwards water district bill may go down legislative drain," *San Antonio Express-News*, May 14, 1995; Stefanie Scott, "Trouble awaits new aquifer plan," *San Antonio Express-News*, May 9, 1995.

30. Act of May 29, 1995, 75th Leg. R.S. ch. 261, Tex. Gen. Laws 2505.

31. Jim Price and James Coburn, "It's official: Dry spell at an end; Aquifer

has jumped foot a day," *San Antonio Express-News,* May 31, 1995; Sierra Club v. Babbitt, "Order on summer 1995 emergency withdrawal reductions," June 14, 1995.

32. In re: The State of Texas and Danny McFadden, Tommy Walker, and Carl Muecke Jr., "Petition for writ of mandamus to the United States District Court Western District of Texas," June 19, 1995.

33. Deval Patrick, assistant attorney general, Civil Rights Division, to the Honorable Antonio O. Garza, Texas secretary of state, August 8, 1995.

34. Medina County Underground Water Conservation District v. Barshop, "Plaintiffs' original petition for declaratory judgment, temporary restraining order and temporary and permanent injunctive relief," August 23, 1995.

35. Mike Todd, "Judge strikes down aquifer authority; Ruling says Edwards agency deprived people of property rights," *Austin American-Statesman,* October 28, 1995.

36. Medina County Underground Water Conservation District v. Barshop, "Temporary injunction and order setting trial on the merits," No. 95–08–13471-CV (38th Dist. Ct., Medina County, Tex., September 1, 1995).

37. Medina County Underground Water Conservation District v. Barshop, "Final judgment," No. 95–08–13471-CV (38th Dist. Ct., Medina County, Tex., October 28, 1995).

38. Sierra Club v. Babbitt, "Order setting status and scheduling conference," October 6, 1995, 1. See also Rick Casey, "Feds to run aquifer by January," *San Antonio Express-News,* October 12, 1995.

39. Sierra Club v. Babbitt, *slip op.,* at 7 (5th Cir. October 18, 1995),

40. Ibid., 4. See also "Agriculture commissioner cheers Edwards Aquifer ruling; He says Texas will resolve case in wake of appeals court limits on federal judge," *Dallas Morning News,* October 21, 1995.

41. Sierra Club v. Babbitt, "Order to take effect if the Fifth Circuit lifts its stay," November 29, 1995.

42. Sierra Club v. Babbitt, "Findings of fact and conclusions of law," November 29, 1995, 2, 23–31.

43. US Fish and Wildlife Service, "San Marcos & Comal Springs & Associated Aquatic Ecosystems (revised) recovery plan," February 14, 1996.

44. Sierra Club v. Babbitt, "Appeal from the United States District Court for the Western District of Texas (CA-MO-91–69)," 5th Cir., February 26, 1996, 12–14.

45. Johnson quoted in Jerry Needham and Stefanie Scott, "Court takes feds off aquifer's back," *San Antonio Express-News,* February 27, 1996.

46. Barshop v. Medina County Underground Conservation District, 925 S.W.2d 618 (Tex. 1996).

47. Sierra Club v. San Antonio, "Order," August 23, 1996, 4.

48. Ibid.

49. Ibid.

50. Sierra Club v. City of San Antonio, 112 F.3d 789 (5th Cir. 1997).

51. "State briefs," *San Antonio Express-News,* May 26, 2000; Jerry Needham, "Judge near ruling on Sierra Club aquifer case; 1996 lawsuit targets S.A., other pumpers," *San Antonio Express-News,* March 28, 2002.

52. Jerry Needham, "Judge sinks aquifer lawsuit; Sierra Club lawyer ponders new action," *San Antonio Express-News,* May 11, 2002.

53. Carmina Danini, "Judge Bunton, 76, dies; Aquifer decision was monumental," *San Antonio Express-News,* January 18, 2001.

54. Todd Votteler, interview by author, Seguin, Tex., March 7, 2014.

Chapter 6. Attempts by the Edwards Aquifer Authority to Tackle the Edwards Issue

1. See, e.g., Sierra Club to Edwards Aquifer Authority and Department of the Interior, "Notice of violation of Federal Endangered Species Act and notice of intent to sue," August 14, 1998" (alleging, among other things, failure to impose meaningful limits on pumping).

2. David C. Fredrick, supervisor, US Fish and Wildlife Service Ecological Services' Austin field office, to Mr. Greg Ellis, general manager, Edwards Aquifer Authority, September 18, 2000.

3. See app. 2 regarding the requirements for an incidental take permit.

4. Memorandum, "EAA habitat conservation meeting," August 2, 2000.

5. Alisa Shull and Carrie Thompson, notes from EAA HCP meeting, January 7, 2003, 2–3.

6. Andy Donnelly, LBG Guyton, memorandum to Roy Frye, Hicks and Company, "Scope of additional model runs for the drought of record," February 7, 2003; Roy Frye, email to Carrie Thompson, "Additional drought of record model runs for HCP/EIS," February 19, 2003 (reporting the Edwards Aquifer Authority approval of the scope of work); Carrie Thompson, US Fish and Wildlife Service, Ecological Services' Austin field office, email to Roy G. Frye, "March 4th meeting regarding new model runs," March 3, 2003.

7. Meeting of the House Natural Resources Committee, video recording, April 23, 2003.

8. Alisa Shull and Carrie Thompson, notes from "EAA HCP meeting, January 7, 2003, 3.

9. Edwards Aquifer Authority, "Draft Edwards Aquifer Authority habitat conservation plan, July 2004, as amended on September 21, 2004," 4–27, table 4–1 of appendix H.

10. Ibid., 4–29.

11. See, e.g., Tom Taggart, director of water and wastewater utilities for the City of San Marcos, to Robert Potts, general manager, Edwards Aquifer Authority, "Comments on proposed habitat conservation plan," January 20, 2005; W. E. West Jr., general manager, Guadalupe-Blanco River Authority, to Robert Potts, general manager, Edwards Aquifer Authority, December 3, 2004; Ken Kramer, "Comments of the Lone Star Chapter of the Sierra Club on the draft Edwards

Aquifer Authority habitat conservation plan and draft environmental impact statement," December 3, 2004.

12. Ken Kramer, "Comments of the Lone Star Chapter of the Sierra Club on the draft Edwards Aquifer Authority habitat conservation plan and draft environmental impact statement," December 3, 2004, 2.

13. Alexander E. Briseño, interim president/chief executive officer, to Mr. Robert Potts, general manager, Edwards Aquifer Authority, December 3, 2004.

14. Edwards Aquifer Authority, memorandum, "Authority response to public comments on the September 21, 2004, amended draft HCP," February 25, 2005.

15. Edwards Aquifer Staff, memorandum, "Revised HCP approach," February, 23, 2005; Jerry Needham, "EAA approves plan for troubled critters," *San Antonio Express-News*, March 9, 2005.

16. Edwards Aquifer Authority Board of Directors meeting, audio recordings, March 8, 2005.

17. Robert Potts, general manager, Edwards Aquifer Authority, to Mr. Robert Pine, supervisor, US Fish and Wildlife Service, Ecological Services' Austin field office, March 11, 2005 (transmitting the draft habitat conservation plan).

18. James quoted in "River flow should not be sacrificed for endangered species, coalition says," *Victoria Advocate*, March 10, 2005.

19. Edwards Aquifer Authority Board of Directors meeting, audio recordings, March 8, 2005.

20. Chardavoyne quoted in Jerry Needham, "EAA approves plan for troubled critters; It describes actions to save species in aquifer or spring openings," *San Antonio Express-News*, March 9, 2005.

21. Carrie Thompson, US Fish and Wildlife Service Ecological Services' Austin field office, email to Alisa Shull, US Fish and Wildlife Service, Ecological Services' Austin field office, "Parting notes on the Edwards Aquifer Authority HCP," March 3, 2006 (hereafter cited as Thompson email to Shull, March 3, 2006).

22. Thompson email to Shull, March 3, 2006. Fish and Wildlife Service rules require that an application must be complete before the review can begin. See 50 C.F.R. § 13.11 (an application is considered abandoned if information is not provided for an incomplete application within forty-five days).

23. Thompson email to Shull, March 3, 2006.

24. William Sewall, for the supervisor of the US Fish and Wildlife Service, Austin field office, to Rick Illgner, Edwards Aquifer Authority, May 22, 1998.

25. Dr. Randall E. Moss, chair, Biological Advisory Team, to Robert J. Potts, general manager, Edwards Aquifer Authority, January 31, 2005.

26. "Answers to questions raised at the July 23 special board meeting," July 28, 2004, 2.

27. See app. 2.

28. 65 Fed. Reg. 56,916, 56,919 (September 20, 2000).

29. Tex. Admin. Code § 711.176 (b)(6) (2000).

30. Meeting of the House Natural Resources Committee, video recording, April 23, 2003. See also Hicks & Company, "Regulatory impact assessment for proposed rules, chapter 711, E (Groundwater Withdrawal Permits), G (Groundwater Available for Permitting: Proportional Adjustment; Equal Percentage Reduction), and K (Additional Groundwater Supplies)," December 2003.

31. Beldon quoted in Jerry Needham, "EAA gives legislature water woe; Board fails to reach recommendation on pumping permits," *San Antonio Express-News,* February 4, 2003.

32. Chuck McCollough, "Water officials seek changes in law; Edwards Aquifer Authority is seeking a solution to contradictory provisions in the current legislation," *San Antonio Express-News,* March 26, 2003.

33. Puente quoted in Jerry Needham, "Aquifer bill would delay pumping cap deadline," *San Antonio Express-News,* April 29, 2003.

34. The initial regular permits issued during a year did not become effective until January 1 of the following year.

35. Resolution and Order No. 12–03–478, attached to the Minutes of the Board of Directors of the Edwards Aquifer Authority, December 16, 2003.

36. Edwards Aquifer Authority Rules § 711.164 (2004).

37. The South Central Texas Water Advisory Committee can ask the aquifer authority board to reconsider any action that may harm downstream users. EAA Act § 1.10(f). If the board review does not result in a resolution satisfactory to the advisory committee, the advisory committee may, by resolution, request the Texas Commission on Environmental Quality to review the action. Edwards Aquifer Authority Rules § 711.164 (2004).

38. Gary Middleton, chair, South Central Texas Water Advisory Committee, to Kathleen Harnett White, chair, and R. B. "Ralph" Marquez and Larry R. Soward, commissioners, Texas Commission on Environmental Quality, June 3, 2004.

39. Regarding "measurable impact," see Robert E. Mace and Shirley Wade, Texas Water Development Board, "Open file report 05–02: The effect of bifurcated permits on spring flow in the San Antonio segment of the Edwards Aquifer," August 2005, which states that, "according to the model, flow at Comal Springs could be reduced as much as seven percent of peak flows and flow at San Marcos Springs could be reduced as much as one percent when spring flows are at their highest levels when bifurcated permits are used. During a drought similar to the one of the 1950s, flow in Comal Springs may be as much as one cubic feet per second lower when bifurcated permits are used." But see LBG-Guyton, on behalf of the Edwards Aquifer Authority, "LBG-Guyton's review of Texas Commission on Environmental Quality's evaluation of Edwards Aquifer Authority's permitting of bifurcated water rights and potential impact on downstream interests," October 21, 2005. Regarding the downstream surface water rights holders and other downstream interests, see Texas Commission on Environmental Quality, "Resolution regarding the request by the South Central Texas

Water Advisory Committee concerning the Edwards Aquifer Authority Board of Director's action: TCEQ Docket No. 2004–1705-MIS," January 11, 2006.

40. Harvey Hilderbran, chair of the House Committee on Culture, Recreation, and Tourism, and co-chair of the Edwards Aquifer Legislative Oversight Committee, to the Honorable Greg Abbott, attorney general of Texas, March 16, 2006.

41. 21 Tex. Reg. 8,337 (September 3, 1996).

42. 23 Tex. Reg. 112 (January 28, 1997).

43. Living Waters Artesian Springs, Ltd. v. Edwards Aquifer Auth., No. 98–02644 (353rd Dist. Ct., Travis County, Tex.).

44. Living Waters Artesian Springs, Ltd. v. Edwards Aquifer Auth., No. 98–02644, *slip op.* at 1 (353rd Dist. Ct. Travis County, Tex. August 5, 1998).

45. Living Waters Artesian Springs v. Edwards Aquifer Auth., No. 98–02644, *slip op.* (353rd Dist. Ct. Travis County, December 17, 1998).

46. 25 Tex. Reg. 7,184 (July 28, 2000).

47. 25 Tex. Reg. 4,397 (May 19, 2000).

48. Todd Votteler, "Chronology of Edwards Aquifer developments beginning July 2003," August 2005.

49. Puente quoted in Bruce Davidson, "Without a crisis, water issue sinks," *San Antonio Express-News,* June 5, 2005.

50. Ken Kramer, director, Lone Star Chapter, Sierra Club, "Raising the cap on Edwards pumping solves nothing," Alamo Group of the Sierra Club, http://www .texas.sierraclub.org/alamo/water.htm (emphasis in original).

51. Christopher Anderson, "Water contract almost dunked; 3 way pact cuts aquifer demand," *San Antonio Express-News,* May 19, 2001.

52. Jerry Needham, "SAWS set to join SARA in Guadalupe water deal," *San Antonio Express-News,* January 15, 2001.

53. Jerry Needham, "Water project muddied again; GBRA spat with SAWS bubbles up in letters," *San Antonio Express-News,* August 26, 2004.

54. See San Antonio Water System, "Water resource plan update," June 21, 2005, 4–5; Jerry Needham, "SAWS won't dip deeper into the aquifer," *San Antonio Express-News,* August 17, 2005.

55. Jerry Needham, "Another SAWS project facing ax," *San Antonio Express-News,* June 16, 2005.

56. West quoted in Greg Bowen, "SAWS chief recommends canceling water project," *Victoria Advocate,* May 24, 2005.

57. "According to a presentation by the U.S. Department of the Interior, the Recovery Implementation Program is a voluntary effort by all interested parties, who create a long-term plan based on science, ultimately signed by the U.S. secretary of the interior and eligible for congressional funding." "Compromise possible in water battle," *Austin American-Statesman,* February 26, 2007. Such programs were developed under Interior secretary Bruce Babbitt to blunt efforts in 1995 to substantially amend the Endangered Species Act. John D. Echeverria, "No success like failure: The Platte River collaborative watershed planning pro-

cess," *William & Mary Environmental Law and Policy Review* 25 (2001): 559, 567; Joseph L. Sax, "Environmental law at the turn of the century: A reportorial fragment of contemporary history," *California Law Review* 88 (2000): 2,375, 2,381.

58. Todd Votteler, telephone interview by author, September 2, 2013.

59. Ibid.

60. Those attending the meetings included Bob Cook, executive director, and Larry McKinney, deputy executive director, Texas Parks and Wildlife Department; Kevin Ward, executive director, Texas Water Development Board; Kathleen White, chair of the Texas Commission on Environmental Quality; and Robert Potts, general manager, Edwards Aquifer Authority. Votteler interview, September 2, 2003.

61. Those attending the meetings included Senator Kip Averitt; Representative Robert Puente; Senator Jeff Wentworth; Guadalupe Basin Coalition; Myron Hess, National Wildlife Federation; Amy Hardberger, Environmental Defense Fund; Ken Kramer and Tyson Broad, Sierra Club; and David Chardavoyne, chief executive officer, San Antonio Water System. Votteler interview, September 2, 2013.

62. Joy Nicholopoulos, email to Bill West, copy to Todd Votteler, "Great mtng with Chairman White yesterday," March 23, 2006.

63. Joy Nicholopoulos, email to Robert Cook, "Hello and request for a meeting to discuss water issues in TX," June 2, 2006. Anna Munoz was a graduate student of Dr. Tarla Rai Peterson at Texas A&M. Earlier, as an employee of the Fish and Wildlife Service, she had worked with Nicholopoulos on the Middle Rio Grande Recovery Implementation Program.

64. Joy Nicholopoulos, email to Todd Votteler, "Imperiled critters to get protection," July 18, 2006.

65. Anna Munoz, interview by author, Austin, Tex., September 5, 2013; Colette Barron, Texas Parks and Wildlife Department, interview by author, Austin, Tex., December 5, 2013.

66. South Central Texas Water Advisory Committee, "Fifth biennial report on the effectiveness of the Edwards Aquifer Authority," October 2006, 3–11.

67. Joy Nicholopoulos, presentation to Edwards Aquifer Authority Board of Directors, audio recording, October 10, 2006.

68. The reason for including the third provision in the legislative agenda is difficult to discern because, if the cap were raised to cover the full amount of the permitted rights, there would be no need for a buy-down. According to Todd Votteler, the provision was intended to discourage a subsequent suit to have the cap reduced. Dr. Todd Votteler, interview by author, San Antonio, Tex., February 23, 2014.

69. Larry Zinn, chief of staff of former mayor Phil Hardberger, interview by author, San Antonio, Tex., October 31, 2013.

70. Joint meeting of the House and Senate Natural Resources Committees, San Antonio, video recording, September 22, 2006.

71. According to the Texas Water Development Board, "The South Central Texas Region used 340,000 AFY as the groundwater availability for the San Antonio segment of the Edwards aquifer. This is a temporary value until a better value is attained through the process of developing the Habitat Conservation Plan required by U.S. Fish and Wildlife Service." Texas Water Development Board, "Water for Texas—2002," January 2002, 43. The Region L Plan stated, "For planning purposes, an estimate of 340,000 acft/yr of available supply during a drought of record from the Edwards Aquifer was agreed upon by the South Central Texas Regional Water Planning Group and the staff of the Texas Water Development Board. This quantity was adopted as a placeholder number until the EAA completes and acquires approval from the U.S. Fish and Wildlife Service for a Habitat Conservation Plan (HCP)." South Central Texas Regional Planning Group, "South Central Regional Water Planning Area regional water plan," 2001, vol. 1, 3–4.

72. In referring to a recovery implementation program Nicholopoulos used the term "cooperative agreement" in her presentations to the various stakeholders. The term "cooperative agreement" is used in section 6 of the Endangered Species Act in reference to an agreement to allow a state that establishes and maintains an adequate and active program for the conservation of threatened and endangered species to provide assistance in the implementation of the state program. 16 U.S.C. § 1535 (c). The agreement was used to allow funding of earlier recovery implementation programs. She may have had a section 6 cooperative agreement in mind when she approached the Texas Parks and Wildlife Department to take the lead in the recovery implementation program. Later, at the suggestion of Nicholopoulos, Senator Glenn Hegar attempted, mostly successfully, to remove the term "cooperative agreement" from his committee substitute that formed the basis for Senate Bill 3. Lisa Craven, chief of staff for Senator Hegar, email to Tom Taggart, Jerry James, Billy Howe, Bill West, Todd Votteler, Robert Potts, Wendy Foster, David Chardavoyne, Janelle Okorie, Michael Booth, Wil Galloway, Tris Castañeda, Donovan Burton, Steve Holzheauser, D. Pearson, Jay Howard, Christina Wisdom, Frank Santo, C. McGarah, Darcy Frownfelter, Doug Miller, "Update . . . EAA bill," April 25, 2007; Tyson Broad, notes on the EARIP meeting, May 10, 2007.

73. Joint Legislative Committee on the Oversight of the Edwards Aquifer, video recording, October 5, 2006.

74. Guadalupe Basin Coalition, "Resolution 2006–1: A resolution expressing the Guadalupe Basin Coalition's position on possible amendments to the Edwards Aquifer Authority Act," November 9, 2006.

75. Guadalupe-Blanco River Authority, "GBRA endorses use of U.S. Fish and Wildlife process for springflow management," press release, November 20, 2006.

76. GBRA statement quoted in Jerry Needham, "Edwards pumping battle is revived," *San Antonio Express-News,* December 24, 2006; Molly Bloom, "Limits on aquifer pumping debated," *Austin American-Statesman,* January 1, 2007.

77. Finch quoted in Molly Bloom, "Limits on aquifer pumping debated," *Austin American-Statesman,* January 1, 2007 (discussing the scheduled meeting of the proposed Edwards Aquifer Recovery Implementation Program sponsored by the US Fish and Wildlife Service on January 17, 2007).

78. Bruce Davidson, "Region's water battle looms large," *San Antonio Express-News,* December 10, 2006.

79. Greg Abbott to the Honorable Harvey Hilderbran, Opinion No. GA 0498, dated January 9, 2007.

80. Jerry Needham, "Edwards pumping bill revived," *San Antonio Express-News,* December 24, 2006; Office of State Senator Glenn Hegar, District 18, "Senator Hegar files Edwards Aquifer legislation," press release, dated March 7, 2007; "San Antonio seeks more pumping; Drought-protection more limited than environmentalists wanted," *Austin American-Statesman,* May 25, 2007; Roddy Stinson, "Forget gold, double your pleasure (and money) by buying H2O rights," *San Antonio Express-News,* February 19, 2007.

81. Jerry Needham, "Aquifer system to limit pumping is ruled in error," *San Antonio Express-News,* January 10, 2007.

82. Robert Mace, Texas Water Development Board, "GAM RUN 06–33a," February 12, 2007; Representative Patrick M. Rose to Mr. Kevin Ward, executive administrator, Texas Water Development Board, and Glenn Shankle, executive director, Texas Commission on Environmental Quality, October 12, 2006. According to Todd Votteler, the Guadalupe-Blanco River Authority suggested to Representative Rose that he request the modeling. Votteler interview, February 23, 2014.

83. Puente and Hegar quoted in Laylan Copelin, "Drought may stop Comal Springs," *Austin American-Statesman,* March 15, 2007.

84. Hegar quote recalled in Votteler interview, September 2, 2013.

85. House Committee Report for the House Natural Resources Committee, Witness list for hearing on March 21, 2007.

86. Senator Wentworth's district extended from San Antonio to Austin, giving him constituents on both sides of the debate. Molly Bloom, "Limits on aquifer pumping debated," *Austin American-Statesman,* January 1, 2007.

87. Office of State Senator Glenn Hegar, District 18, "Senator Hegar files Edwards Aquifer legislation," press release, March 7, 2007. Hegar stated in the release, "I have a lot of concerns over raising the pumping cap without addressing critical management (drought) issues." Ibid.

88. Guadalupe Basin Coalition, "Guadalupe-Blanco River Authority and Guadalupe Basin Coalition endorse Edwards Aquifer legislation sponsored by Senator Glenn Hegar," March 8, 2007.

89. Pauline Villagran, executive assistant to the Board of Trustees, San Antonio Water System, email to Jerry James, director of environmental services, "Edwards pumping cap meeting," March 9, 2007.

90. "Officials seek common ground on water needs," *San Antonio Express-*

News, March 22, 2007; David Tewes, "Working towards a water deal," *Victoria Advocate,* May 21, 2007.

91. See, e.g., Jerry James, director of environmental services, City of Victoria, email to Alex Briseño, chair of the San Antonio Water System Board of Trustees, "Items for consideration," March 23, 2007. James wrote in the email, "I have spent time with my Mayor and Council members this week to ensure that we want to continue our discussions with an intent to resolve this and we do. With that in mind I would like to offer some items for your consideration in how we can resolve this situation in this session of the legislature."

92. Hegar quoted in Laylan Copelin, "Legislation on pumping limits advances," *Austin American-Statesman,* April 28, 2007. According to this article, the environmental community complained that they were not included in the negotiations.

93. Jerry Needham, "Aquifer pumping measure in Senate receives praise," *San Antonio Express-News,* April 28, 2007. After attending the first meeting of the proposed Edwards Aquifer Recovery Implementation Program sponsored by the Fish and Wildlife Service, Senator Wentworth recognized the potential benefits of such a program. "I left the meeting more optimistic that we could work towards a cooperative answer," he said. Quoted in "Compromise possible in water battle," *Austin American-Statesman,* February 26, 2007.

94. House Research Organization Bill Analysis, "House Bill 1292 (CSHB 1292 by Puente)," May 10, 2007.

95. Glenn Hegar, email to Michael Booth, Jerry James, Lisa Craven, and J. A. Lazarus, "EAA bill Chairman Puente's changes to Senator Hegar's engrossed version," May 15, 2007.

96. Glenn Hegar, email to Lisa Craven, J. A. Lazarus, Michael Booth, and Wil Galloway, "Today," May 22, 2007.

97. Puente interview.

98. "Gov. Rick Perry's remarks at the signing of water legislation," San Antonio, June 19, 2007, http://governor.state.tx.us/news/speech/5469.

99. Senate Bill 3 §§ 1.26A(a), 1.26A(d).

100. Ibid., §§ 1.26A(d)(1), 1.26A(d)(3). On July 12, 2007, Senator Hegar spoke to the EARIP, and the minutes of the meeting state that "Sen. Hegar wants a successful RIP, and through conversations with Joy Nicholopoulos (USFWS), he came to realize that the RIP process can take a long time and thus, he saw the need for legislation as an incentive to get [the] process moving. His intent was to fashion something in the political arena to help this process move forward." Minutes of the EARIP meeting, July 12, 2007. On several occasions, Senator Hegar told the author that he considered the December 31, 2012, deadline to be an important part of the bargain for raising the withdrawal caps.

101. Senate Bill 3 §§ 1.26A(e), 1.26A(p).

102. Senator Hegar spoke to the EARIP about the deadlines. "The RIP should be an open process where everyone has a say in the decisions. [Hegar] can't tell

the federal government what to do, but he could set up a structure conducive to get things moving. This was done by providing benchmarks. He doesn't want to be stuck in this same place 2 years from now [the next session of the legislature] and believes that the legislation will help the process arrive at a quicker solution, including the creation of an HCP." Minutes of the EARIP meeting, July 12, 2007.

Chapter 7. Organizing the Program

1. On July 31, 1990, Bob Price, from the Soil Conservation Service of the US Department of Agriculture, testified before the Special Committee on the Edwards Aquifer that some crops in the region might require as much as two acre-feet of water per acre of land. Special Committee on the Edwards Aquifer, Report to the 72nd Legislature, 1.

2. Senate Bill 1477 § 1.31.

3. In Senate Bill 1477, the fees that the Edwards Aquifer Authority was allowed to charge agricultural users were based on the volume of water withdrawn and could not be more than 20 percent of the fee rate for municipal use. Senate Bill 1477 § 1.29(e). In 2001 the Edwards Aquifer Authority board set the rate for municipal pumpers at $20.00/permitted acre-feet. The irrigators' fees, however, were capped at $3.00 for the first acre-foot pumped (instead of $4.00/acre-foot) and, after that, $4.70/acre-foot or 20 percent of the municipal fee. Rick Casey, "Legislators give farmers 'double butter' on their bread," *San Antonio Express-News,* June 22, 2001. Not to be outdone, in the 2001 legislative session, Representative Tracy King introduced in committee an amendment to Senate Bill 2 that capped the fee at $2.00/acre-foot of water pumped. Representative Puente tried unsuccessfully tried to have the amendment removed on the floor. Ibid. Thus, in 2007, when aquifer management fees for municipal pumpers were almost $40.00/acre-feet of permitted water, agricultural users were paying only $2.00/acre-foot of permitted water that they actually used.

4. Senate Bill 3 §1.26(a)(5).

5. See the discussion of the jeopardy standard in app. 2.

6. On December 26, 2006, Nancy J. Glomar, acting regional director of the US Fish and Wildlife Service Region 2, wrote a letter inviting stakeholders to "the first meeting of the proposed Edwards Aquifer Recovery Implementation Program" at the San Marcos City Activity Center. The meeting was canceled due to an ice storm, however, and rescheduled for February 16.

7. There were also discussions on the relationship of the voluntary EARIP and the process created by Senate Bill 3 and on hiring the project manager. Many of the concerns regarding the relationship of the voluntary process and the legislated process focused on the composition of the steering committee. Nicholopoulos expressed concern that the legislation posed a problem for a recovery implementation program because such programs must be voluntary and inclusive, while the legislation mandated participation by some and could

exclude others. Steering committee membership was mandated and exclusionary. EARIP meeting notes, May 10, 2007.

8. Gregg Walker and Steve Daniels, "The basics of collaborative learning," http://oregonstate.edu/instruct/comm440–540/CL2pager.htm.

9. Minutes of the EARIP meeting, February 28, 2007.

10. Minutes of the EARIP meeting, April 5, 2007. See also Summary, Statements of interest, June 7, 2007, http://www.eahcp.org/files/uploads/EARIP InterestStatements2.pdf.

11. However, see John M. Donahue, "Anthropological insights into stakeholder participation in water management of the Edwards Aquifer in Texas," in *The social life of water*, ed. John R. Wagner (New York: Berghahn Books, 2013).

12. Edwards Aquifer Recovery Implementation Program, "Draft memorandum of understanding," February 28–March 1, 2007.

13. Minutes of the EARIP meeting on July 12, 2007. Those who volunteered to serve on the committee were Con Mims (Nueces River Authority), Dan Laroe Jr. (stakeholder), Mary Q. Kelly (stakeholder), Jenny Sanders (stakeholder), Patrick Shriver (San Antonio Water System), Joe Cole (San Antonio Water System), Mark Taylor (City of San Marcos), Colette Barron (Texas Parks and Wildlife Department), Carol Patterson (Regional Clean Air & Water), Kirk Patterson (Regional Clean Air & Water), George Ozuna (US Geological Survey), Myron Hess (National Wildlife Federation), and Larry Hoffmann (stakeholder). Myron Hess chaired this committee. Jim Bower (City of Garden Ridge) later joined the committee.

14. Minutes of the EARIP meeting, September 6, 2007.

15. "Draft memorandum of agreement for the Edwards Aquifer Recovery Implementation Program," September 6, 2007, section 2.1.

16. Ibid., section 4.1. Mary Q. Kelly, representing the Greater San Antonio Chamber of Commerce and working through an ad hoc committee, circulated a draft set of operating rules for the non–steering committee members of the EARIP (referred to as the "Group of Edwards Aquifer Region Stakeholders"). "Group of Edwards Aquifer region stakeholders proposed rules of operation," July 11, 2007, attachment to EARIP minutes for July 12, 2007 meeting. The original draft contemplated separate meetings of the steering committee and the other stakeholders. The draft was discussed again in August, but the EARIP team generally agreed that Kelly's guidelines set up parallel processes and did not believe her operating rules were necessary because the memorandum of agreement adequately addressed the relationship of the steering committee and the stakeholders. Tyson Broad, notes regarding the EARIP meeting, August 9, 2007. Kelly's document was never adopted.

17. Myron Hess, memorandum to EARIP stakeholders, "Draft of MOA for EARIP Process," September 4, 2007.

18. A copy of the final memorandum of agreement that was executed by the steering committee and stakeholders can be found on the website of the Ed-

wards Aquifer Habitat Conservation Plan, http://www.eahcp.org/files/uploads/
EARIPFinalMOA.12.18.075.pdf.

19. See app. 1. At the EARIP meeting in March 2008, a draft of the procedural rules called for by the memorandum of agreement was circulated for review and comment. Minutes of the EARIP meeting, March 13, 2008. These rules were intended to provide specific details on the procedures described in general terms in the memorandum of agreement. After further discussion, the procedural operating rules were approved by the steering committee at its meeting on April 10, 2008. Minutes of the EARIP meeting, April 10, 2008.

20. Myron Hess, interview by author, Austin, Tex., December 5, 2013; Colette Barron, interview by author, Austin, Tex., December 5, 2013.

21. Barron interview.

22. "Q&A with Senator Hegar," Minutes of the EARIP meeting, July 12, 2007.

23. Rice comment during "Q&A with Senator Hegar," Minutes of the EARIP meeting, July 12, 2007; Tyson Broad, notes on EARIP meeting, June 12, 2007.

24. Senate Bill 3 § 1.26(p).

25. "Memorandum of agreement for Edwards Aquifer Recovery Implementation Program," December 13, 2007, section 4.2.

26. Minutes of the EARIP meeting, February 14, 2008.

27. Minutes of the EARIP meeting, March 13, 2008.

28. Minutes of the EARIP meeting, April 10, 2008.

29. "Memorandum of agreement for Edwards Aquifer Recovery Implementation Program," December 13, 2007, section 5.5 (identifying the Tier I decisions) and section 5.6.

30. "Memorandum of agreement for Edwards Aquifer Recovery Implementation Program," December 13, 2007, section 5.2.

31. See "Memorandum of agreement for Edwards Aquifer Recovery Implementation Program," December 13, 2007, section 5.3.

32. See "Revised procedural operating rules," section 7.11.

33. "Report of the additional studies issues team," November 4, 2009.

34. Minutes of the EARIP meeting, November 12, 2009.

35. Bruce Alexander, representing the utility interests in the western sector of the aquifer region, objected, not because of concerns with the habitat conservation plan itself but because of the method of paying for implementation of the plan.

36. Calvin Finch, interview by author, San Antonio, Tex., September 23, 2013. The City of Garden Ridge and the representatives of agricultural interests often attended the meetings but did not always vote with this bloc. Ibid.

37. The San Antonio Water System committed nine staff members to the EARIP—far more than the other steering committee members or stakeholders. They met weekly internally to work through the issues, formulate the position of the San Antonio Water System, and develop support for that position behind the scenes.

38. EAA Act § 1.26A(i).

39. Minutes of the EARIP meeting, September 6, 2007.

40. Handout distributed at the EARIP meeting, November 8, 2007.

41. Minutes of the EARIP meeting, January 10, 2008.

42. Dutton resigned from the subcommittee in October 2009 because of his increased responsibilities at his university. His slot was filled by Shirley Wade, a hydrologist/modeler at the Texas Water Development Board.

43. Edwards resigned his position in April 2008. Minutes of the EARIP meeting, March 13, 2008. Based on the recommendation of the science subcommittee, the steering committee replaced Edwards with Doyle Mosier. Minutes of the EARIP meeting, May 8, 2008.

44. Brooks soon resigned from the subcommittee. Based on the recommendation of the science subcommittee, the steering committee replaced Brooks with Mike Gonzales, from the San Antonio River Authority. Minutes of the EARIP meeting, May 8, 2008.

45. Minutes of the EARIP meeting, February 14, 2007.

46. Ibid. Subsequently, Kreitler was added to the science subcommittee as a voting member when in early 2009 the US Geological Survey said that Susan Aragon-Long could not serve as a voting member but allowed her to participate as a paid program manager for the science subcommittee.

47. EAA Act § 1.26A(k).

48. The Edwards Aquifer Area Expert Science Subcommittee for the Edwards Aquifer Recovery Implementation Program, *Evaluation of designating a San Marcos pool, maintaining minimum spring flows at Comal and San Marcos Springs, and adjusting the critical period management triggers for the San Marcos Springs,* November 13, 2008, 4, 36, 63.

49. Sustainable Ecosystems Institute, "Peer review of the Edwards Aquifer Recovery Implementation Program's Science Subcommittee's 'k' charge recommendations," March 2009.

50. The Edwards Aquifer Area Expert Science Subcommittee for the Edwards Aquifer Recovery Implementation Program, *Analysis of species requirements in relation to spring discharge rates and associated withdrawal reductions and stages for critical period management of the Edwards Aquifer,* December 28, 2009, vi, 85.

51. Annear Associates, LLC, "Peer review of the Edwards Aquifer Recovery Implementation Program's Science Subcommittee recommendations and the Hardy Study," May 28, 2010.

52. Ibid., Executive summary.

Chapter 8. Tackling the Minimum Flow Issue

1. The Edwards Aquifer Area Expert Science Subcommittee for the Edwards Aquifer Recovery Implementation Program, *Evaluation of designating a San Marcos pool, maintaining minimum spring flows at Comal and San Marcos*

Springs, and adjusting the critical period management triggers for the San Marcos Springs, November 13, 2008, 35.

2. Ibid.

3. See app. 2 for a discussion of "take" and "jeopardy."

4. The US Geological Survey has a relatively modest appropriated budget for the scientific initiatives it undertakes. In the water area, it "partners" with state and private entities (referred to as "cooperators") to collect and disseminate reliable, impartial information. The role of the cooperator involves in large part initiating and funding the project. In effect, the USGS acts as a contractor except that it does not go through a competitive bidding process for projects.

5. Adam Zerrenner, supervisor, US Fish and Wildlife Service Ecological Services' Austin field office, presentation to the EARP team, February 14, 2008.

6. See, e.g., Minutes of the EARIP meetings, February 14, April 10, May 8, 2008; Lee Failing, Compass Resource Management, to Robert L. Gulley, "Preliminary proposal for decision-support services for the Edwards Aquifer Recovery Implementation Program," May 29, 2008.

7. Minutes of the EARIP meeting, April 10, 2008.

8. Minutes of the EARIP meeting, May 8, 2008, attachment 7, "Recommendations of the Biological Work Group."

9. Minutes of the EARIP meeting, May 8, 2008.

10. George Ozuna, email to Robert Gulley, "EARIP," May 14, 2008.

11. EARIP meeting agenda, June 8, 2008, attachment 4, "Report of the Biological Work Group."

12. Dr. Thom Hardy was at that time director of the Institute for Natural Systems Engineering and associate director of the Utah Water Research Laboratory at Utah State University. He was the principal author on one study on the impacts of in-stream flows on the fountain darter at Comal and San Marcos Springs and another on the fountain darter at Comal Springs. Hardy was, at that time, in discussions with the River Systems Institute at Texas State University and the Texas Parks and Wildlife Department about making a move to Texas State University.

13. EARIP meeting agenda, June 8, 2008, attachment 4, "Report of the Biological Work Group."

14. Ibid.

15. Joy Nicholopoulos, US Fish and Wildlife Service, "Biological modeling for the Edwards Aquifer Recovery Implementation Program," June 12, 2008.

16. Joy E. Nicholopoulos, Texas state administrator, US Fish and Wildlife Service, to the Honorable Glenn Hegar, July 16, 2008.

17. Robert L. Gulley to David Carter, Texas Water Development Board, "Application for a grant from the Texas Water Development Board," July 17, 2008.

18. Ibid.; Robert L. Gulley, memorandum to Biological Modeling Work Group, "Update regarding the Hardy and SDM biological modeling projects," June 27, 2008. The four state agencies (Texas Parks and Wildlife Department, Texas

Commission on Environmental Quality, and Texas Department of Agriculture), in addition to the Texas Water Development Board, had agreed to contribute $25,000 annually toward project management costs.

19. The team undertaking the study included scientists from the Texas Parks and Wildlife Department, Texas State University, Edwards Aquifer Authority, Bio-West, Inc., Texas A&M University, and the US Fish and Wildlife Service. As part of the engineering solutions study being conducted by HDR Engineering, a request was made for Ed Oborny of Bio-West to design a flow regime that would allow the listed species to survive during a ten-year severe drought, similar in nature to the 1950s drought of record, with the potential for recovery following that event. See Bio-West, Inc., "Technical memorandum: Engineered solutions—Biological technical services drought of record flow regime development," March 31, 2010.

20. Minutes of the EARIP meeting, July 10, 2008.

21. See, e.g., EARIP habitat conservation plan, fig. 4.5a.

22. Minutes of EARIP meeting, July 27, 2010.

23. Ibid.

24. Robert L. Gulley, memorandum to EARIP Steering Committee members and stakeholders, "Support information for September 9–10, 2010 EARIP meeting," August 10, 2010, 3.

25. Edwards Aquifer Habitat Conservation Plan, "Comal simulated flows," http://www.eahcp.org/files/uploads/09-11-10HardyPresentation.pdf. The final report on the study was submitted to the EARIP on December 29, 2010. See Dr. Thomas B. Hardy, "Technical assessments in support of the Edwards Aquifer Science Committee 'J charge' flow regime evaluation for Comal and San Marcos River systems," December 29, 2010.

26. Minutes of the EARIP meeting, September 9, 2010. See also the Edwards Aquifer Area Expert Science Subcommittee for the Edwards Aquifer Recovery Implementation Program, "Analysis of species requirements in relation to spring discharge rates and associated withdrawal reductions and stages for critical period management of the Edwards Aquifer," December 28, 2009, 29 (finding a minimum one-month average flow of thirty cubic feet per second with no flow below five cubic feet per second as the lowest flow threshold for the Comal system); and ibid., 63 (finding a minimum one-month average flow of sixty cubic feet per second with a minimum flow of fifty-two cubic feet per second as the lowest flow threshold for San Marcos Springs).

27. Robert L. Gulley, memorandum to EARIP Steering Committee members and stakeholders, "Support information for September 23–24, 2010 EARIP meeting," September 21, 2010.

28. Minutes of the EARIP meeting, September 23, 2010.

29. HDR Engineering, Inc., subsequently developed a correction factor that could be applied to the minimum flows to derive the monthly averages that would result in daily average flows of at least thirty cubic feet per second

at Comal Springs and forty-five at San Marcos Springs. To manage to a daily average for Comal Springs, one would have to apply a correction factor of approximately fifteen cubic feet per second to the monthly average number. For San Marcos Springs, the correction factor would be approximately eight cubic feet per second. HDR Engineering, Inc., and Todd Engineers, *Evaluation of water management programs and alternatives for springflow protection of endangered species at Comal and San Marcos Springs,* October 2011, 3–21. Thus, the recommended minimum flow targets, if daily averages were used, would be forty-five cubic feet per second at Comal Springs and fifty-three at San Marcos Springs.

30. Hess and Barron interviews; Calvin Finch, interview by author, San Antonio, Tex., December 9, 2013; Jerry James, interview by author, San Antonio, Tex., March 13, 2014.

31. Minutes of the EARIP meeting, September 24, 2010.

32. Finch interview, December 9, 2013; James interview.

33. Weir Labatt, email to Carter Smith, "EARIP Meetings on Sept 23 and 24," September 25, 2010.

34. See, e.g., Todd Engineers, *Recharge and recirculation Edwards Aquifer optimization program: Phase III/IV report,* December 2008.

35. Minutes of the EARIP meeting, November 12, 2009.

36. See Report of the Additional Studies Issues Team, November 4, 2009.

37. Minutes of the EARIP meeting, February 10, 2010.

38. HDR Engineering, Inc., and Todd Engineers, *Evaluation of water management programs and alternatives for springflow protection of endangered species at Comal and San Marcos Springs,* October 2011, 4–19.

39. Maureen Reilly and Phyllis Stanin, Todd Engineers, "Recharge & recirculation (R&R) modeling," June 14, 2014.

40. HDR Engineering, Inc., "Preliminary cost estimates of Edwards Aquifer recharge & recirculation springflow protection alternative," June 4, 2010.

41. Minutes of the EARIP meeting, June 14, 2010.

42. Ibid. Larry Land and Sam Vaugh, HDR Engineering, Inc., technical memorandum, "Revised fundamental assumptions for technical evaluation of three programs and two trade offs," July 7, 2010. With respect to brush management, see generally Minutes of the EARIP meeting, September 9, 2010, attachment 3, "Report and recommendation of the project work group regarding rangeland restoration project subgroup," September 3, 2010.

43. HDR Engineering, Inc., and Todd Engineering, "Technical evaluation of springflow protection programs," presentation at the EARIP meeting, September 9, 2010.

44. Ibid.

45. Under the Senate committee substitute in article V of Senate Bill 3–2005, the withdrawal reduction floor would have been dropped to 288,000 acre-feet in 2020.

46. Minutes of the EARIP meeting, September 9, 2010.

47. Cindy Loeffler, "Notes on the conference call of the San Antonio Water System Aquifer Storage and Recovery Work Group on September 16, 2010."

48. Minutes of the EARIP meeting, September 23, 2010; Colin McDonald, "Stage 5 drought limits eyed," *San Antonio Express-News,* September 24, 2010; and Larry Land and Sam Vaugh, HDR Engineering, technical memorandum to Dr. Robert L. Gulley, "Fundamental assumptions for technical evaluation of bottom-up program," October 7, 2010.

49. Larry Land and Sam Vaugh, HDR, technical memorandum to Dr. Robert L. Gulley, "Fundamental assumptions for technical evaluation of bottom-up program," October 12, 2010. The brush management option, which had support among the EARIP stakeholders, particularly among the agricultural interests, was determined not to be feasible, because the Texas Commission on Environmental Quality would require a lengthy demonstration project before it would permit the removal of water from Canyon Lake.

50. Sam Vaugh and Larry Land, HDR, and Phyllis Stanin and Maureen Reilly, Todd Engineers, "Technical evaluation of the bottom-up program for springflow protection," October 21, 2010.

51. Minutes of the EARIP meeting, October 21, November 11, 2010; Robert L. Gulley, memorandum to EARIP Steering Committee and stakeholders, "Support information for the November 11, 2010[,] EARIP Meeting," November 7, 2010.

52. Minutes of the EARIP meeting, January 28, 2011.

53. See T. B. Hardy, K. Kollaus, and K. Tower, "Evaluation of the proposed Edwards Aquifer Recovery Implementation Program drought of record minimum flow regimes in the Comal and San Marcos River systems," December 28, 2010.

54. Robert L. Gulley, memorandum to EARIP Steering Committee members and stakeholders, "Memorandum regarding item 2 and the first bullet of item 3 of the agenda for the February 10, 2011[,] EARIP Meeting," February 9, 2011.

55. Agenda for EARIP meeting, February 10, 2011, attachment 3; Minutes of EARIP meeting, February 10, 2011. A brief description of each of the flow protection measures in the bottom-up package is in attachment 4 of the February meeting agenda and is described in more detail in chapter 5 of the habitat conservation plan.

56. See app. 2 for a description of the issuance criteria.

57. See 31 Tex. Admin. Code § 57.901.

58. For a description of these measures, see chapter 5 of the habitat conservation plan, www.eahcp.org.

59. 65 Fed. Reg. 35,242, 35,250 (June 1, 2000).

60. Minutes of the EARIP meeting, February 28, 2011.

61. Minutes of the EARIP meeting, May 17, 2011.

62. Habitat conservation plan, § 4.1, www.eahcp.org.

63. Minutes of the EARIP meeting, June 9, 2007.

64. HDR Engineering, Inc., and Todd Engineers, *Evaluation of water manage-*

ment programs and alternatives for springflow protection of endangered species at Comal and San Marcos Springs, October 2011.

Chapter 9. Funding and Allocating Costs

1. Minutes of the EARIP meeting, August 9, 2007.

2. Senate Bill 3 § 1.29(i).

3. Minutes of the EARIP meeting, September 6, 2007.

4. Texas A&M University tried, unsuccessfully, to obtain a $1.5 million increase for the US Geological Survey Water Resources Program for FY 2009. This request would have funded the EARIP process for two years, including the salary of the project manager, and allowed the stakeholders to ensure that the best science was used in their decision making. Agenda for the EARIP meeting, February 14, 2008, attachment 4.

5. Minutes of the EARIP meetings, July 10, 2008, May 14, 2009.

6. Robert L. Gulley, memorandum to EARIP, "Report on meetings pursuant to the operational rules for the funding work group," March 19, 2009; Robert L. Gulley, memorandum to EARIP, "Meeting with Daniel Mezza, regional director for Senator John Cornyn," October 27, 2008.

7. Agenda for the EARIP meeting, February 12, 2009, attachment 3; Minutes of the EARIP meeting, February 12, 2009.

8. Robert L. Gulley, memorandum to EARIP, "Report on meetings pursuant to the operational rules for the funding work group," March 19, 2009.

9. During the session we met with many legislators and staff from the House, including Shelly Botkin, senior natural resources policy advisor, and Clyde Alexander, chief of staff for Speaker Joe Straus; Representatives Mike Villarreal (Bexar County) and Doug Miller (Bandera, Comal, Gillespie, and Kendall Counties); and staff for Representatives Ruth McClendon Jones (Bexar County) and Brandon Creighton (Montgomery County). Robert L. Gulley, memorandum to EARIP, "Report on meetings pursuant to the operational rules for the funding work group," February 27, April 25, 2009.

10. Robert L. Gulley, memorandum to EARIP, "Report on meetings pursuant to the operational rules for the funding work group," April 25, 2009.

11. Ibid.

12. Robert L. Gulley, memorandum to EARIP, "Report on meetings pursuant to the operational rules for the funding work group," May 2, 2009.

13. General Appropriation Bill, article VI, May 29, 2009.

14. The Region 2 staff attending the meeting included Jennifer Fowler Probst, FWS Fisheries; Mike Montagne, Fisheries; Mark Jacobson, acting assistant regional director for Ecological Services; Mike Oetler, Fisheries; and Marty Tuegle, Ecological Services. Adam Zerrenner and Lesli Gray, public affairs specialist, participated by telephone.

15. Weir Labatt, Karl Dreher, Calvin Finch, Jerry James, Todd Votteler, and I attended the meeting on behalf of the EARIP.

16. Ultimately, with a lot of work and refinement, those estimated costs were reduced to just over $18.5 million per year.

17. Minutes of the EARIP meeting, October 12, 2010.

18. Tom Taggart, "Issues involving growth in the Edwards Aquifer dependent region and possible mitigation initiatives," attachment 4 to agenda for the EARIP meeting, October 21, 2010.

19. See EAA Act § 1.29.

20. "Report of the funding work group to the EARIP," January 14, 2011.

21. Minutes of the EARIP meeting, January 28, 2011.

22. "Outline of a general structure for a bill for a sales tax distributed through the Texas Water Development Board," January 28, 2011.

23. "Report of the issues team," February 4, 2011.

24. Minutes of the EARIP meeting, February 10, 2011.

25. HDR Engineering, Inc., "Changes in spring discharge and associated groundwater and surface water supplies," January 17, 2011; revised and included in HDR Engineering, Inc., *Evaluation of water management programs and alternatives for springflow protection of endangered species at Comal and San Marcos Springs,* October 2011, at 3–23–29.

26. Minutes of the funding work group meeting, March 15, 2011.

27. Ibid.

28. Finch interview, December 9, 2013.

29. Minutes of the funding work group meeting, March 15, 2011.

30. Agenda for the EARIP meeting, attachment 2, "Considerations related to delaying the completion of the habitat conservation plan until after the 2013 legislative session," April 29, 2011.

31. Steve Raabe, notes on EARIP meeting, April 29, 2011.

32. Ibid.

33. Minutes of the EARIP meeting, April 29, 2011.

34. Minutes of the EARIP meeting, May 17, 2011.

35. Con Mims, "Prepared remarks," May 16, 2011.

36. Steve Raabe, notes regarding the EARIP meeting, May 17, 2007.

37. Ibid.

38. The assertion that the aquifer management fees might treble was misleading. Most of the fee increase Dreher was referring to came from the Edwards Aquifer Authority rebate program—not the actual cost of the habitat conservation plan. The actual difference in the aquifer management fees would have been only a doubling of the current fee.

39. Sam Vaugh, email to Robert Gulley and Karl Dreher, "EARIP—alternative CPM concepts," April 4, 2011; Robert L. Gulley, memorandum to EARIP Steering Committee members and stakeholders, "Memorandum to assist in preparing for the June 9, 2011[,] EARIP meeting," May 21, 2011. Later, Dreher admitted that his cost estimates also assumed that the Regional Water Conservation Program in the habitat conservation plan would also be abandoned. However, if this were

true, the stage IV and V pumping cuts required to replace the VISPO and conservation programs in stage IV cuts would have to be increased from 35 percent to 45.7 percent for the Uvalde pool and from 40 percent to 44.2 percent for the San Antonio pool. Stage V cuts would be 48.2 percent for both pools. Sam Vaugh, email to Robert Gulley, "EARIP—CPM withdrawal reduction alternative to VISPO and conservation in [bottom-up] program," May 23, 2011.

40. Downstream surface water rights holders who benefit from the increased springflow from the aquifer will contribute $736,000 annually toward the cost of implementing the habitat conservation plan.

41. Robert L. Gulley, memorandum to EARIP steering committee and stakeholders, "Strawman to provide a basis for discussion at the June 9, 2011 EARIP meeting," June 8, 2011.

42. Steve Raabe, "Minute notes for the joint meeting of the steering committee and stakeholders of the Edwards Aquifer Recovery Implementation Program on June 9, 2011," June 9, 2011.

43. Ibid.

44. Minutes of the EARIP meeting, June 9, 2007.

45. Finch interview December 9, 2013; Puente interview.

46. Finch interview, December 9, 2013.

47. Ibid.

48. Calvin Finch, email to representatives of City Public Service, Bexar Metropolitan Water District, San Antonio River Authority, agricultural interests, City of Victoria, City of San Marcos, New Braunfels Utilities, and the Guadalupe-Blanco River Authority, "SAWS supports EARIP bottom up package," June 22, 2011.

49. Karl Dreher, "Funding phase I of the Edwards Aquifer habitat conservation plan while minimizing the increase in aquifer management fees," June 10, 2011.

50. Edwards Aquifer Authority board workshop, audio recording, June 24–26.

51. Ibid.

52. Ibid.

53. Ibid.

54. Edwards Aquifer Authority, "EAA keeps aquifer management fee rebate program intact, plans to explore more conservation options," press release, September 13, 2011.

55. Darcy Alan Frownfelter, general counsel, and Deborah Clarke Trejo, Kemp Smith LLP, memorandum, "Rebate of aquifer management fees EARIP funding and management agreement," November 9, 2011.

56. Brian R. Pietruszewski, email to Mary Q. Kelly, "EARIP legal issue," November 23, 2011.

57. Minutes of the regular board meeting of the Edwards Aquifer Authority, December 13, 2011; Colin McDonald, "Vote sinks aquifer funding," *San Antonio Express-News,* December 14, 2011; "EAA OKs habitat conservation plan," *New Braunfels Herald-Zeitung,* December 14, 2011.

58. See Tracy Idell Hamilton, "Aquifer plan's last part approved," *San Antonio Express-News,* December 29, 2011.

59. The habitat conservation plan approved by the Fish and Wildlife Service can be found on the documents page of the Edwards Aquifer Authority website: http://www.eahcp.org/files/uploads/Fina120HCP.pdf.

Chapter 10. Reflections

1. See, e.g., US Fish and Wildlife Service San Marcos National Fish Hatchery and Technology Center and Bio-West, Inc., "Effectiveness of host snail removal in the Comal River, Texas and its impact on densities of the gill parasite *Centrocestus formosanus* (Tremotada: Heterophyidae)," February 2011; Halff Associates, Inc., "Initial study on the recreational impacts to protected species and habitats in the Comal and San Marcos Springs ecosystem," November 3, 2010.

2. Hegar quoted in Laylan Copelin, "Key part of battle? Springs," *Austin American-Statesman,* May 25, 2007.

3. The Fish and Wildlife Service strongly encourages applicants for an incidental take permit to include an adaptive management process in their habitat conservation plan to address uncertainties and create more flexibility in the implementation of the plan. 65 Fed. Reg. 35,242, 35,245 (June 1, 2000). The EARIP habitat conservation plan contains a robust adaptive management program accompanied by an applied research program, and together they narrow the uncertainties and test the assumptions underlying both the biological goals and the development of a mechanistic ecological model to evaluate the impacts on the listed species and their habitat.

4. Minutes of the EARIP meeting, March 12, 2009.

5. Agenda for the EARIP meeting, June 14, 2010, attachment 2.

6. Jerry James, interview by author, San Antonio, Tex., August 27, 2013.

7. See, e.g., Joy Nicholopoulos, PowerPoint presentation to the Guadalupe-Blanco River Authority Board of Directors, "Balancing water needs in the Edwards Aquifer: The collaborative approach of recovery implementation programs," November 15, 2006, slide 3.

8. Agenda, San Antonio Water System Board of Trustees meeting, November 7, 2006, item 43.

9. Finch interview, September 23, 2013. See also, "Sierra Club proposal on Edward Aquifer pumping caps," February 2007, 5 (describing Nicholopoulos's PowerPoint presentation with respect to the prospects for federal funding).

10. Senate Natural Resources Committee meeting, video recording, April 10, 2007.

11. Senator Hegar comments as reported in Minutes of the EARIP meeting, July 12, 2007.

12. Puente quoted in Bruce Davidson, "Without a crisis, water issue sinks," *San Antonio Express-News,* June 5, 2005.

13. See John E. Birdwell, commissioner, Texas Water Commission, to

Michael J. Spear, regional director, US Fish and Wildlife Service Region 2, August 3, 1990.

14. See John W. Nielsen-Gammon, "The 2011 Texas Drought," *Texas Water Journal* 3 (2012): 59.

15. Gulley quoted in Colin McDonald, "Panel OKs proposal to manage the aquifer," *San Antonio Express-News,* November 8, 2011.

16. Editorial Board, "Aquifer plan a major success," *San Antonio Express-News,* December 29, 2011.

Appendix 2. The Endangered Species Act

1. Endangered Species Act, Pub. L. No. 93–205, 87 Stat. 884 (1973), codified at 16 U.S.C. §§ 1531–44.

2. 16 U.S.C. § 1533; 50 C.F.R. § 222.101 and 50 C.F.R. § 17.01. The species at the Comal and San Marcos Springs are regulated by the Fish and Wildlife Service, which is within the Department of the Interior. Thus, the use of the term "secretary" herein refers to the secretary of the interior.

3. 16 U.S.C. § 1538(a)(1).

4. 16 U.S.C. § 1532(19).

5. 50 C.F.R. § 17.3; Babbitt v. Sweet Home Chapter of Communities for a Great Oregon, 515 U.S. 687 (1995).

6. Babbitt v. Sweet Home Chapter of Communities for a Great Oregon, 515 U.S. 687 (1995).

7. 16 U.S.C. § 1538(a)(2).

8. 16 U.S.C. § 1540.

9. 16 U.S.C. § 1540(b).

10. 16 U.S.C. § 1540(g).

11. Strahan v. Coxe, 127 F.3d 155, 166 (1st Cir. 1997); Palila v. Hawaii Department of Land and Natural Resources, 639 F.2d 495 (9th Cir. 1981) (Hawaii Department of Land and Natural Resources liable for "take" of the palila bird by failing to manage herds of feral sheep and goats); Loggerhead Turtle v. County Council of Volusia County, 148 F.3d 123, 1251 (11th Cir. 1998) (Volusia County may be liable for take resulting from its regulatory actions). See also Sierra Club v. Yeutter, 926 F.2d 429 (5th Cir. 1991) (US Forest Service even-aged management practices violated section 9 of the ESA); Defenders of Wildlife v. Administrator, EPA, 882 F.2d 1294 (8th Cir. 1989) (Environmental Protection Agency liable for take of the endangered black-footed ferret due to the pesticide registration program of the agency); but see Aransas Project v. Shaw, slip op. (5th Cir. June 30, 2014).

12. Strahan v. Coxe, 127 F.3d 155, 166 (1st Cir. 1997).

13. Ibid., 159.

14. Ibid., 163, citing 16 U.S.C. § §1538(a)(1)(B).

15. 16 U.S.C. § 1539(a)(1)(B).

16. Ibid.

17. 16 U.S.C. § 1539(a)(2)(A)(i)–(iv); 50 C.F.R. § 17.22(b)(iii).

18. 16 U.S.C. § 1539(a)(2)(B); 50 C.F.R. §§ 17.22(b)(2) and 17.32(b)(2).

19. 16 U.S.C. § 1536(c).

20. 50 C.F.R. §§ 17.32(b)(5)(iii)(B).

21. 50 C.F.R. § 402.02. The term "recovery" means "improvement in the status of a listed species to the point at which listing is no longer appropriate."

22. 16 U.S.C. § 1532(5)(A)(i).

23. 50 C.F.R. § 424.12.

Appendix 3. Texas Water Law

1. See Ronald Kaiser, "Conjunctive management and use of surface and groundwater resources," in *Essentials of Texas water resources,* ed. Mary K. Sahs, 2nd ed. (Austin: State Bar of Texas, 2012), 5–1.

2. Russell S. Johnson, "Groundwater law and regulation," in *Essentials of Texas water resources,* ed. Mary K. Sahs, 2nd ed. (Austin: State Bar of Texas, 2012), 4–3.

3. Texas Co. v. Burkett, 296 S.W. 273, 278 (Tex. 1927); Pecos County Water Control & Improvement District No. 1 v. Williams, 271 S.W.2d 503 (Tex. Civ. App.—El Paso 1954, writ ref'd n.r.e.).

4. Texas Const. art. III, § 59(a). On the change that occurred in 2012, see Edwards Aquifer Authority v. Day and McDaniel, 55 Tex. Sup. Ct. J. 343, 369 S.W.3d 814 (Tex. 2012) (landowner has an interest in groundwater in place that cannot be taken for public use without compensation).

5. Act of June 2, 1949, 51st Leg., R.S., ch. 306 (codified at Tex. Rev. Civ. Stat. art. 7880–3c), *repealed by* Act of April 12, 1971, 62d Leg., R.S., ch. 58, § 2.

6. Texas Water Code § 11.021(a).

7. Water Rights Adjudication Act, Tex. Water Code §§ 11.301–41.

8. See Ronald Kaiser, "Texas water law and organizations," in *Water policy in Texas: Responding to the rise of scarcity,* ed. Ronald C. Griffin (Washington, D.C.: RFF Press, 2011), 24–27.

9. Ibid., 25.

Appendix 4. Elements of the Bottom-Up Approach

1. Keith O. Keplinger and Bruce A. McCarl, "The 1997 irrigation suspension program for the Edwards Aquifer: Evaluation and alternatives," February 1998. See also Jerry Needham, "40 farmers win an irrigation gamble," *San Antonio Express-News,* July 15, 1997.

2. Edwards Aquifer Authority, "Document describing pilot irrigation suspension program for 1997," 41.

3. Keith O. Keplinger and Bruce A. McCarl, "The 1997 irrigation suspension program for the Edwards Aquifer: Evaluation and alternatives," February 1998.

4. Jerry Needham, "No irrigation payments for farmers start," *San Antonio Express-News,* February 7, 2007.

5. See San Antonio Water System, "Twin Oaks: Aquifer recovery & storage," http://www.saws.org/Your_Water/WaterResources/projects/asr.cfm.

INDEX

critical period management: and Edwards Aquifer Authority plan, 68, 78–79; bottom-up package, discussion on, 124, 125, 126, 130; Edwards Aquifer Authority draft habitat conservation plan, discussion on, 71, 72; expert science subcommittee, report on, 110, 111; House Bill 41, 81; Senate Bill 1914, 77; Senate Bill 1477, 57; Senate Bill 3 (2005), 80; Senate Bill 1341, 92. *See also* Senate Bill 3 (2007)

Cuero dam and reservoir, 7, 74

Cullinan, Steve, 36

Doggett, Lloyd, 132, 134

Donahue, John M., 214n11

Dow Chemical, 107, 142

Dreher, Karl, 126, 146, 150, 151–56, *passim*, 162, 221n15, 222nn38–39

drought of record: description of, 3, 185n3; Edwards Aquifer Authority draft habitat conservation plan, consideration of , 71–72; Texas Water Commission 1992 aquifer management plans, treatment of, 29, 30, 32, 35, 36, 37; Senate Bill 1341, 91–92; Senate Bill 3 (2007), 95, 158; Sierra Club v. Babbitt, 60, 61

dry year option, 29, 31, 181

Dutton, Alan, 109, 216n42

East Medina County Special Utility District, 107, 144, 158

Edwards Aquifer Authority (EAA): authority background, xvii; catfish farm, permit for, 190n81; creation of, xii, 53; draft habitat conservation plan, 71–76, *passim*, 165, 100; legislative mandates, xii, 53, 70, 76, 78–79; Living Waters Artesian Springs, Ltd. v. Edwards Aquifer Authority, 79; Medina County

Underground Water Conservation District v. Barshop, constitutionality of, 65–66, 67; notices of intent to sue, received by, 70; Senate Bill 1292, supported by, 90; Sierra Club v. City of San Antonio, 67, 68; withdrawal caps, attorney general opinion on, 78, 207n39; withdrawal caps, legislative efforts to raise by, 76–77, 79–81. *See also* Senate Bill 1477; Senate Bill 3 (2007)

Edwards Aquifer Authority workshop in Bandera Texas, 151–153

Edwards Aquifer Habitat Conservation Plan: biological goals and objectives, 128–130; bottom-up package, 125, 127, 151, 180–83; measures, minimization, 120, 128, 166; phased approach, 120–21, 123, 130–31, 148, 162–63; regional water conservation program, 180–81; SAWS aquifer storage and recovery program, 124–27, *passim*, 148, 182–83; stage V withdrawal reductions, 126, 127, 130, 146, 148, 180,183, 222–23n39; state scientific areas, 128; Voluntary Irrigation Suspension Program Option (VISPO), 148, 150, 151, 153, 181–82, 223n39

Edwards Aquifer Recovery Implementation Program (EARIP), 105–107, 127–28, 139, 160, 163–65. *See also* Senate Bill 1341; Senate Bill 3 (2007)

Edwards Underground Water District (EUWD): district background, xvii, 12, 188n45; drought management plan, 13, 18, 24, 188n45, 191n98, Regional Water Resources Plan, 10–18 *passim*; secession of Medina and Uvalde counties from, 15–18, *passim*; Senate Bill 1477, dissolution of, 50

Edwards, Robert, 109

Ellis, Greg, 71, 76
emergency withdrawal reduction plans in Sierra Club v. Babbitt, 60, 61, 64, 65, 67, 68, 203n24
Endangered Species Act, 67, 175–78, 210n72, 225n11. *See also* jeopardy; take
Environmental Defense Fund, 70, 209n61
expert science subcommittee, 93, 95, 108–11, 159–60. *See also* Senate Bill 3 (2007)

federal funding, attempts to obtain, 132, 136–37, 166–68
Field, Patrick, 164
Finch, Calvin, 88, 104, 136, 137, 147, 150, 151, 161, 162, 167
Folk-Williams, John, 22–23
Forbes, Tom, 28,
Frownfelter, Darcy, 154, 155
Funding and Management Agreement, 154, 155, 156
funding compromise regarding habitat conservation plan costs, 147–49

Garden Ridge, City of, 105, 137, 162, 214n13, 215n36
Garza, John, 40
Goliad dam, 7
Gonzales, Charles, 132, 134
Gonzales, Henry B., 18
Gonzales, Mike, 216n44
Griffin, Charles, 15
Green, Ron, 109
Guadalupe Basin Coalition, 80, 87, 88, 89, 90, 105, 107, 137, 209n61
Guadalupe River, xi, 2, 3, 8, 19, 22, 35, 50, 51, 179
Guadalupe-Blanco River Authority (GBRA): Applewhite reservoir, comments by, 62; authority background, xvii–xviii; creation of

EARIP option, role of, 83, 84, 87, 88; joint projects attempted with the City of San Antonio, 6–7, 11, 82, 83; notices of intent to sue, 19, 189n76; Sierra Club v. Babbitt, motivation for joining suit, 198n1; Regional Water Resources Plan, participation in, 14; Texas Water Commission 1992 aquifer management plans, opposition by, 29, 36, 37; threat to dissolve board of, 53–54
Guadalupe-Blanco River Authority underground river lawsuit, 20–22, 189n78, 190n79

habitat conservation plan in Sierra Club v. Babbitt, 63, 203n21
Hall, Dale, 83
Hall, John, 27–42, *passim*, 49, 55, 69, 158
Hannah, John, 57
Hardberger, Phil, xvii, 90, 91, 104, 179
Hardy, Thom, 115–129, *passim*, 159, 160, 217n12
Hardy study costs, contributions to, 118, 119
Hartman, Glen, 9–10
Hasslocher, Robert, 12, 13, 15, 16, 17
Hays County, 19, 22, 24, 49, 53
HDR Engineering, Inc., 123, 124, 125, 126, 130, 141, 159, 218n19, 218n20
Hegar, Glenn: and EARIP, 160; assistance with lowering indirect costs of program management funding, 133; assistance with state funding, 134, 135; letter from Joy Nicholopoulos to, 116; meeting regarding delaying the habitat conservation plan, 145; on EARIP deadlines, 115, 143, 212n100; on federal funding, 167; on steering committee composition, 103–104; Senate Bill 3 (2007), 89, 210n72; Senate Bill 1341, 90–94, *passim*

Henry, Stuart, 37
Hess, Myron, 122, 161, 214n13
Hilderbran, Harvey, 78, 87
Houston Chronicle, 42
Hutchison, Kay Bailey, 132

Illgner, Rick, 74, 136
irrigated agriculture: and EARIP, 99–
100, 213n3; and permit allocation
for, 99, 42, 36, 37; aquifer management fees, cap for, 99; crop in the
ground, 93, 99–100; House Bill 1792,
opposition by, 51; regional authority, opposition by, 23, 28–29, 31,
36,-37, 38, 39; Regional Water Resources Plan, opposition by, 15, 16,
17; Senate Bill 1477, opposition by,
51, 52

J-17 index well, 2, 50, 92, 95, 146, 182,
183
J-27 index well, 2, 53, 78, 92, 95, 183
Jacaman, Kerim, 132
James, Jerry, 73, 132, 134, 135, 137, 161,
165
jeopardy: and Edwards Aquifer Authority draft habitat conservation
plan, 72, 73, 75; and FWS determinations, 44–46; definition, 177–78;
Sierra Club v. City of San Antonio,
67; structured decision-making,
113–18, *passim*; Texas Water Commission 1992 aquifer management
plans, 31–32, 38, 40–41
Johnson, Russell, 33, 67
Joint Committee on Water Resources,
12
Judson, M.C., 5

Kazan, Abraham "Chick," Jr., 8
Kelly, Mary Q., 155, 214n13, 214n16
Knippa Gap, 2
Kramer, Ken, 209n61

Kreitler, Charles, 110, 216n46
Krier, Cyndi, 21, 22

Labatt, Weir, 21, 28–29, 61, 122, 132, 134,
135, 136, 161–62
Laney, Pete, 51
legislative session in 1989, 18
legislative session in 2007, preparation
for, 85–89, 99–100, 211n82, 212n91
Legislation: House Bill 1942 (1987), 13,
17; House Bill 2540 (1993), 200n6;
House Bill 3189 (1995), 65; House
Bill 3586 (2003), 77, 85; House Bill
1292 (2007), 90; House Bill 2760
(2011), 90; House Bill 41(2005), 80;
House Bill 1792 (1993), 49–51, 52, 69;
Senate Bill 1, Article VI (2009), 135–
36; Senate Bill 1341, 90, 91–94; Sen-
ate Bill 1477 (1993), 49, 51–57, 65, 70,
75, 78, 197n71, 200n6, 213n3; Senate
Bill 1595 (2011), 140; Senate Bill 1914
(2003), 77; Senate Bill 24 (2005), 80;
Senate Bill 3 (2005), 79–81; Senate
Bill 3 (2007), 94–96 (*see also* Senate
Bill 1341)
Lewis, Gib, 18
Lewis, Ron, 52
Linebarger, Libby, 49
Lohoefener, Renne, 83
Longley, Glenn, 109
Luna, Gregory, 49
Lytle, Curtis, 29

Mace, Robert, 109, 112, 207n39
Macias, Robert, 147
Madla, Frank, 50, 52
McAllister, Walter W., xvii, 7
McDermott, Robert, 33
McMahon, Joseph, 164
Medina County, 16, 17, 36, 53, 54, 63,
65, 78, 153
Medina County Water Protection and
Conservation Association, 36

Richardson, Gene, 153
Rodriguez, Ciro, 132, 134
Rose, Patrick, 89, 211n82
rule of capture, xii, 15, 18, 19, 20, 24, 42, 63, 158, 179

sales tax option for funding the habitat conservation plan, 138–140
San Antonio, City of: and Applewhite reservoir, 10–11, 25–26, 61–63; and Regional Water Resources Plan, 12, 18, 19; and Texas Water Commission 1992 aquifer management plans, 28, 30, 31, 33, 34, 35, 37, 38, 41; House Bill 1292, supported by, 90; Senate Bill 1792, supported by, 50, 51; Sierra Club v. Babbitt, 60, 199n8; Sierra Club v. City of San Antonio, 67, 68, 69; water supplies, efforts to diversify by, 5, 6, 7, 8, 9, 11, 185n6
San Antonio City Council, 9, 10, 11, 12, 16, 18, 25, 26, 33
San Antonio City Planning Commission, 11–12
San Antonio City Public Service, 18, 107, 141, 142
San Antonio City Water Board, xviii, 7, 8, 9, 25
San Antonio Express-News, 33, 185
San Antonio Light, 21, 185
San Antonio pool, 2, 80, 87, 110, 146, 183, 222n39
San Antonio River, xviii, 5, 82, 139
San Antonio River Authority (SARA), xviii, 7, 8, 20, 63, 82, 86, 93
San Antonio Water System (SAWS): and bottom-up package, 125, 130, 182–83; catfish farm acquisition of water rights by, 190n81; discussions with Dreher, 150, 151; dispute with GBRA over joint water project, 82, 83; Edwards Aquifer Authority

draft habitat conservation plan, supported by, 73, 74; eight hundred pound gorilla, 161, 162, 215n37; funding work group, 133, 137, 141, 142, 143; habitat conservation plan decision, threat to delay by, 143, 144, 145, 146; House Bill 1292, supported by, 90; organization background, xviii, Senate Bill 1341, 93; Sierra Club v. City of San Antonio, 67; steering committee expansion, 104
San Marcos, City of, 18, 20, 22, 38, 128, 154, 155, 156, 180
San Marcos pool, 110
San Marcos River, xi, 2, 3, 12
San Marcos River Foundation, 105, 107
San Marcos Springs: 2, 3, 45, 80, 110–11, 119–22, 129, 130–31
SAWS/2050 Committee Water Resources Plan, 61, 62
Schaefer, John, 8–9
science in the decision-making process, state support for, 118–19, 134–36
science, peer review of, 109, 110, 111, 136, 160
science, role in EARIP decision-making, 159–60
section 6 grant to support development of the habitat conservation plan, 133–34, 135
Shull, Alisa, 40
Sierra Club, xii, 32, 36, 37, 43, 70, 81, 209n1
Sierra Club v. Babbitt, 43–48, 59–61, 63–67, 69, 74–75, 86, 198nn1–2, 199n8
Sierra Club v. City of San Antonio, 67–69
Sims, Bill, 51, 52
Smith, Carter, 122

Smith, Lamar, 134

Smith, Terral, 22

South Central Texas Water Advisory Committee, 53, 65, 78, 79, 201n18, 207n37

Sparks, Sam, 69

Spear, Michael J., 24, 25, 31, 32, 37, 40, 41, 75, 158

Specht, John, 21, 36, 53, 54, 198n1

Special Committee on the Edwards Aquifer, 22–23, 24

Special Committee on the Edwards Aquifer, facilitated negotiations sponsored by, 22–23

springflow targets, 45–46, 80, 119, 121–24, 125, 218–19n 29

statutory minimums, 54

steering committee, membership, 92, 93–94, 171–74

steering committee, voting blocs in, 107

structured decision-making, 113–18, 163, 164, 166

Taggart, Tom, 137

Take: definition, 175; measures, minimization of, 128; Sierra Club v. Babbitt, 43, 44, 45, 46; Sierra Club v. City of San Antonio, 67, 68; structured decision-making, 114–18, *passim*; Texas Water Commission 1992 aquifer management plans, 37, 38. *See also* Endangered Species Act, 175–76

Texas A&M University, xi, 93, 100, 101, 133

Texas Bass Federation, 107

Texas Commission on Water Quality, xix, 2

Texas Farm Bureau, 18, 32, 39, 49, 52, 153

Texas Living Waters Project, 107

Texas Natural Resource Conservation Committee, xix, 65

Texas Parks and Wildlife Department, xviii, 84, 128, 129, 209n60, 210n72, 218n19

Texas State University, xi, 109, 128, 154, 165, 217n12, 218n19

Texas State Water Plans, 5, 8

Texas Water Commission: and 1992 aquifer management plans, 27–42, 46–48, 192nn8–9, 197n71; commission background, xviii-ix; emergency measures plan, 23, 24, 25, 168, 191n98

Texas Water Commission Plan in Sierra Club v. Babbitt, 46–48

Texas Water Development Board, xix, 89, 109, 112, 137, 138, 207n39, 209n60, 210n7, 216n42

Thompson, Carrie, 74

Todd Engineers, 124, 159

Todd, Bruce, 28

Tuggle, Benjamin, 136, 166

underground river, Texas Water Commission designation of the Edwards Aquifer as, 32–40

underground river, Texas Water Commission compromise with City of San Antonio, 33–34, 35, 38, 195n45

United States Army Corps of Engineers, 6, 25, 83

United States Commission report, 5

United States Department of Defense, 60, 67, 136, 167

United States Fish and Wildlife Service (FWS): agency background, xix; and EARIP, 165–66; and EARIP initial startup, 100, 102, 109, 213n6; emergency measures action plan, letter to Texas Water Commission, 24; EARIP creation, role in, 83, 85,

United States Fish and Wildlife Service (FWS) (*cont.*)
86, 87, 88, 209n63; Edwards Aquifer Authority draft habitat conservation plan, 71–73, 74, 75, 76, 206n22; Edwards Aquifer habitat conservation plan, approval by, xiii, 129, 156, 160, 210n71, 224n3; Edwards Aquifer Authority, threat to sue, by, 70; failure of federal funding, 167; measures, minimization, 128; section 6 grant, 133–34, 135; Sierra Club v. Babbitt, xii–xii, 43, 64, 66, 67, 198n1, 199n8; springflow determinations, 45–46, 199n15, 218n19; structured decision-making, supported by, 113–19, *passim*; Texas Water Commission 1992 aquifer management plans, communications regarding, 31–32, 36, 37–38, 40–41

United States Geological Survey, 109, 112, 114–16, *passim*, 117, 118, 119, 214n13, 216n46

Uresti, Carlos, 93, 134

Uvalde County: Regional Water Resources Plan, opposition by, 15, 16; secession from Edwards Underground Water District by, 15–18, *passim*; Senate Bill 1477, opposition by, 49, 52; Sierra Club v. Babbitt, 63; Texas Water Commission 1992 aquifer management plans, opposition by, 23, 36, 53

Uvalde County Underground Water Conservation Association, 51

Uvalde County Underground Water Conservation District, 53, 54, 63

Uvalde Leader News, 36

Van de Putte, Leticia, 49, 86, 93, 134

Vaugh, Sam, 109, 146

Victoria, City of, xi, 80, 90, 91, 137, 142, 161

Voting Rights Act of 1965, 57–58, 64–65

Votteler, Todd, 67, 69, 83, 84, 132, 136, 137, 147, 209n68, 211n82

Water Resources Task Force, 10

Waugh, John, 109

Wentworth, Jeff: assistance with state funding, 134; district represented, 211n86; meeting on legislative strategy for San Antonio, 86; sales tax 140; Senate Bill 1792, introduced by, 50; Senate Bill 1477, introduced by, 52; Senate Bill 1914, introduced by, 77; Senate Bill 659, introduced by, 90; Senate Bill 1341, 93, 212n, 209n61

West, Bill, 82, 83, 84, 86, 87, 117, 149

Windwehen, Charles, 91

withdrawal caps, 54–55, 76–78

Wolff, Nelson W., xvii, 17, 32, 33, 38, 61, 86, 91

Wynne, Buck, 21, 23, 27, 190n84

Yablonski, Adam, 137, 152–53

Zaffirini, Judith, 52, 134

Zerrenner, Adam, 115, 133, 221n14

Zinn, Larry, 86

Other Books in the

Money for the Cause: A Complete Guide to Event Fundraising
Rudolph A. Rosen

On Politics and Parks
George L. Bristol

Hillingdon Ranch: Four Seasons, Six Generations
David K. Langford and Lorie Woodward Cantu

Green in Gridlock: Common Goals, Common Ground, and Compromise
Paul W. Hansen